THE COMMON GROWL

I0809714

FORDHAM UNIVERSITY PRESS NEW YORK 2016

COMMONALITIES
Timothy C. Campbell, series editor

THE COMMON GROWL

Toward a Poetics of Precarious Community

THOMAS CLAVIEZ

Editor

Copyright © 2016 Fordham University Press

All rights reserved. No part of this publication may be reproduced, stored in a retrieval system, or transmitted in any form or by any means—electronic, mechanical, photocopy, recording, or any other—except for brief quotations in printed reviews, without the prior permission of the publisher.

Fordham University Press has no responsibility for the persistence or accuracy of URLs for external or third-party Internet websites referred to in this publication and does not guarantee that any content on such websites is, or will remain, accurate or appropriate.

Fordham University Press also publishes its books in a variety of electronic formats. Some content that appears in print may not be available in electronic books.

Visit us online at www.fordhampress.com.

Library of Congress Cataloging-in-Publication Data available online at catalog.loc.gov.

Printed in the United States of America

18 17 16 5 4 3 2 1

First edition

CONTENTS

The Politics of Aesthetics

Sociological Reflections

FOREWORD: THE COMMON GROWL

JEAN-LUC NANCY

Of politics, today, nothing remains.

Of politics, today, everything remains.

Nothing remains because what defined the content of the word *politics* has been swept away by a history that there can be no question of reviving or probably even of revisiting.

First, this was the history that saw the birth of the *polis*, that is to say, the form that a gathered collectivity gave itself, one governed by itself and not by a divine authority. The Greek city, like the Roman one, depended on a shattering of theocratic or tribal forms of organization (which were often interlinked), but not without retaining essential aspects of the rigid hierarchies that structured traditional societies, as well as the displacement of a part of social sacredness onto what we can (anachronistically) call civil religion.

The general design of the ancient city no longer makes any sense to us since it unraveled of itself. The *polis* was formed, transformed, and deformed with the movement of a civilization profoundly in flux, leaving behind the reproduction of life based solely on agriculture to initiate forms of production and commerce Marx called "pre-capitalist." The representation of another city ended up being invented, that of a God resolutely outside the world and before whom the hierarchies and forms of domination that structured society no longer obtained.

The task of making the world—in the sense of a space for circulation of sense—to which the city was supposed to respond, became divided in two: on the one hand, the transfiguration of the world into God's kingdom; on the other, the configuration of the world of humans. "Politics" thus became the name of a space to be invented: It will be called "Republic" (in all the successive values of the word, at least since Jean Bodin), a space for the creation of sense (of the world), whose consistency and stability (the *State*) are assured through sovereignty (the quality of origin and of founding "public law"). When sovereignty ceased to be identified with a figure (a royal one, for example) and became that of the "people," it adopted the task of configuring the space of this "people." This is what goes by the name of democracy.

At this point, politics suffered a profound dehiscence. On the one hand, it remained identified with the Republic and with the State, at the same time that its scope of practice and legitimacy came to be determined as the "nation"—an assumed or fashioned identity. On the other hand, preserving the traits of a figural, authoritarian, and separate organizational function (*instance*), it was destined to cancel its own separation and to disappear as a distinct sphere in order to re-emerge immersed in all spheres of common existence, beginning with the exercise of decision (council, direct democracy).

The separation of "politics" has neither been abolished nor really maintained. What has effectively occurred is an impregnation of all spheres of common existence (that is to say, tendentially, of existence *tout court*, the common of existing, both human and non-human, that with which the word *communism* was supposed to be charged) by infrapolitical as well as suprapolitical schemata. These involve mythical and affective representations of collective destinies (which at the same time shelter enormous techno-economic machines) or else the representation of the generalized management of comfort within the general equivalence of market value—in one way or another, a world of completeness or of indefinite saturation.

This is the point at which nothing remains of politics, and thereby everything of it remains: The question of the configuration of a space for circulation of sense (one can also say: of sense, thus of circulation without completeness) is fully posed, open, gaping.

In this opening, at least one signal flickers: All forms of completeness or of saturation, ideological or techno-economic, engender inequalities—inhumanities, insensibilities, insanities—that are not only as onerous as those sustained by former hierarchies and forms of sacredness, but that are also henceforth clearly devoid of any appearance of natural or supernatural justification.

That is why politics subsists at least as revolt—when necessary, as a revolt against politics. "Revolt" does not mean "revolution" to the extent that this latter term has come to bear the projection either of an overturning of the basis of politics—with the conservation of its structure—or of a complete abolition of the separation of its organizational function. Neither does revolt promise as much by way of great risks, which is why it may become suspicious even of revolutionary politics. But it protests that existence is untenable if it does not open up spaces of sense; that this opening up of sense is impossible so long as what reigns instead of circulation is the pitiless circularity in which everything-amounts-to-the-same; and that this "reign" itself is devoid of any kind of glory or grace, whereas the other reign, that of the heavens, no longer flutters except exsanguinate and grimacing.

Subsisting as revolt, politics perhaps no longer subsists at all; but perhaps it is not necessary to think in terms of subsistence, of remainder, or of survival. It is above all necessary not to wait for anything from "politics," as if it were the mysterious reservoir of who knows what hidden resource of meaning.

Revolt still denounces "the spirit of a world without spirit," even if it does not intend these words entirely in the same way. Without spirit: not without "spirituality" but without the brio (*vif*) of signs and acts by which, alone, one *exists*.

Revolt, however, does not make clear what the élan (*vif*) of an existence open to its possibilities might be. Revolt does not discourse, it *growls* (*gronde*). What does "growl" mean? It's almost an onomatopoeia. It means to grunt, bellow, and roar. It means to yell together, to murmur, mumble, grouse, become indignant, protest, become enraged together. One tends to grumble alone, but people growl in common. The common growl is a subterranean torrent: It passes underneath, making everything tremble.

Translated by Steven Corcoran

THE COMMON GROWL

INTRODUCTION: TOWARD A POETICS OF COMMUNITY

THOMAS CLAVIEZ

In the "Overture" to his 2001 book with the programmatic title *Community: Seeking Safety in an Insecure World*, the renowned sociologist Zygmunt Bauman sketches a startlingly nostalgic scenario of community as "a cosy and comfortable place," "a roof under which we shelter in heavy rain, like a fireplace at which we warm our hands on a frosty day," a place where "we are safe most of the time and hardly ever puzzled or taken aback" (1–2). This view—stated, admittedly, in a kind of hyperbolic tongue-in-cheek manner—is, needless to say, strongly indebted not only to the romantic nostalgia that characterizes similar descriptions in Ferdinand Tönnies' famous 1887 *Community and Society*, but to a story that we've been telling ourselves for quite some time. However, although Bauman readily admits that this concept "stands for a kind of world that is, regrettably, not available to us" (3) (and presumably never has been), in the chapters that follow, Bauman has no qualms using it as the backdrop against which, again in a manner reminiscent of Tönnies, to diagnose and measure all the evils haunting our contemporary existence—an existence that, consequently, manifests itself rather melancholically as a perpetual betrayal of this story.

Two sets of questions arise at this point: What kind of story is this? Is it a consoling fiction? A necessary narrative? An elusive myth? A combination of all of the above? The second set arises once we venture our reservations to subscribe to either that story/fiction/narrative/myth, or to the attempt to describe our world today as simply a betrayal of these. Granted, however, that we *do* need some form of narrative to tell ourselves how we see and interact with each other, what would such a story look like? What kind of fiction might it be? Need it be a fiction? What other "poetic" devices do we have available not only to describe, but maybe also to conceptualize the communities we live in?

The esteemed scholars invited to contribute to this collection on a "poetics of community" were asked to interpret this theme in a rather broad manner: They could either address the relationship of community and "poetics" in gauging the former's dependency on myth, narrative, central metaphors, tropes, and single works of literature, or engage in attempts to actually think community in poetic terms. The idea of this collection was to offer a counterweight to a widespread tendency in sociology to supplant a former (and other) myth—that of "social engineering"—with the even more ambitious project of "rational choice." These rationalistic schools, however, seem to be hard put to address at least two social phenomena that have gained increased prominence since modernity and beyond: those of a heightened feeling of contingency, and that of a growing precariousness of existence. The "new complexity" (*Neue Unübersichtlichkeit*) that Jürgen Habermas in 1985 diagnosed and addressed in a book with this title has, if anything, gained both in extensity and intensity, propelled forward by globalization and its concomitant processes such as deregulation, massive population movements, an acceleration of travel and information, diasporic communities, and the like. In the face of these processes, it seems rather odd to relegate, as Anthony Appiah does, migration, nomadism, and diaspora to a past practically overcome, in order to celebrate a diversity created by free wills and voluntary movement.[1] More than ever, community itself—traditionally considered one of the bulwarks against contingency—has become increasingly contingent: Our neighbors seem to be less and less "necessary" than they were in earlier, more tightly knit and homogeneous communities—if, that is, such communities, as projected by the last Romantic sociologist, Ferdinand Tönnies, ever existed in the first place, which seems doubtful.[2]

In order to address such contingencies and precarious communities, we could, of course, simply argue that we can describe our contemporary experience only in terms of a both/and (instead of an either/or), as another famous scholar on cosmopolitanism, Ulrich Beck, does. In his *Cosmopolitan Vision*, he suggests replacing "universalism, relativism and nationalism [which] are based on the either/or principle" with a "cosmopolitanism [that] rests on the both/and principle" (57). This we can certainly do; he would have to be aware, however, that in so doing we are kissing the basic premise of syllogistic thinking—the law of noncontradiction—good-bye and are approaching the structure of myth.[3] We might, however, also diagnose such a state of affairs in less optimistic terms, as Herbert Marcuse did 50 years ago, when he considered "the grand unification of opposites which counteracts qualitative change" as "pertain[ing] to a thoroughly hopeless or thoroughly preconditioned existence that has made its home in a world where even the irrational is Reason" (*One-Dimensional Man*, 230). Whether, that is, the irrational has made its home in what still claims to be a reasonable world, or whether it offers us a reconciliatory, cosmopolitan stance toward a contingent, globalized world which simply defies being measured by the yardstick of syllogistic reason, what both assessments show is that we might need discourses other than that of reason to come to terms with our highly contingent environment—myth maybe being one of them and, as its successor (according to Hans Blumenberg[4]), poetics perhaps being another candidate.

This is why a "poetics of community" might offer us alternative and innovative views on newly emerging forms of community that cannot be read productively anymore against either the backdrop of older concepts of community colored by a romantic nostalgia for homogeneity, closeness, and sameness (as suggested by Tönnies or Bauman) or the myth of rational choice. Should we, as Raymond Williams once urged us to do, "search out and counterpose an alternative tradition taken from the neglected works left in the wide margin of the century, a tradition which may address itself . . . to a modern *future* in which community may be imagined again" (in Jessica Berman, *Modernist Fiction*, 2)? Or are we more and more forced to tell ourselves "different" narratives and stories about what constitutes such newly wrought communities? Can we resort to existing forms—be they literary, mytho-poetic, narrative, tropological, or otherwise—to help us envisage or imagine new forms of community that avoid what Roberto Esposito (2011) has identified as the "immunizing" reflexes of communities? Reflexes that have characterized almost all conceptualizations of community from Aristotle via Thomas Hobbes, Jean-Jacques Rousseau, and John Locke to Tönnies, Martin Heidegger, and beyond?

To venture an answer to these and related questions is what the contributions collected in this volume attempt to do—if, needless to say, with widely differing strategies and results. The short essay by Jean-Luc Nancy, which serves as a prologue to the collection, sets the tone. "The Common Growl" addresses what might be called the "white noise" that both digital technology and a sociology of "rational choice" try either to suppress or to ignore; a "growl" that spells, in Nancy's words, a last remnant of *the* political that revolts against *a* political that, by saturating society, has lost itself, and thus the capability to "make sense." The revolt is a *re-volte*, a reminder of a beginning—a beginning, however, not in the sense of a nostalgic *arkhē*, but of an endless re-beginning—and re-beginnings are always rife with "potentialities." The political, then, does not serve to "saturate" everything with meaning, in that this saturation spells the end of all potentialities. The political, in Nancy's view, is designed to keep open and alive the tension between the potential and its actualization, since the taking place of the potential in its actualization always engenders the danger of closure. It is, in fact, in this very gap that sense *has* a place. That is why the "growl" itself involves no specific, clear-cut aim; it seems to signify nothing but its own (as yet impotent) *potentia*. Nor can this "common growl" have anything "in common" but itself, as Nancy reminds us in *The Inoperative Community*.[5] There is no common objective, no work, no harmony implied in it, or to be achieved by it, as all immanence spells death—and death is the end of all potentiality.

The "trembling" that the growl causes can thus be interpreted in many ways: It might spell "fear and trembling" for those who consider sense as something to be actualized, and thus finally achievable; and, once achieved, something to be defended. The tremble might also refer to the perpetual inquietude of the potential itself, of a creative force at the moment shortly before bursting out: The quiver of a community that is, to use Jacques Derrida's words, always "to come," and that takes, to use another memorable sentence of Derrida, "the formless, mute, infant, and terrifying form of *monstrosity*" ("Structure, Sign and Play," 293).

One way to think of the coming community is how Giorgio Agamben sketches it in his book of the same title. And, indeed, to some readers the scenario that he develops there certainly carries aspects of the monstrous. Tropologically speaking, as Robert Young argues in his contribution, Agamben "reformulates community away from the vertical synchrony of metaphor, from sharing and substitutability, to the horizontal prospectiveness of metonymy, of *clinamen*, a relation of leaning or contiguity and therefore also of contingency, a narrative always in process or temporality of unfinished becoming," a thought that my contribution takes up and tries to systematize.

The central question raised by Agamben—as well as by Maurice Blanchot's (1983) and Jean-Luc Nancy's reflections on the topic of community—is, to put it rather simply, whether "being in common" necessarily implies "having something in common." This assumption characterizes an entire tradition of theories of community. As paradigmatic examples of such a merger, usually the Greek *polis* and the nation state are mentioned, a fact which, in Young's view, "has had the unfortunate effect of distorting the community into the image of the nation." Young traces this history along the names of Stalin and Benedict Anderson, pointing out that, paradoxically, the "imagined community of the nation has historically been a destroyer of actual communities," a fact that strongly inflects Tönnies' argument in *Community and Society.* In order to carve out the paradoxes of this merger, Young then turns to James Joyce's *Ulysses*, where, in a pivotal scene, in an exchange with John Wyse, Bloom defines a nation as "the same people living in the same place"—or, as he adds, "living in different places." What is not being discussed is a third option: "different people living in the same place," which would come closest to a globalized, metonymic society. If anything, metropolitan Dublin is exactly such a space, while "the same people living in different places" might define the Jewish exilic experience; and one is unthinkable without the other. In such a scenario, Moses Maimonides' *The Guide for the Perplexed* might indeed be a good book to turn to, as Young suggests.

As already mentioned, my own contribution tries to further pursue, and to systematize, the idea of a "metonymic community" which, I argue, can be traced in many contemporary contributions on the topic of community, covering such diverse thinkers as Judith Butler, Agamben, Nancy, but also Jacques Rancière. It takes its start from the assumption that, traditionally, community was designed to safeguard us against various forms of contingency; as such, it features in the central works on political theory and community already mentioned above. This, however, opens numerous questions: Are not then other forms of contingency by default included and enclosed into the walls of the *polis* and the nation, respectively? And why is it that contingency has acquired such a bad reputation in the first place? Clearly, humankind has spent almost its entire history trying to overcome (some of) it; on the other hand, why is it that, when we tell the story of our life, it will usually turn out an assemblage of things that just so happened to us—that is, events that were, if anything, contingent, unforeseen, incalculable? Our birth, our first kiss, meeting the person(s) we love, our first job, our illnesses, our important encounters—all of which happened more or less accidentally? Sketching the rather troublesome etymological and logical history of the concept of contingency, and locating its status in modern and contemporary theory and literature, I am arguing for a reassessment of the term, as it threatens to become functionalized by the immunizing strategies that Esposito has so convincingly described, and that are fueled further by the heightened emphasis on the precariousness that surrounds us.

If contingency is what causes us to develop more and more so-called contingency plans in order to avoid being exposed to it, 9/11 has shown us that we cannot be prepared for the worst. The American government was keen on identifying the attacks as such—that is, as contingent—which implies that they constituted something unforeseeable, incalculable, unprecedented, and irrational. This, in turn, served as the occasion to increase measures of immunization (in the sense of Esposito) to an unprecedented (and this time, the attribute fits) pitch: Everybody with a "strange" look came under a general suspicion. Moreover, the "thing in itself" seemed to defy representation; that is why some commentators compared it to an aesthetics of the sublime.[6]

Homi Bhabha's essay, "Poetics of Anxiety and Security," challenges these assumptions, in reconnecting the experience we shared endlessly on TV with W. H. Auden's poem "September 1, 1939"—which was referred to and quoted immediately and repeatedly in the aftermath of the attacks. Auden's poem manages, in a unique manner, to capture the mood, the symbolic and emotional impact, of the outbreak of the Second World War. In so doing, Bhabha argues, he "keeps redrawing the contingent boundary between what we represent as 'public' and what we designate as 'private,'" thus creating a poetry that captures the uneasy, and hard-to-delineate, porous borders between anxiety and security that defy being put into rigorous political statements and action plans. The poet sketches a third space that, according to Bhabha, moves "restlessly in this mediatory mongrel space in-between what Auden calls the 'public space of commonality' and the 'inner space of private ownership,' keeping both Eros and Agape in play." The "moral asymmetric souls"—one of the finest poetic pictures ever devised to describe the gray expanse between the private, the communal, and the universal—must, and can only, find agency in this third space that "Auden's design of proximity *within* the polarized, or contingency in the midst of contradiction," evokes, as Bhabha, referring to Walter Benjamin, puts it. If, as Hannah Arendt emphasizes (whom Bhabha also quotes), "Everything that exists amongst a plurality of things is not simply what it is, in its identity, but it is also different from others; this being different belongs to its very nature," then her conclusion—"When we try to get hold of it in thought, wanting to define it, we must take this otherness (*alteritas*) or difference into account"—certainly holds. This alterity, as Arendt and Bhabha know all too well, cannot be integrated into the holism that a metaphoric concept of community implies.

Can literature offer us access to this (contingent) other? And would that access have to be metonymic, to expose us to its contingency? Djelal Kadir's essay "Literature, the World, and You" starts out with a quote from Quintillian's *Institutio Oratoria* that seems to point in a different direction, as the famous orator identifies metaphor as "the commonest and by far the most beautiful of *tropes*"—a rather rare instance of something being both "commonest" *and* "most beautiful." Kadir, however, locates our theorizing about the connection between literature and the world in the contingent realm of "the tussle between poetics and community, or the paronomasia of anomalous construct, on the one hand, and normative structure on the other," or "the counterpoint between Aristotle's *Poetics* and his *Nichomachean Ethics*." The "worlding" which we are all involved in who use—and translate—texts historically or geographically far away from us, is part and parcel of the *theoria* which, as Kadir reminds us, "means to witness for oneself and for one's own city-state the rituals of others." This witnessing is itself inscribed in the counterpoint mentioned above, that is, between a poetics that translates between "ourselves" (and our *polis*) and the others, and an ethics that makes us apply our own moral yardsticks to those others. Thus the Derridean project of *mondialisation*, too, that Kadir evokes in connection with "world literature," is located in this gap; and the *metaphorein*, the acts of translation we are involved in, are in fact twofold: We not only have to translate between our own poetics and our ethics, we also have to translate the others' poetics and ethics. What *littérature-monde*, then, can offer is just this double act of translation: a mediation between different ethics by means of poetic translation. In order to do so, Kadir argues, "there remains the need for a dual discernment—what we might call a requisite literacy on the one hand, and a worldliness on the other, for the reading and understanding of world literature." Worldliness here acquires a rather un-Heideggerian facet: that of the exposure to otherness, an exposure which—as again literature can remind us—has been simply the story of human coexistence as such. Kadir traces such "exposures" through the works of three authors—the Chinese writer Lu Chi, the English metaphysical poet Andrew Marvell, and the 20th-century Argentine author Jorge Luis Borges—in all cases discerning "a frame of reference turning into a frame of difference": a process that any translation worth its name is designed to achieve. Literature itself thus serves as rehearsing "a performative function as projection from the realm of literature into the lifeworld, or a morphing *translatio* from the poetic to the pragmatic."

For Jacques Rancière, this translation between the poetic and the pragmatic is also of key interest since, as he puts it, a "literary community exists whenever human beings are gathered by the power of certain words." The power of these words, however, is highly ambivalent. In his view, the poetic can never be translated entirely into the pragmatic—at least in what he calls the "aesthetic regime"; in fact, literature proper, which only emerges within this regime, has to disentangle itself from the "world" in order to be able to change it. Although especially the realistic novel "has no walls separating the inside from the outside," as it defies the social and artistic hierarchies set up by the "representative regime" (whose origins he locates in Aristotle), it also defies the didacticism of the latter. Accordingly, for the representative regime, Rancière would challenge the very gap between the poetics and the ethics of Aristotle, where Kadir begins. What, in fact, the aesthetic regime—whose origin he locates in Schiller's *Letters on the Education of Man*—achieves is exactly that: to disentangle art from the mimesis of the social hierarchies that it has in Aristotle. If, in the representative regime, action and control are in the hands of those in power, and are ascribed to certain genres exclusively, the aesthetic regime opens the stage to "people to whom events just happen." What literature freed from mimesis stages, consequently, is a disruption of the normal distributions of forms of life. "Normal" in this connection refers to an allegedly natural social hierarchy which is disrupted by the *demos*, and by democracy: by those who have no part in the distribution of the visible, sayable, and doable. By undermining the representative regime's emphasis on narrative probability and causality, the aesthetic regime offers a glimpse of what lies below the political order: sheer contingency.

What *Madame Bovary* dramatizes is just that: "a random combination of impersonal events"—that which happens to all of us, and what will later make up our CV. The poetics of the aesthetic regime thus expose us to the very contingency that, on the one hand, characterizes the real as political and communal but that, on the other hand, we try by all means to keep at bay. It shows us the very singularities in the midst of the immanence that Young also alludes to. It is thus located, as Rancière puts it, "in the flood of the micro-events that produce those affirmations as singular forms of crystallization of the Impersonal. Literature turns the power of disidentification into the power of writing itself, the power of dissolving . . . the rigid forms of social identity and relationships to produce its own events in the breath of sentences. . . ." Below the surface of identification that literature serves to disidentify with, there lurks the "community of the atoms," for the illustration of which Rancière refers to two works of Virginia Woolf: the short story "An Unwritten Novel," and her novel *To the Lighthouse.* While the former takes its cue from the meeting with an anonymous woman on a train, *To the Lighthouse* manages to turn anonymous life into one of its main protagonists, which, in turn, prevents the other *personae* from achieving "predatory identities." The clash between such identities is further developed in Woolf's later novel *Mrs. Dalloway.* There, however, Septimus, the "man of books," goes mad; indeed, as Rancière argues, has to go mad, as the "tyranny of the plot"—an inheritance from the representative regime—reasserts its dominance. The contingency of madness (or the madness of contingency) is sacrificed on the altar of the social and narrative order; to be continued. . . .

Hardly anyone has addressed the contingency—if not the madness—of the colonial encounter in clearer terms than Franz Fanon, whose new or "reparative" humanism Paul Gilroy sets out to vindicate in his contribution to this collection. Gilroy, too, urges us to reconceptualize the encounter with the other not exclusively in terms of immunization, as he evokes the "need to appreciate and perhaps also cultivate exposure to alterity as something beyond mere plurality and something apart from loss, anxiety, and risk." The post-racial humanism that he sees advocated by Fanon, however, should not be read as a last-ditch attempt to return to or vouchsafe a rational universalism that, if anything, has been sufficiently discredited by the colonial atrocities committed in its name. To reach beyond "humanity's epidermalization" would, in his view, require a wholesale reassessment of both the history and the status quo of political ontology, if not "a revision of modernity understood as epistemology, *techne,* and aesthetics as well as the historic union of capitalism with democracy." In order to do so, however, we have to become aware that even our newest technological achievements—implemented by an allegedly "post"-colonial policy—might serve to perpetuate a racialized humanism that Fanon so emphatically tried to unmask. However, it might, in the form of biometric technology, also specify "a degree of 'somatic individualism'" that "therefore points in a different direction from approaches to security that can be straightforwardly premised upon the logics of racial type and group profile."

Whether and how a racialized politics—or, for that matter, the political ontology that has so far sustained it—can be reformed is hard to judge. This might be not only a philosophical task, but also an aesthetic one—provided that these aesthetics allow us to have encounters with alterity that, at the same time, simultaneously acknowledge it and defuse our potentially allergic strategies to immunize ourselves against it. And I would argue that postcolonial literature provides us with a large array of narrative instances that offer us a glimpse into just this direction. Not least, Franz Fanon's own writings, especially *Black Skin, White Masks* and *The Wretched of the Earth,* are clearly written with and within a modernist poetics of alienation that undergirds his more philosophical-political arguments.

Nancy Fraser, in her essay, "Can Society Be Commodities All the Way Down?," raises a point not unconnected to that of Gilroy: whether there exists a vocabulary that offers us an alternative to that of the status quo. Among the three crises that she distinguishes as the most pressing—the ecological strand, the financialization strand, and the social reproduction strand—the latter is the one that is most relevant to the topic of community—although Fraser rightly points out that a contemporary "critical theory . . . must encompass all three of these crisis dimensions." The third—social reproduction—she more broadly defines as "the human capacities available to create and maintain social bonds, which includes the work of socializing the young, building communities, of reproducing the shared meanings, affective dispositions, and horizons of value that underpin social cooperation." What characterizes contemporary approaches to said crises is that they proceed from a strongly "departmentalized" point of view, which is to say that they are not able or willing to orchestrate a theoretical encounter between all three—an encounter that would acknowledge, and account for, the cross-connections and mutual dependencies of all these strands, and still be geared toward an emancipatory resolution. In order to overcome this impasse, she identifies Karl Polanyi's 1944 book *The Great Transformation* as one of the works that tries to do just that. At the heart of Polanyi's account is—a fiction: the fictitious commodification of all strands of communal life. "Society, morals, ethics, and politics . . . subordinated to, even modeled on, markets." The term "fictitious," needless to say, here implies an untruth, but one that has had (and still has) enormous ramifications for our contemporary malaise. While Polanyi's book offers, according to Fraser, a certain kind of de-mystification of this fiction, it contains some flaws, as its tendency to demonize marketization "neglects injustices *within* communities, including injustices, such as slavery, feudalism, and patriarchy, that depend on social constructions of labor, land, and money precisely as *non*-commodities. Demonizing marketization, the book tends to idealize social protection, as it fails to note that protections have often served to entrench hierarchies and exclusions."

Tracing Polanyi's critique along these lines, Fraser shows us that, for Polanyi, this "fiction" evaded—indeed, was juxtaposed to—what he considered to be a communal reality. For him, to conceive of society as "commodities all the way down" is "entirely fictitious," a fiction that, however, in the last 150 years has created its own reality. The classical "as if" problem arises with a vengeance: If society is being *treated* as a commodity (even though it might not think of itself and its members as such, and considers such an assumption fictitious), does it then nevertheless not *become* just such a commodity? Can Nancy's "growl" be heard here? Do we need a de-fictionalization of a fictitious commodification that has already become "real"? And how powerful would a "counterfiction" have to be in order to upset not only the previous fiction, but its reification in/as reality? Fraser's modification of Polanyi's approach points in this direction: Identifying the "blind spots" in Polanyi's thought, she argues for a critical holism that defies the departmentalization of old, and admits to these different strands being "inextricably interwoven." According to Fraser, a "critical theory for the 21st century must develop a conception of the grammar of social struggle that goes beyond Polanyi's idea of a double movement"—a grammar that, however, would have to be amended by a complex normative perspective that tries to "integrate the legitimate interests in solidarity and social security that motivate social protectionists with the fundamental interest in non-domination that is paramount for emancipation movements, without neglecting the valid concern for negative liberty that animates the most principled and consistent free-market liberals." A rather demanding counterfiction that would be, and in its interdisciplinary comprehensiveness and discursive diversity, a poetic enterprise. But now that we know about the inherent power of fictions, one certainly worth pursuing.

Two contemporary movements that try to overcome the dominance of (the fictions of) marketization and the commodification of community by means of a strategy that one could call spontaneous "communification" are the focus of Dietmar Wetzel's essay. Contrary to an encompassing "counterfiction," these movements—"Occupy" and "Sharing Economy"—try to disturb the common narrative logic of order and domination, thus constituting what Rancière would call "scenes" of emancipation where the order of the doable, thinkable, and makeable is interrupted and challenged. Wetzel argues that these moments indeed could be termed (with due qualification) "metonymic" communities, in that they assemble spontaneously in one space and disseminate again, being organized around punctual needs and interests, and defying an economy of institutional organization and exchange. They thus do not instigate any new "master narrative" in the Lyotardian sense, but see themselves as interrupting, rather than claiming to replace, the existing order. They thus also lead us back to Nancy's "common growl," which, in his words, exposes "the pitiless circularity in which everything-amounts-to-the-same; and that this 'reign' itself is devoid of all sorts of glory and of grace."

Overall, the contributions assembled here testify to the fact that a poetic view of community in all its facets can generate new and exciting angles on this topic. Since their inception, communities have felt the need to resort to stories, narratives, tropes, myths, and have, in turn, been read accordingly. Newly emerging forms of community, as we witness them today, might need not only new narratives to assert themselves, but maybe also innovative poetic and narrative forms and strategies to be deciphered. The contributions to this collection hopefully offer some new ideas on how to do just that.

NOTES

1. Thus Appiah writes: "The cosmopolitan patriot can entertain the possibility of a world in which everyone is a rooted cosmopolitan, attached to a home of his or her own, with its own particularities, but taking pleasure from the presence of other, different, places that are home to other, different people. The cosmopolitan also imagines that in such world not everyone will find it best to stay in their natal patria, so that the circulation of people between different localities will involve not only cultural tourism (which the cosmopolitan admits to enjoying) but migration, nomadism, diaspora. (In the past, these processes have usually been the result of forces we should deplore: the old migrants were often refugees, and older diasporas often began in an involuntary exile. But what can be hateful if coerced can be celebrated when it flows from the free decision of individuals or groups") (Appiah in Martha C. Nussbaum, *For Love of Country?*, 22). I am afraid that those "forces we should deplore" are by no means a phenomenon of the past.

2. Cf. Ferdinand Tönnies, *Community and Society*. While Zygmunt Bauman, in his 2001 volume *Community: Seeking Safety in an Insecure World*, seems to wholeheartedly subscribe to this myth, in *The Inoperative Community* Jean-Luc Nancy asserts that "no *Gesellschaft* has come along to help the State, industry, and capital dissolve a prior *Gemeinschaft*" (11). What did take place at the end of the 19th century was that new "Gesellschaften" arose, namely insurance companies that tried to share the risk of contingencies; these new and partly international corporations were to exert an enormous influence on 20th- and 21st-century economy—not only as protectors against contingency, but as creators of it. Moreover, as Ian Hacking has shown in *Taming Chance*, the very probabilities that were so central for assessing risk became the focus of many different disciplines and discourses.

3. Cf. Thomas Claviez, "Traces of a Metonymic Society in American Literary History."

4. Cf. Hans Blumenberg 1984, 72ff.

5. This is what I take Nancy to mean when he writes: "We 'resemble' together, if you will. That is to say, there is no original or origin of identity. What holds the place of an 'origin' is the sharing of singularities. . . . I do not rediscover myself, nor do I recognize myself in the other: I experience the other's alterity, or I experience alterity in the other together with the alteration that 'in me' sets my singularity outside me and infinitely delimits it" (*The Inoperative Community*, 33–4).

6. Such as the German composer Karlheinz Stockhausen, whose rather unreflected comparison of 9/11 with sublime art brought him a lot of scathing criticism.

The Poetics of Community

COMMUNITY AND *ETHNOS*

ROBERT J. C. YOUNG

What is a community? If we found one would we know it? Would we want to be a part of it? How would we know it if we were? How, in fact, do you know if you're in a community—or if you are, do you always feel fully a part of it? Does a community emerge from shared work, personal contact, friendship, or can you be part of a community without even knowing the people in it? How do we even know if we are a member of a single community or of several interrelated or even distinct ones?

What if, on the other hand, we considered community not from the point of view of the individual as something to which we might equivocally belong, but from the perspective of the community itself, as a subject: "the community"? Instead of uncertainty, things immediately begin to look more definite and restrictive. Communities, it is argued, become closed, with an innate tendency to wish for an undivided social identity—what Jean-Luc Nancy calls "immanentism."[1] If so, this makes the relation of the individual to the community even more problematic than before, though for antithetical reasons: Whereas before you felt uncertain as to whether you were fully a part of it, now the community wants you to belong too much. Moreover, once the community is figured as a subject in its own right in this way, it runs in imminent danger of being metaphorized beyond itself. In recent decades the focus of discussions of community has always, implicitly or explicitly, assumed a relation of community to nation. Philosophers have tended to presuppose the identification between the two that politicians have been keen to promote, so much so that much of the interrogation of community amounts to a covert philosophical analysis of the forms of nationalism and its dangers. In their drive for modes of being-together, it is suggested, the danger of communities is that they are inherently totalitarian.

In response to this, the line of philosophical inquiry that begins with Georges Bataille and develops through Maurice Blanchot, Jean-Luc Nancy, and Giorgio Agamben, has involved an attempt to redefine community against its tendency toward totalization.[2] This interest in redefining community is derived from the apparent relation of community to communism, in which historically, as they see it, community writ large became totalitarian. The descent of communism into totalitarianism means, in this view, that community itself will always be potentially tainted. Articulated through Bataille's notion of sovereignty, philosophers have tried to redefine the form of community in order to create a non-coercive model. Instead of trying to find new ways in which people create communities based on the traditional model of a set of shared features as a group, they have offered a possibility of community constructed on the idea of the singular plural, that is, of individuals who remain singular individuals but in a relation to a community which has no boundaries or lines of exclusion.[3] The question that follows is what relation such singularities may have to each other in a philosophical context in which totalities and essences, and the politics of identity formation founded on sameness and an excluded other, have been disallowed. How do you conceive of a community that is not based on identity, Agamben asks, not based on being something—being French or Muslim or gay—but on being in common, via the notion of the singular plural?[4] How do you theorize a community without closure, without othering, a community which allows the singularity and difference of each of its members? How, in other words, can you reconcile community and difference, a "community without unity," as Nancy puts it?[5] A community of affiliations without collectivity or a sense of belonging is of course an entirely paradoxical idea, which is why philosophers have defined it negatively, particularly through Nancy's term *désoeuvrement*—strictly untranslatable in English, but suggesting the very opposite of a quality that we associate with community, which arguably provides the foundation of community from a conventional view, namely that it is something that works, a working together. *Désoeuvrement*'s inoperativity is what makes any community, in Agamben's formulation, always a community to come—like democracy, it is always in the process of being constructed for the future but not yet in the now. So Agamben reformulates community away from the vertical synchrony of metaphor, from sharing and substitutability, to the horizontal prospectiveness of metonymy, of *clinamen*, a relation of leaning or contiguity and therefore also of contingency, a narrative always in process or an unfinished becoming. This community that is structured temporally rather than spatially, without a sense of belonging or identity, indeed without any shared features at all beyond the conjunction of the moment, as in the Tiananmen Square protests of 1989, becomes a "community without community" as Nancy famously puts it.

What, in practice, could such a community be? The community without community, I want to argue, is less of a paradox than the historic form that many communities have taken. While philosophers have tended to consider community in antithetical terms—that is, either top down, from the total community to the individual person whom it seems to subsume, or from the individual's relation to the totality which threatens her singularity—other theorists and novelists typically work differently, never conceptualizing the community as a subject in its own right, but rather showing how in practice community can never be totalizable, or indeed community itself was never achieved so as to become more than the sum of its parts. From this perspective, the immanent power of community becomes more conflictual, riven, and "disworkly."

The idea of the intrinsic unachievability of community can already be found in Freud's essay known in English as *Civilization and Its Discontents* (1931). A more accurate translation of its original title, *Das Unbehagen in der Kultur*, would be *Unpleasure in Culture*, with the word unpleasure suggesting the uneasiness that the individual feels within his or her own culture or community. The acquisition of a common culture, Freud argues, is achieved through the denial, suppression, renunciation, or repression of the instincts in the individual. The result is good for the community, while by contrast the acquisition of communal norms is always unpleasurable for the individual. This is why communities can never be homogeneous, as even the East German state discovered despite its best efforts. The rather different malaise of contemporary culture or civilization in his own day, Freud argues, comes from too successful a history of sublimation. The paradox is that the more successful sublimation is, the more ambivalent individuals feel about it and the more inclined they are to reject it. In other words, the development of culture produces an increasing tension or dissensus between the community and the individual. For Freud, therefore, becoming adult, becoming part of a community, is something about which at best we can only feel ambivalent. The community's gains are also the losses of its individual members. It is arguable that recent theories of community have been nothing so much as attempts to theorize the basis of this ambivalence as an intrinsic part of community itself. What Freud suggests is that the culture or the community will never succeed in being holistic, because the more it becomes so, the more uneasy its members will feel. The community has its own resistance to itself built in, and this is the reason for its typical heterogeneity: Communities act out a conflictual poetics of dissent, and only exist performatively in that process. The real problem comes when a certain holistic idea of the community, which is how it is imagined that communities should be, is extended to the idea of the nation.

What this suggests is that Nancy, Blanchot, and Agamben's radical attempt to rethink the community backward, without the elements which had previously been regarded as foundational to it, is somewhat skewed by their project to undo the history of totalitarian communism, in the broader context of a perceived failure of secular humanism.[6] If we take the link to the historical practice of communism away from the concept, it is an open question whether community suffers from the holistic paradigm from which Nancy et al. seek to release it. Communities are not imprisoned, their borders are open—even in certain respects the prison itself (like any institution, or community, it is made up of a constantly changing set of people). The widespread use of the term "community" to describe the nation has had the unfortunate effect of distorting the community into the image of the nation, with all the attendant disadvantages of nationalism and totalitarianism. Nancy suggests as much himself when he discusses the seemingly endemic link between community and nostalgia. Just as nationalism is often the long-distance creation of diaspora figures, the idea of community, national or otherwise, is often the creation of those who have moved beyond it, and it is they who nostalgically create the sense of its bounded edenic harmony. The nostalgia is misconceived: community, Nancy himself suggests, is always lost; it is always marked by lack and evanescence, change and disappearance, disruption and strife. Why, though, has it been felt that community is so vulnerable to totalitarian pressures? Historically it is easy to see why, from Bataille onward, French writing on community in particular has been the product of the identification of community with communism and its attempt to enforce the idea of the nation as a homogeneous entity. In the 21st century, however, the correlation may seem less compelling than it used to appear.

The identification of nation with community originates with Joseph Stalin's 1913 essay on "Marxism and the National Question." Here Stalin begins with customary directness by asking the question "What is a nation?" Since as a progressive Marxist he eschews any traditional identification of nation with race, Stalin chooses a definition most compatible with communism: "A nation is primarily a community, a definite community of people."[7] However, Stalin is taking here what is strictly a non-Marxist position, since for Marx a "real community" can only be achieved with the withering of the state after the achievement of communism. Anything before that, he calls "illusory community."[8] Although Stalin does not mention the illusion, for him the community of a nation is nevertheless certainly designed to be a stage that will in time be transcended by a federation of workers of all nationalities. For now, the nation is defined as a community that possesses a common language, territory, economic life, and "psychological make-up manifested in a community of culture."[9] Claims to nationhood are then assessed according to whether the claimant can fulfill these criteria: So the Jews cannot be a nation because they have no territory or common language; small linguistic groups in the Caucasus cannot be nations because they have no literature. It becomes clear that community is not in itself an attribute of a nation, and never offered as a test as such; rather, a nation has to possess one or more common attributes. Nevertheless, the Stalinist identification of nation with community remains unchallenged. In 1983 it was notably endorsed and made more substantial by Benedict Anderson, whose *Imagined Communities* can from one perspective be said not only to be aligning with Stalin's position, but seeking to resolve the major contradiction within Stalin's text, namely that he never analyzes the nature of a community nor demonstrates how a nation is a community as well as an entity possessing a common language, territory, economic life, and so on. According to any definition of community, a nation is too impossibly large ever to be one. Before Stalin, after all, a nation was not a community but "a people," which is a very different concept. Anderson's idea of the "imagined" community, which he argues develops from the "community of culture" that Stalin proposes, a commonality that, according to both Stalin and Anderson, is particularly generated by the development of the newspaper, is designed to resolve the contradiction within Stalin's account. What can a community really be though, if it is only ever imagined? In what sense, in other words, is a nation a community at all?

Anderson's idea of the "imagined community" as the paradigm of the nation follows the logic not of how a community works, but rather of the nationalist fantasy of how a nation should work. If nations are imagined communities, the community has become the basis for a political formation that belies its own material experience—the nation is only imagined; its people achieve communion with each other only through the mediation of technology: "In the minds of each lives the image of their communion."[10] While Stalin brings together community and communism, Anderson offers a further collation of which Stalin would not have approved, namely of community with communion, based on a certain idea of Christian fellowship before God. Insightful as his analysis is, Anderson remains within the ideological formations of the nationalism he describes, while assuming the identification between community and nation first proposed by Stalin. Nationalism, however, is the impulse that destroys community, as the practice of "communalism" suggests. Nation and community, far from being identifiable, are historically antithetical, above all when the nation becomes a nation-state, at which point it is transformed into the governmentalized, disciplinary regime that communities, and theorists of community, have rebelled against. The imagined community of the nation has historically been a destroyer of actual communities, of the historically achieved modes of intercommunal living. If such communities are always plural, existing in complex relations with each other as communities of dissent, then we can begin to see the conjunction of conflict and toleration that necessarily founds any poetics of community.

II

To consider further how the relation of community with nation might work, let us turn to a snatch of community conversation culled from a discussion that took place in Barney Kiernan's pub in Dublin in 1904. An Irish pub, with its regulars presided over by the landlord ("mine host"), intermingling with a casual trade of occasional drinkers, is certainly a community of a sort. It suggests immediately that while theorists anxiously think in terms of ensuring that the community is open rather than closed, totalized, in practice the boundaries of communities are always indeterminate and open, made up of an interaction between inside and outside as much as the individual. The Dublin among whose many pubs Leopold Bloom circulates during the day could also be called a recognizable community ("Dubliners"), for the city too is an open community, made up of smaller urban communities such as pubs, streets, markets, churches—a place where at a micro-level everyone more or less seems to know everyone else, but in a free, open-ended way, that merges at certain incalculable points into anonymity. The community is not necessarily a collectivity: Indeed, the communities of *Ulysses* are so open that Raymond Williams, brought up in a rural community in Wales, declared that the book contained no communities at all.[11] Yet Williams' own community was not homogeneous either—the village in which he grew up was made up of railway workers and farmers, though he continued to argue that community was a wholly positive term.[12] In the light of Williams' own *The Country and the City* (1973), it is tempting to argue that there are two models of community, that of the country and that of the city, and that while nationalism appropriates the former for its nostalgic fantasy of homogeneity, Joyce offers the city as the model of heterogeneous communities that can never correspond to nationalistic fantasy. However, as we shall see, even the rural community has its own kind of heterogeneity.

What we discover in the "Cyclops" episode of Joyce's *Ulysses* is that the city creates the most fluid, open forms of community, juxtaposing communities contingently and creatively against each other in recusant friction. At the same time, something else emerges that appears all too rarely in the many discussions of community that have taken place in the past hundred, even two hundred years, namely that just as much as offering intimate warmth, communities can also be places where communication of emotional warmth and inner experience does not take place: As soap-opera script writers know better than philosophers, communities can also be places of discord and dissension, of breaking up as much as coming together. Like families, another idealized image of the nation, communities are also primary sites of conflict. Among all the nostalgia that has so often marked the evocation of community, how many have fully experienced its torments?

> Bloom was talking and talking with John Wyse and he quite excited with his dunducketymudcoloured mug on him and his old plumeyes rolling about.

—Persecution, says he, all the history of the world is full of it. Perpetuating national hatred among nations.

—But do you know what a nation means? says John Wyse.

—Yes, says Bloom.

—What is it? says John Wyse.

—A nation? says Bloom. A nation is the same people living in the same place.

—By God, then, says Ned, laughing, if that's so I'm a nation for I'm living in the same place for the last five years.

So of course everyone had a laugh at Bloom and says he, trying to muck out of it:

—Or also living in different places.

—That covers my case, says Joe.

—What is your nation if I may ask? says the citizen.

—Ireland, says Bloom. I was born here. Ireland.

The citizen said nothing only cleared the spit out of his gullet and, gob, he spat a Red Bank oyster out of him right in the corner. . . .[13]

In this episode, James Joyce is staging the conflict between community and nation, demonstrating the intrusion into a pluralistic community of the interrelated ideologies of nation, of *ethnos* and race. Bloom's adversary, known simply as "the citizen," is a fierce Fenian with little pity for other oppressed nations. His militant Irish nationalism has no interest in other disempowered communities, indeed he deploys his antisemitism to attack them because the minority, the immigrant, is regarded as alien to the nation. Historically, the citizen is a portrait of the founder of Sinn Féin, Arthur Griffith, who was an aggressive antisemite as well as a republican revolutionary. Years before Griffith became one of the 1922 signatories of the Anglo-Irish agreement establishing Irish independence, Joyce presents his republicanism not as radical, progressive, or even, despite republicanism's historical association with ideas of liberal egalitarianism, supporting human rights, but as narrow bigotry—the insularity in fact that would become the hallmark of the numbing grip of de Valera's independent Ireland.

Sinn Fein, *Swadeshi*, our own: This account of the nation turns it into a form of property that has been expropriated by the colonial power. Perhaps that is why nationalism of the anticolonial type is most problematic, since it typically defines itself as a form of property that invokes the totality of possession.

Bloom is doubly exposed not only by his reluctance to endorse fully the Fenian position, but also by his Jewishness. He begins by referring to the persecution of others, of minorities, that perpetuates "national hatred among nations." Repeating the word nation, John Wyse demands to know if he knows what a nation really is. Bloom responds with what, technically in relation to the Greek ἔθνος, usually translated as "nation," is a correct definition of a nation—the same people living in the same place.[14] The pub community's laugh at Bloom after Ned's humorous response involves another mode of behavior that conjures community, friendship, and intimacy—having a laugh together. But laughter is an ambivalent form of socialization; it can also be, and often is, teasing, hostile. Laughter hurts, producing the response of attempted reassurance—"I'm only joking." What makes community, bonds people together, involves an activity that often produces hurt in the jokee, even if it bonds the joker and his audience.

Community is not only created by constituting an outside, as is often remarked; it is created by bonding against someone within, through the creation of a scapegoat. This is not necessarily seriously malign—as Freud points out, it happens almost every time someone tells a joke. To be part of a community, you have to learn to "take a joke." But it can become more sinister. In response to the laughter half directed against him, Bloom modifies his definition of a nation with an alternative which alludes to a different kind of nation, the diasporic nation of Israel—the same people living in different places. It is at this point that the citizen pointedly asks him "what is your nation, if I may ask?" Bloom's immediate response, "Ireland," receives no joking riposte; instead, the citizen spits contemptuously. Bloom may be a native of Ireland but he is not Irish so far as the citizen is concerned. He does not share with the citizen what Charles Darwin, in *The Origin of Species* (1859), called "community of descent." His *ethnos* is both a nation and what would now be called a race or ethnicity, and for Bloom, the Jew in Ireland, according to the citizen's nationalist logic, which identifies nation with race, the two do not coincide. A nation, according to the citizen, may be the same people living in the same place, but it is not different people living in the same place, even if they were all born there and interact as part of interrelated communities. The narrowness of the citizen's myopic opinions, the rage that is scarcely hidden below the surface before it erupts into violence, is focused here on the fact that Bloom has a double loyalty, to his country and to his persecuted people. Any double loyalty among citizens was and continues to be regarded as dangerous—in earlier centuries in the British Isles, being a Catholic or a Jew was always regarded as suspect, because your loyalties were also placed in a community beyond the nation.

Today the same logic is applied to Muslims. In the logic of nationalism, everything must be streamlined to produce homogeneity, a single focus and self-identity. There is little room for liberal tolerance or negotiation with difference. The nation moves with uncanny speed, as *ethnos* in the Greek, from a people to the people to whom they are opposed, *ethnikos*.[15] But *ethnikos* only articulates a dialectic that is there already within *ethnos*: It is *ethnos* that is divided within itself, like the nation, like community.

Bloom's definition of nation deliberately eschews the benign ideologies of nationalism, Ernest Renan's characterization of the nation as a soul, for example, with a more banal pragmatic and contingent account—the same people who happen to be living in the same place, as in the city. Bloom's quick-witted response to John Wyse's demand for a description follows closely the first meaning to be found in Liddell and Scott's entry for *ethnos*: "A number of people living together."[16] Ned's joke in response, however, points to the ambiguity in Bloom's definition, introducing the question of temporality, and of sameness and identity. Bloom's use of "the same" rather than Liddell and Scott's "a number of" people introduces a certain ambiguity—are they the same people in the Leibnitzian sense of identity through time, that is, either individuals who remain the same over time by being in the same place (as Ned suggests) or the same unchanging group of people, whose members do not change as they stay in the same place through time? Or is a nation, as the citizen's Sinn Féin slogan—"we ourselves, we ourselves alone!"—implies, the same people in the sense of people who are the same in the sense of the same identity, for example, of the same culture, religion, or ethnicity, whose members may, or may not, individually change? Alongside the question of whether some of those people can come and go, the Greek definition of *ethnos* also leaves out any unit of temporality, that is, of how long the same people have to be in the same place, or how long someone has to live in the same place to become one of "the same"—for example, an outsider such as Bloom.

In the face of the citizen's contempt for his claimed Irishness, Bloom responds more aggressively, deliberately confronting him with his Jewishness:

> —And I belong to a race too, says Bloom, that is hated and persecuted. Also now. This very moment. This very instant. . . . Robbed, says he. Plundered. Insulted. Persecuted. Taking what belongs to us by right. . . .
>
> —Are you talking about the new Jerusalem? says the citizen.
>
> —I'm talking about injustice, says Bloom. . . . But it's no use, says he. Force, hatred, history, all that. That's not life for men and women, insult and hatred. And everybody knows that it's the very opposite of that that is really life.
>
> —What? Says Alf.
>
> —Love, says Bloom. I mean the opposite of hatred.[17]

In the political context of 1904, Bloom argues provocatively that nationalism produces not justice but injustice, that it is energized by hatred—of the English, in the Irish case—and violence, whether the violence, force, of the nationalist state or a revolutionary violence of "the people" that creates it in the first place.[18] Speaking in 1904, in the epoch of rampant antisemitism, Bloom forcefully allies this hatred and violence of nationalism to racism, to the persecution of the Jews. Yet even today racism and nationalism, perversely and provocatively merging in the Greek term *ethnos*, for which there is no modern translation that is not an anachronism, are not generally placed together in their unsavory alliance. The sign of that intimate union historically was the increasing violence with which nationalism transformed community into communalism and produced the destructive dismantling of a system of tolerance within and between communities that had operated for hundreds of years.

"What is your nation if I may ask?" The citizen's pointed question is a more aggressive version of the question that is often asked of migrants who are visibly different from the majority: "Where do you come from?" And even if the answer is like Bloom's, "from here, I was born here," it is followed by another question: "No, I mean where are you really from?" If nation and ethnicity merge into each other, are often identified with each other, so too the minority will often be, or be characterized as, a migrant. And it is as a migrant that Joyce offers a parodic farewell to an imaginary Bloom who is now leaving Ireland to return to the Jewish quarter in Budapest from which his grandfather Lipóti Virag originally came, written in the overwritten celebratory style of a newspaper account. It is at this point that the only use of the word "community" in *Ulysses* occurs—broached provocatively in the language of journalistic platitude: "The ceremony which went off with great *éclat* was characterized by the most affecting cordiality. An illuminated scroll of ancient Irish vellum, the work of Irish artists, was presented to the distinguished phenomenologist on behalf of a large section of the community. . . ."[19]

III

Sicherheit schaffen—to create security: Against the foreground of Bloom's expulsion from the pub by the nationalist citizen who threatens to crucify him, Joyce places a long ironic farewell description in which the fugitive Bloom is deported and repatriated to the land of his immigrant grandfather, to "Szazharminczbrojugulyas-Dugulas (Meadow of Murmuring Waters)." Here Joyce throws in a wild card that takes us in a different but provocative direction. The parenthesis after the Hungarian name leads us to assume that it offers a translation into English, but here this is not the case. Szazharminczbrojugulyas-Dugulas has been literally translated as "constipation caused by one hundred and thirty portions of veal goulash,"[20] but its more genial false translation, "Meadow of Murmuring Waters," transports us in a very different direction to an earlier location of the wandering Jew, the city of Córdoba in the 10th century—described by a British historian in 1900 as "the most beautiful, the most magnificent, the most luxurious, the most civilized city of Medieval Europe in the tenth century."[21] The "Meadow of Murmuring Waters" was one of the many gardens of the city. The extraordinary cultural, scientific, and intellectual world of Córdoba has already been evoked earlier in *Ulysses* by Stephen Dedalus when, while proving by algebra that Shakespeare's ghost was Hamlet's grandfather, he thinks of the Islamic culture from which algebra sprang, and thence of Córdoba's two most famous philosophers, the Arab philosopher Averroes, author of *The Incoherence of the Incoherence*, and the Jewish philosopher Moses Maimonides, author of *The Guide for the Perplexed*.

Joyce's allusions to the material and intellectual splendors of Al-Andalus in the context of Bloom's experience of antisemitism in contemporary Ireland is particularly pertinent as part of an episode demonstrating the perils of a community where nationalist sentiments begin to intrude. Bloom's return to the Meadow of Murmuring Waters reminds the reader of an often-forgotten part of European history that remains particularly relevant today with respect to relations between different communities, the same but different people living in the same place. Joyce was unusual in the early part of the 20th century in invoking the image of the golden age of Al-Andalus under the rule of the Caliphate of Córdoba (929–1031).[22] In fact, the remnants of the Islamic culture that had created it were, at the time of the writing of *Ulysses*, just about to be dismantled. Today, when liberal tolerance is associated with Western values and intolerant fanaticism with the Islamic world, it is rarely acknowledged that Europe's greatest achievement in communities living together at peace occurred under the Caliphates and subsequent Ottoman rule that lasted for over a thousand years.

The cultural pluralism of, in today's terms, multiethnic living-together constituted in Al-Andalus an unparalleled instance of a tolerant society. The distinction of the Umayyad, Abbasid, and Ottoman empires was to produce cities of cultural mixture. Given its often vast geographic extent, the task of empire has typically been to manage diversity rather than to attempt to impose homogeneity on the lines of the nation. Although Christians and Jews, the "people of the book," did not live in a state of full equality with Muslims, and had to pay specific taxes, the conditions for Jews, for example, under the Caliphates were far more generous and more tolerant than any that could be found in the Christian world of that time, or long after. In Joyce's day Córdoba had long since been subsumed within a Christian Spain whose religious diversity had been remorselessly diminished by the expulsion of the Jews, Muslims, and even Marranos, policed and enforced by the Spanish Inquisition. But a version of that culture still existed even then in the great cosmopolitan cities of the Mediterranean, Alexandria, Baghdad, Salonica, Smyrna. All those cities would be transformed by the principles of the ethnic homogeneity of the nation between 1919 and the 1950s, involving in most cases the expulsion of ethnic minorities, forced migration of millions of people, in order to produce the appropriate sameness of the nation state. Nowhere more so than in this enforced ethnicization of the nation state were the historical realities of community living more opposed to the imaginary community of the nation.

What can we learn from Islamic practices of cultural diversity and tolerance? Diversity involves tolerance, and tolerance involves a certain amount of suffering: putting up with others' differences, even having to suffer them. The idea of the nation, on the other hand, whether nationalist or Stalinist, presumes an essential non-conflictual compatibility that makes tolerance unnecessary and redundant. It is also radically at odds with the idea of democracy, the institutional basis of which is constituted by a formal procedure for mediating conflict, dissent, and difference of opinion: the election. For this reason, the idea of tolerance within a structure of difference is also necessarily fundamental to democracy. As George Simmel argued, even "conflict could be a basis of social integration in modern society" leading to the formation of "a web or network of diverse group affiliations which does not depend on common values."[23] The problem with nationalism and its idea of nation has been that by conflating "a people" with "a community," the idea of a necessary homogeneity was then forced onto states made up of multiple, heterogeneous communities so as to create the new nations of ethnic nationalism. All this Joyce anticipates in his unpacking of the charged antithesis between community and *ethnos* when the latter has been subsumed into the modern idea of the nation. By 1922, the time of the publication of *Ulysses*, the ideology of the nation and its ethnic homogeneity was in full flow: After the Armenian genocide, and the chaos of refugees in postwar Europe who were the wrong people in the wrong place for their new nation,[24] the Treaty of Lausanne the following year in 1923 could be said to have formed the high, or perhaps the low, point of ethnic nationalism, for the treaty involved an agreement between Greece and Turkey to give up territorial claims based on the location of their respective ethnic communities and instead to institute the first international agreement to forcibly transport different ethnic groups into the same place as their own "communities": Greece and Turkey engaged in an exchange of populations—over a million Greeks moved from Turkey, and around 400,000 Turks left Greece.[25]

The Treaty of Lausanne created the possibility of artificially creating nations by engineering a forced mass movement of their populations—a procedure that would become the hallmark of the creation of many nation-states. The agreement constituted the legal prototype for the communal ethnicization of nations in the 20th century—the Nazi extermination of the Jews of Europe, the partitions of India, Israel-Palestine, Cyprus, the more recent forms of "ethnic cleansing" following the breakup of Yugoslavia, the state-sponsored pogrom of Muslims in Gujarat in 2002, the almost continuous persecution of the Roma in Europe since the Nazi era. The treaty of Lausanne gave international legal sanction to the ideology and practice of ethnic cleansing, with its underlying assumption that different communities could not live together, and that any community could only exist happily in the larger imagined community of a nation-state constructed in its own image. The cities of Salonica in Greece and Smyrna in Turkey, which had existed with mixed populations for many hundreds of years, were transformed from multicultural into monocultural cities. In the ashes of Smyrna, burned down in 1922, and the fire of ethnic identifications, went the memory of centuries of the lived intercultural *milieu* of the Ottoman and Islamic systems.[26] The community of dissent had been challenged, and vanquished, by nationalism's community of descent in which community was identified solely with ethnicity.

In relation to colonial Ireland, Joyce also articulates the discrepancy between practices of community and the imagined nation: As Partha Chatterjee suggests, this was articulated in the colonial period when the idea that subject peoples could not constitute a nation was based on the assumption that they were made up of a set of incompatible communities or tribes.[27] Instead of the singular imagined community of the European nation, differences within and between communities in the colony came to justify, rather in the manner of Stalin's disqualifications, the rejection of any claim to nationhood. The subsequent partition of British India was arguably the result of the fact that British Indian nationalists, in the period after the Treaty of Lausanne, themselves came to believe in the nationalist imaginary identification of a nation with a single community. In practice, this colonial attitude continues unabated today, even in the subcontinent: While "the nation" is still imagined as a singular unity, it is nevertheless qualified by the presence of those who do not belong to this singularity and are classified according to different ethnic communities (in Europe) or Scheduled Castes, tribes, and "backward castes" (in India). The state then attempts to rule, as in the colonial period, by liaising with a number of assumed "leaders of the community." Yet even here, there is no logical reason why all members of a particular ethnicity make up a single community; it is just that the state itself or the media enforces their membership on the assumption that they must ipso facto be different from the homogeneous majority.

While the historical documentation of many earlier historical events or processes, such as the destruction of the great cosmopolitan cities of the Ottoman Empire, is well established, the discrepant relation of community to the creation of new nations has received far less analysis. No one, however, has better shown the ways in which communities of different peoples who, despite their inevitable conflicts, had evolved a way of living together, sharing their lives together, then slowly hardened in their attitudes toward each other and transformed their relations under the aegis of nationalist ideology, than the writers of the Partition novels about the creation of India and Pakistan. To mention but two, Kushwat Singh's *Train to Pakistan* (1956) and Bapsi Sidwa's *Ice Candy Man* (1991), both patiently chart the destructive effect on two communities of the communal division of the nation. Both novels present portraits of specific small communities, one rural, one urban. Despite differences of religion between Sikhs, Muslims, and Hindus, in each case the individuals who make up such communities operate in workable and effective ways in which difference is known and acknowledged but not regarded as a signal of incompatibility or incommensurability in the everyday practices of village or local city life. In fact, as the novels show, many of the personal relationships cross over any such boundaries: The communities are constituted through the accepted differences between individuals and families, even if they are conflictual. However, as the time draws near when the two new nations, divided according to religions, are created, individuals within each community feel pressured to affiliate themselves with one side or the other, and the equitable personal relations that have hitherto obtained between them begin to break down and quickly turn to violence. These novels do not idealize the community in relation to the nation, but powerfully show that community's conflictual politics was essentially workable, whereas community identified with nation is fundamentally unworkable, or inoperative, *désoeuvrement*.

IV

If we deny the Stalinist tendency, and separate community from nation, how do they work (or diswork) without that misidentification? In this context, I want to conclude by considering the work of another Irish writer, the contemporary Irish poet Bernard O'Donoghue. O'Donoghue suggests that while communities do work, after a fashion, they only become self-conscious about themselves through interruptions. It is only the common interruption that paradoxically creates the community around specific events. As can often be found in fiction, the narrative of a community falters, hinges on moments of life and death, accident and disaster, leaving and undoing. Everyone who is part of a community in a sense exists in a precarious and tangential relation to it because the community itself is a space of disturbance, disjunction, and dissolution. It is as much about discontinuity as continuity, separation and disconnection as union, conflict as harmony, silence as speech. Community is the interruption of silence, of moments of inarticulacy, of stuttering, the things you cannot say, of non-communication.

O'Donoghue writes much, though not exclusively, about the community in which he grew up, Cullen, near Cork in Ireland. At one level, his poetry is dedicated to celebrating the lives, the knowledge, the emotions, of those who for the most part slip in and out of history, leaving no trace, and who, certainly from the perspective of academic knowledge, remain invisible, or at most objects of a certain kind of statistical knowledge. Much of his poetry is preoccupied with memory, and memorializing the living and the dead, the dear departed, as the phrase goes, those who arrive and then suddenly take their leave according to the incidental moments of birth and death. In general, readers of his poems have never heard of those who are being memorialized before reading the poem. These are, as it were, anonymous people, subalterns to use the way academics might now describe them, people not without history but whose history does not get recorded.

Their immediate context is very clear: They are the people of Dev's—de Valera's—Ireland, the severe, pinched, and impoverished Ireland that followed for many decades after independence. O'Donoghue offers us in his poems people—not just the individual observing eye which has become the norm for much contemporary poetry which records a series of moments in the poet's individual and special sensibility. O'Donoghue does offer us that, but there is more than just the individual isolated poet in his poetry. He writes about others and manages to make them subjects in both senses, at once public and private.

We might imagine too quickly that O'Donoghue is a poet of community in a traditional sense, as in the rich warmth of many of Seamus Heaney's poems. O'Donoghue celebrates, without in any sense sentimentalizing, the richness, poverty, wisdom, foolishness, and humor of the lives of ordinary people, but also presents to us in a matter-of-fact way their struggles and moments of defeat, the violence of hardship, the frequent violence of masculinity that accompanies it, the emotional repression, punctuated with sudden violent moments of emotional expression, together with the long communal wealth of shared lives. His poems are not only peopled but also unusual because they are peopled in moments of unanticipated drama, which provides the focal point and *raison d'être* of the story that is being told. Within the poem this is its function, but we are also told that it is precisely the dramatic interruption which constitutes the community as a series of moments, not a processual reciprocal organism. This is the eventful rather than the uneventful community, and it is the interruptive event itself which creates the community according to its arbitrary staccato rhythm. Take a poem like "Ceo Draiochta (Magic Mist)," which narrates the story of the day Matt Bridgie fell into the threshing drum during harvest time. The slow lead-up to the moment of the accident when Bridgie's scream heard two miles away is followed by an anticlimax of deliberate bathos:

> That was it really. A man passing
> From town tied a belt around the leg
> And administered a cigarette.
> Pieces of rubber from the Wellington
> And clots of sock were scraped
> From the hopper. Ultimately
> Some compensation was paid, enough
> For a rudimentary false leg
> And a few rounds of drinks.
> Matt showed signs of a latent
> Family talent for composing verse,
> And often sang well past closing time.[28]

The poem is presented as a narrative of the community, a local legend. You are halfway into the poem before you are told that the poet himself was one of those at school two miles away, and so experienced "that famous day" only in hearing the scream. All the detail which we are given has been recounted from other retellings, a communal perspective which reabsorbs Matt himself as his accident gives him a certain stature which he subsequently develops as a poet and singer in the local pub. It is not a tragic event in anyone's eyes, however much anyone feels the shock at the time. Rather, it is part of an intermittent violence that does not so much reanimate the community and communal feeling as create the community, becoming part of its mythology, the common in which everyone shares, which is both public and private at once. The mythologizing might lead us to think of the community as a continuous narrative, but what the poem offers is one of a series of disasters—and it is these that, as is said, paradoxically "bring the community together" at its moment of interruption, and perform the space of the common. What is unstated in that clichéd phrase is that the community only realizes itself momentarily in such traumatic moments that create its narrative of creation and dissolution. The community is brought together and then, in an inevitable systolic rhythm, opens its valves and moves apart again.

It is poems like "Ceo Draiochta (Magic Mist)," "Concordiam in Populo," or "The Mule Duignan" that make us realize that what is really necessary is not so much to deconstruct the community but rather to start to understand the complex structures of emotion and behavior that community involves. Rather as people tend to associate India with nonviolence because of Gandhi, without realizing that Gandhi's doctrine of nonviolence was necessary and only meaningful because India was and is such a violent country, our idea of the nonviolence and coziness of community misunderstands what community is trying to achieve—to alleviate the violence intrinsic to its social formation. This is what O'Donoghue perceives so tellingly. He writes frequently about the larger everyday violence of life, which some people, such as "O'Regan the Amateur Anatomist," the subject of an early poem, intermittently repeat, or others, as in the portrait of the father saving the crow or the wounded rabbit in "Gunpowder," attempt to ameliorate and assuage. In every case, O'Donoghue also makes us aware of a certain unethical relation to others that forms part of living in a community—especially in relation to those on its fringes, and here we are reminded of Bloom in *Ulysses*. One poem, "Unknownst to the People," is especially compelling in this regard, where the poet focuses on the appearance of a family of travelers camping at the edge of the village, who come and go without trace, unwelcomed, unembraced, and unknown. Their exclusion is lightly compared to the notorious Catholic Penal Laws in the reference to Art O'Leary, who, in a complicated story, was lawfully shot in 1773 because he had refused to sell his horse to a Protestant for five pounds. The compassion and interest shown here in this traveling family, the lived details of their ordinary lives as well as their elusive coming and going, the sense of embarrassment that the locals feel when speaking about them, conjures an important ethical and political challenge. This moving poem questions how individuals and communities can sustain themselves through denial and an unethical relation to the world outside themselves that has such a long provenance in colonial history.

But the point is that it is not just that those in the community do not reach out to those who live at the fringes of their world. They do not reach out to each other. A final poem, "Ter Conatus (Three Times He Made the Attempt)," is the story of a sister and brother who have farmed together for sixty years, "never touching once." In old age she develops cancer, but it is diagnosed too late, and the brother, living so long without expressing himself, finds himself altogether inexperienced in the emotional intimacy and support that should be the foundation of his new role of carer for his sister. After she has died, the neighbors notice sympathetically that the farm is being neglected:

> . . . the rolled-up bales, standing
> Silent in the fields, with the aftergrass
> Growing into them, and wondered what he could
> Be thinking of: which was that evening when,
> Almost breaking with a lifetime of
> Taking real things for shadows,
> He might have embraced her with a brother's arms.[29]

"With the aftergrass / Growing into them": While celebrating the common of the communal, O'Donoghue's poetry never lets us forget that its warmth comes often at the cost of its lack and denial, its repression and emotion unexpressed and unsaid. That is also community—the hesitation, deferment, emotional denial, the moment of stuttering inarticulacy, in the unspoken common.

NOTES

1. Jean-Luc Nancy, *The Inoperative Community*, 3.

2. Giorgio Agamben, *The Coming Community*; Georges Bataille, *The Obsessions of Georges Bataille: Community and Communication* and *Visions of Excess: Selected*

Writings, 1927–1939; Maurice Blanchot, *The Unavowable Community*; Jean-Luc Nancy, *The Inoperative Community*, *Being Singular Plural*, and "The Confronted Community."

3. Cf. Nancy, *Being Singular Plural.*

4. Agamben, *The Coming Community*, 85.

5. Nancy, *The Inoperative Community*, 156.

6. Cf. Stefanos Geroulanos, *An Atheism That Is Not Humanist Emerges in French Thought.*

7. Joseph Stalin, *Marxism and the National and Colonial Question*, 5. It could be argued that Stalin is invoking a longer tradition of identification of community and state that goes back to Hegel's *Elements of the Philosophy of Right* (1820). While there is not space to elaborate this further here, it should be remarked that while Stalin identifies community with the nation in the realm of the prepolitical (for it is only in becoming a nation that the community achieves the right of self-determination), Hegel does not identify the state with the community, arguing instead that the civic community, as the realm of difference intermediate between the family and the state, is itself a product of the state. It is this conception that allowed later commentators, notably Karl Popper, to criticize Hegel for anticipating 20th-century totalitarianism. Cf. Z. A. Pelczynski, *The State and Civil Society.*

8. Karl Marx and Frederick Engels, *The German Ideology*, 83. Cf. Kenneth A. Megill, "The Community in Marx's Philosophy."

9. Stalin, *Marxism and the National Question*, 8.

10. Benedict Anderson, *Imaginary Communities: Reflections on the Origins and Spread of Nationalism*, 6.

11. Cf. Emer Nolan, *James Joyce and Nationalism*, 85.

12. Cf. Raymond Williams, *Keywords: A Vocabulary of Culture and Society* and "The Importance of Community."

13. James Joyce, *Ulysses*, 429–30.

14. The entry for the Greek ἔθνος in Liddell and Scott gives

> A number of people living together.
> 2. after Homer, nation, people
> b. later, foreign, barbarous nations, opp. to Hellenes
> 3. class of men, caste, tribe
> II. Of a single person, a relation

15. Cf. Gayatri C. Spivak, *Death of a Discipline*, 82.

16. Henry George Liddell and Robert Scott, *A Greek-English Lexicon.*

17. Joyce, *Ulysses*, 431–32.

18. Cf. Georges Sorel, *Reflections on Violence*; Nikolaj Lübecker, *Community, Myth and Recognition in Twentieth-Century French Literature and Thought*, 7.

19. Joyce, *Ulysses*, 445.

20. Andrew Gibson, *Joyce's Revenge: History, Politics and Aesthetics in Ulysses*, 122.

21. Ulick Ralph Burke, *A History of Spain, from the Earliest Times to the Death of Ferdinand the Great*, 167.

22. Tolerance and the culture of Al-Andalus is discussed in a related context in my "Postcolonial Remains." On the Ottoman Empire, see Suraiya Faroqhi, *The Ottoman Empire and the World Around It.*

23. Gerard Delanty, *Community*, 53; George Simmel, "Conflict and the Structure of the Group."

24. Cf. Hannah Arendt, *The Origins of Totalitarianism*, 269–90.

25. Cf. Bruce Clark, *Twice a Stranger: How Mass Expulsion Forged Modern Greece and Turkey.*

26. Marjorie Housepian Dobkin, *Smyrna 1922: The Destruction of a City*; Giles Milton, *Paradise Lost: Smyrna 1922—The Destruction of Islam's City of Tolerance*; Mark Mazower, *Salonica, City of Ghosts: Christians, Muslims and Jews.*

27. Partha Chatterjee, *The Nation and Its Fragments: Colonial and Postcolonial Histories*, 224. Cf. Chatterjee, "Community in the East."

28. Bernard O'Donoghue, *Selected Poems*, 50.

29. Ibid., 89.

A METONYMIC COMMUNITY? TOWARD A POETICS OF CONTINGENCY

THOMAS CLAVIEZ

INTRODUCTION

In his 2001 book with the programmatic title *Community: Seeking Safety in an Insecure World*, Zygmunt Bauman sketches in an almost stereotypical way a concept of community, one that not only seems to be far away, sunken into history, but that, for all that we know, might never actually have existed: a community that is both "distinctive" and "indistinct" (or even "undistinguished") in that it (a) distinguishes itself from all other groups around it, but (b) does not evince any noticeable distinctions within itself: "[T]here are no 'betwixt and between' cases left, it is crystal clear who is 'one of us' and who is not, there is no muddle and no cause for confusion—no cognitive ambiguity, and so no behavioural ambivalence" (12). And a short glance into the history of political theory—from Aristotle's *Politics* to Hobbes' *Leviathan*, Rousseau's *Social Contract* and Locke's *Two Treatises on Government* to Tönnies' *Community and Society*—confirms this dialectic. Community, be it conceived as *polis*, commonwealth, or the state, finds its justification in its alleged ability to overcome what are, in fact, *two contingencies*: One contingency—exposure to an imagined or real *outside* enemy, who might strike at any point—is overcome by a presumed simultaneous reduction of a second contingency *within* the community; it is this latter contingency that Bauman subsumes under "cognitive ambiguity" and "behavioural ambivalence."

The concepts of *communitas* and *immunitas*, as developed by Roberto Esposito,[1] are two intricately (in fact, dialectically) connected phenomena as regards our social life, as all communities try to immunize themselves against contingencies from within and from without. Whether, as I pointed out above, such a community "without muddle or cause for confusion" ever existed, begs the question: Indeed, especially Tönnies' reflections on the topic—which, if one only looks closely enough, are simply a rehash of Aristotle with a few Romantic ingredients—should by now be read for their symptomatic, rather than analytic, quality. But whether or not we take the existence or possibility of such a community for granted, or whether we simply add it to the Derridean folder of the "myth of the engineer," what remains is that community is still being conceived as one of the bulwarks against contingency. Ironically, the well-known strategies of "social engineering" and "rational choice," which have become the leading paradigms within sociology, try to restore, by rational means, what the myth of the "ur-community" considered as a given: a certain homogeneity that, however, seems lost forever, as even Bauman feels forced to admit—if, as I said, it ever existed.

What I would like to do in what follows is to pursue this topic of contingency, by means of three observations that pertain to it—three aspects that will hopefully allow me to carve out, and to throw into relief, its significance for an assessment of what I would like to call a post-subjective or post-identitarian community. If, as Jock Young claims—whom Bauman quotes—"as community collapses, identity is invented,"[2] we have reached a point where not only has the concept of identity, in turn, come under pressure, but where the relationship between identity and (new forms of) community is being reassessed. And both the reassessments of the single terms, as well as their relationship, can be defined along the concept of contingency that—if in different shades, and with different emphases—in my view has to date informed a whole range of approaches and philosophical enterprises; its traces can be discerned not only in the work of Esposito, but also in the oeuvres of Jean-Luc Nancy, Giorgio Agamben, Judith Butler, and Maurice Blanchot, to name just a few.

COMMUNITY AND/AS CONTINGENCY

Before I attempt to identify, collect, and eventually combine these traces, let me return to the three phenomena mentioned above. The first is the rather paradoxical role that contingency has played throughout human history: paradoxical because, on the one hand, at least since the advent of the Enlightenment, we have narrated human history as the genealogy and succession of presumably ever more successful and sophisticated strategies to overcome contingency—usually along the trajectory of myth, monotheism, and reason, each one claiming a larger explanatory power than its predecessors as regards our environment. On the other hand, if there exists any term that is evoked in relation to, and captures our experience of, modernity, it *is* contingency. And just a short glimpse of the titles of works that have tried, in the last two decades, to address or diagnose the status quo of a modern, postmodern, and globalizing world suffices to realize that the feeling of an increased and increasing contingency is the order of the day. Besides Bauman's *Community: Seeking Safety in an Insecure World*, what comes to mind is Pierre Bourdieu's work on *précarité*,[3] as well as Ulrich Beck's *Risk Society* or Judith Butler's *Precarious Life*.

Now, if we take these two observations together—the narrative of the succession of allegedly ever more powerful strategies to overcome contingency, and the rise of an ever more acute, felt contingency—then we are forced either to declare human history a huge failure, or to reconceptualize the role that contingency plays within it. One such reconceptualization may imply that some of the strategies we have devised to overcome contingencies might have actively created, or unwittingly led to, even more, though different, contingencies in other walks of life. What we, in the light of what I said above, may also take into account is that, besides the three master strategies mentioned—myth, religion, and reason—community itself constitutes another strategy to overcome contingency in its own right; whether it is more or less successful than the others is a question I will come back to.

Before I do, I would like to address the second paradox correlated to contingency: that of its definition, and of its status within the Western metaphysical tradition. Here is how the *Oxford Dictionary of Philosophy* defines necessary and contingent truth:

> A necessary truth is one that could not have been otherwise. It would have been true under all circumstances. A contingent truth is one that is true, but could have been false. A necessary truth is one that must be true; a contingent truth is one that is true as it happens, or as things are, but that did not have to be true. . . .

> A permanent philosophical urge is to diagnose contingency as disguised necessity . . . although especially in the 20th century there have been equally powerful movements, especially associated with Quine, denying that there are substantive necessary truths, instead regarding necessity as disguised contingency. (257)[4]

This wonderful definition captures, in a nutshell, the troublesome role that contingency has played, and continues to play, in our theoretical considerations. Though rather inconspicuous, a closer look at this definition makes one realize that it actually *performs* rather than describes contingency, as two mutually exclusive definitions of contingency (and definitions always imply a truth claim) are contingent upon each other, and in fact cancel each other out. It is as if contingency seems to contaminate the very truth that, in this definition, it is both juxtaposed with and, *qua* definition, claims to endorse.

This brings me to the third paradox, which is neither a historical nor an epistemological, but rather a semantic one. And here, too, we notice contingency's almost uncanny ability to evade being nailed down to any truth(s). Its Latin root *contingo* comprises, according to the *PONS Online Dictionary*, the following meanings: to touch, to moisten, to grasp, to eat, to enjoy, to reach one's goal, to bounce against something, to be concerned about something, to be poisoned or contaminated by something, to blemish or to stain something, something that "occurs" to me (also in the German sense of "*widerfahren*"), and something that just so happens. Moreover, *contingo* is etymologically contiguous with, and "contaminated" by, *contagio*, which, in turn, can mean to contaminate, to touch, to influence, to approach, to infect, or to serve as a bad example.[5]

Thus, all definitional "examples" of *contingo* or *contagio* not only mean, but *are* "bad examples," as they touch, contaminate, infect, blemish, and bounce against each other in an abysmal and contradictory semantic vertigo. Again, contingency thus not only designates the concept "contingency"—it genuinely *performs* it. And *vis-à-vis* its great antagonist—necessary truth—it retains and performs its own truth/untruth, serving, as it does, as the crutch, a stand-in, for all the occasions where truth simply cannot (at least as yet) be ascertained.

Now, what has all of that to do with community? Well, first of all, community, as I have already pointed out, serves, and has always been considered to serve, as a counterforce against "contingencies" of all sorts: either, in its Aristotelian variety, to safeguard us against the barbarians before the gates or, in its Hobbesian variety, to tame the wolves that we are to each other with the help of an overwolf called Leviathan. If, however, one thing has become clear, it is that, in Aristotle's *polis*, the exclusion of those diagnosed with *apaideusia*—that is, with not "doing things as they are usually done," which Bauman calls "behavioural ambivalence"—by no means serves to make the community in the *polis* coherent and homogeneous, as still about 80 percent of its inhabitants are excluded from having a say in the city.[6] And it is quite striking that even Jacques Rancière (so intent on providing those who have no part in society with a voice) prefers to exclude the *phaulos*—the warmongering stranger who, in Aristotle's view, threatens the community of the *polis*—from his consideration.[7]

Nor can we, with Hobbes, be sure, as Esposito has so brilliantly shown, that all wolfishness disappears under the auspices of an omnipotent Leviathan to whom, if anything, the community subjects itself to then re-invoke the Aristotelian scenario of the spectral enemy outside (while, interestingly, the most spectral cause for contingency is now the overwolf Leviathan itself). Both attempts to exclude the other, the stranger, them, from "us" and our confines—our shared borders—not only fail to provide security from contingency, they also "close" or "wall us in" with strangers or wolves, and thus heighten rather than lower the potential contingencies within. That is why for Aristotle, Rousseau, Hobbes, and, to an extent, even Locke, consensus is the sine qua non of any community.

In order to overcome this potential source of contingency that, especially in the era of the national state, has been at its roots right from the start, we have tended to tell ourselves narratives that allegedly prove a common ground, a shared history, or even a "destiny"—a term that Heidegger also falls back upon. Heidegger is of importance here because he is the most prominent philosophical voice to remind us that being is always also—and already—Being-with. Now, Heidegger's Being-with—that is, being contiguous, and thus contingent upon—lays the ground for thinking of our being (and being in general) as by default contingent. Indeed, he forces us to think ontology as co-ontology, or even "con-tology," if the neologism be permitted. In *Being and Time*, Heidegger states:

> By reason of this *with-like* [*mithaften*] Being-in-the-world, the world is always the one that I share with Others. The world of Dasein is a *with-world* [*Mitwelt*]. Being-in is Being-with Others. Their Being-in-themselves within-the-world is *Dasein-with* [*Mit-dasein*]. (155).

As Esposito has convincingly shown in *Communitas*, this means that the community of Being-with that Heidegger evokes has to be thought of in a radically negative, nonessential, and nonsubstantial vein:

> . . . [T]he community needs to be understood literally as "coincidence" [that is, as contingency, T.C.], as a falling *together* . . . , with the warning that such a fall, the "being-thrown" . . . , is not to be taken as the precipitous fall from a condition of prior fullness but as the sole and original condition of our existence. (95)

—the condition that Jean-Luc Nancy defines as "exposure."[8] What is so pertinent to our case at hand is that the ethics of "letting be" that Heidegger proposes refers to the very potentiality of those we are with:

> Dasein's resoluteness towards itself is what first makes it possible to let the Others who are with it "be" in their ownmost potentiality-for-Being, and to co-disclose this potentiality in the solicitude which leaps forth and liberates. When Dasein is resolute, it can become the "conscience" of Others. (344)

This potentiality, I would argue, has to be read in the vicinity of contingency, as the not-yet of potentiality embraces the may-be but may-be-not of contingency, and in turn takes place in a context of a "co-incidence" of these potentialities. However, as I have shown elsewhere, Heidgger's concept of "conscience" is deeply compromised, as it does not extend to the other, but only to the truthfulness toward one's own authentic potentiality of being, that is, to the heritage of the community. That is why Heidegger himself seems unable to bear the sheer and pure contingency and potentiality of a community of being-with; and in this, he continues the romantic thread of Tönnies. Indeed, he feels forced, at the end of *Being and Time*, to resort to contingency as the "destiny" that we have encountered above (note that in the German original "fate" means *Schicksal*, while "destiny" translates as *Geschick*):

> But if fateful Dasein, as Being-in-the-world, exists essentially in Being-with Others, its historizing is a co-historizing and is determinative for it

> as *destiny* [*Geschick*]. This is how we designate the historizing of the community, of a people. Destiny is not something that puts itself together out of individual fates. . . . (436)

—*à propos* of which Esposito remarks: "We know the unforeseen and indeed utterly ruinous consequences that Heidegger will suffer some years later, when that destined community will take on the national traits of a 'true German community'" (*Communitas*, 98).[9] That we do; but what is at stake here is also the transformation of "fate" (as contingent potentiality) into "destiny" (as teleological narrative); and only this destiny, in Heidegger's view, constitutes the "full authentic historizing of Dasein" (436). For a community to "occur"—that is, for it to have left its state of contingent possibility and achieved actuality—it has to narrate its own, contingent roots and original *potentia* as a teleological narrative designed to overcome contingency by means of (which means to reformulate it as) necessity, which turns the passive *Schicksal* (fate) into active *Geschick* (destiny). This term *Geschick*, too, comprises a rather ambiguous semantic field, as it combines the two etymologies of *geschickt*, one being the passive one that something has been sent to me, the other designating being skilled or artful.[10]

If anything, in a globalized world like ours, and after the abuses of the Nazi regime, such destiny has become thoroughly questionable; and indeed, more and more, our neighbors are not as "necessary" as they might have been in earlier, more tightly-knit communities. Our neighbors have become less "destined" than "fateful" or "accidental"—contingent, that is—constituting what Judith Butler, in a recent article, has called "populations living in conditions of unwilled adjacency" ("Precarious Life, Vulnerability, and the Ethics of Cohabitation," 134). This globalized world, according to Esposito, is characterized by another paradox: On the one hand, while "[t]he more human beings, as well as ideas, languages, and technologies, communicate and are bound up with one another, the more necessary preventative immunization as a counterweight becomes" (*Terms of the Political*, 60); on the other hand, "globalization also expresses the definitive closure of the immunitary system onto itself" (*Terms of the Political*, 46). This paradox might explain why such closure is far from achieved. As regards the concept of contingency, this immunitary system has succeeded in reducing the rich semantic field surrounding contingency to its contaminating, poisoning, infectious connotations, ridding it of its more positive ones such as touch, newness, concern, or enjoyment.

A new concept of community would have to turn this semantic usurpation around; I am not sure, however, if all the exclusively negative emphasis on risk, precariousness, and an insecure world that are being evoked so incessantly are at all helpful in this regard. If we live, as we increasingly do, in "conditions of unwilled adjacency," I would suggest that we start thinking about community as metonymic.

THE METONYMIC COMMUNITY

In such metonymic communities, we share nothing but the sheer space of the earth's surface—something that Kant already knew we did—in which we are contiguous and contingent upon each other; we do not, as traditional, metaphoric conceptualizations suggest, share a third that implies either a transcendent abstraction, an essence, or a dynastic and patriarchic genealogy.[11] Contrary to metaphor, in which the tenor and the vehicle retain their purity by means of this third which connects one to the other, in the case of metonymy, as a short glimpse into poetry and prose reveals, tenor and vehicle in fact contaminate each other, and neither retains its "purity." That is why, whereas a radical metaphor might be hard to decipher, a radical metonymy is simply unthinkable. This might be one reason for the fact that a community, conceived along the lines of metonymy, is indeed "unavowable," as Maurice Blanchot has called it. In metonymy, the outside is indeed also the inside, as both tenor and vehicle share, but also occupy and *are* the space that they share. This is what I take Esposito to mean when he talks about the "metonymical contagion that is spread [*si comunica*] to all the members of the community and to the community as a whole" (*Communitas*, 122).

As I have argued elsewhere,[12] no poet has given a more metonymic description of modern society than the godfather of modernist poetry, Walt Whitman, whose endless lists dramatize, if anything, the contiguity and contingency that characterize our modern experience, and whose "imperial self"—the one metaphorical remnant in his poetry—is stretched to the limit to contain the contagious co-presence of sheer difference.[13] It can come as no surprise that Gilles Deleuze chose Whitman as the potential poet to evoke a non-totalizing whole that leaves the fragments that constitute it intact.[14] I would argue, however, that this is only part of the truth, in that the one reason why these fragments do *not* seem to contaminate each other—as they are prone to do in a metonymy—is that the omnivorous poetic self of Whitman immunizes them against each other. However, Whitman indeed often comes close to what Deleuze and Guattari, in *A Thousand Plateaus*, have called "a fascination for the pack" (to which Esposito alludes at the end of *Third Person*) and "for multiplicity": "A fascination for the outside? Or is the multiplicity that fascinates us already related to a multiplicity dwelling within us?"[15] To which Esposito adds: "But this also means plurivocity, metamorphosis, contamination—and preventive critique of any claim to hereditary, ethnic, or racial purity" (*Third Person*, 150).

The Whitman of the later *Democratic Vistas*, however, sees such a "contaminated" and impure community in a different light, as he complains about "cities, crowded with petty grotesques, malformations, phantoms, playing meaningless antics" (12). It is indeed useful, as Esposito admonishes us in *Communitas*, "to consider that *communis* (always referring to its earliest meaning) meant, in addition to 'vulgar' and 'of the people,' also 'impure': 'dirty services' [*sordida munera*]" (16). The impurity and the sordidness reappear once the imperial poetic self of Whitman is replaced by Whitman the distant (and disillusioned) observer.

Arguably, another famous literary figure—which recently has received a surprising amount of attention—is Melville's "Bartleby," whose "meaningless antics" and "behavioural ambivalences" do, indeed, create a lot of "cognitive ambiguity" for those around him. It is as if Melville, accidentally, had torn out a name from Whitman's poetic phone book lists and, under a looking glass, magnified this figure, making us aware that there is a lot of maddening "betwixt and between" in the modern day democratic community.

The copyist, as Giorgio Agamben claims, constitutes one of the rare literary examples of sheer contingency. Consequently, metonymic space indeed plays a formidable role in the short story. Contrary to Whitman, who omnisciently sees and hears everything, the attorney shares the same space with Bartleby, hears him, but cannot see him as he is hidden behind a screen. Bartleby is, if anything, an instance of an "unnecessary neighbor." Moreover, Bartleby does not "contain" anything; nor, for that matter, can he be "contained." The entire story revolves around the narrator's attempts to distance himself from Bartleby, first by trying to get him out of the office, then by refraining from entering the office himself, then by moving to another office, and finally by encountering Bartleby in this most striking of spaces or non-spaces, the penitentiary. What makes him so enigmatic, however, is that his notorious "I prefer not to" does not simply denote a personal resistance, as Slavoj Žižek claims,[16] but that these words in themselves resist decipherment by our usual linguistic arsenal. And, as Deleuze remarks—who calls "Bartleby" a "violently comical text" ("Bartleby; or, the Formula," 68)—the undecryptable copyist is far from being the only "mad" figure in the text, because his stubborn insistence that he'd prefer not to elicits even more striking symptoms of madness in the narrator. Writes Deleuze: "With each instance, one has the impression that the madness is growing: not Bartleby's madness in 'particular,' but the madness around him, notably that of the attorney, who launches into strange propositions and even stranger behaviors" (70).

Another pivotal voice of modernism, Franz Kafka, will distill such Whitmanesque malformations and meaningless antics in the memorable figure of Odradek, in the short story "The Cares of a Family Man."[17] Odradek is an instance of total contingency, whose utter purposelessness, combined with the fact that he has "no abode" (does that ring a bell as regards Bartleby?), leads the family man to admit that "the idea that he is likely to survive me I find almost painful" (429). Odradek defies all claims about hereditary, ethnic, or racial purity, as it defies any dynastic third, any transcendence; he—or it—thus comes rather close to what Agamben defined as the exemplars of the "coming community":

> . . . pure singularities [that] communicate only in the empty space of the example, without being tied by any common property, by any identity. They are expropriated of all identity, so as to appropriate belonging itself, the sign ε. Tricksters or fakes, assistants or 'toons, they are the exemplars of the coming community. (10.1)

The fact that Slavoj Žižek, for example, evokes Odradek to exemplify the monstrosity of the Lacanian Real or the "Thing," and that he obliquely ignores the telling last sentence about the father's fear that Odradek might survive him,[18] goes to prove that contingency, and the bad press it has gotten in Western philosophy, might also be connected to a patriarchic discourse keen on extinguishing it by all means, and on establishing clear-cut hereditities—that is, on establishing a metaphoric "third." Odradek's alleged monstrosity does not lie in its/his/her "thingness," but in the sheer fact that this thing is "alive," and thus might not only outlast, but *outlive* the caring father of the house. It emphatically lacks any kind of Heideggerian "resoluteness toward death," and defies all destiny or heritage. Moreover, it defies any metaphoric decipherment via a third, because it *is* this third. It is, if anything, a metaphor for a metonymy that remains radically contingent, a metaphor for life that outlives life. We might indeed think, as Esposito claims Lyotard does, of something like a "pleasurable encounter with the Real,"[19] were it not for the fact that Odradek shatters the dynastic phantasmagorias of the father in bringing, as Blanchot claimed, "the neutral into play."[20] Can such an encounter be envisaged as pleasurable? A question that we might begin to answer with another one: How might the children and the family man's wife deal with Odradek? Surely not by wondering who will survive whom. I'm pretty sure his children would have a ball with him.

Would we, however, be able to tell a story about such a metonymic, contingent community peopled by Odradeks and Bartlebys—or maybe even, dare I say it, a myth? Well, I assume that if there is a narrative comprised of such creatures, it would be—myth! Which brings me back to the historical genealogy of the strategies devised to overcome contingency, of which myth, as our narrative has it, is allegedly the weakest. But again, emphasizing metonymy over metaphor might give us new leverage with regard to myth. Traditionally, myth has always been interpreted as a "mini-metaphor." A closer look at Lévi-Strauss's definition of it, however, clearly shows that nothing could be further from the truth: His structural analysis of the Oedipus myth and others shows that myth by no means solves the irresolvable contradictions it addresses—as, for example, the one between the autochtonous and the non-autochtonous origin of Man—but that, by narrativizing them through successive layers of not-so-irresolvable binaries, and sometimes the introduction of a third term (as, e.g., the trickster) mediates between the two poles without entirely collapsing them.[21] This is as much as to say that the contingency of the coexistence of two mutually exclusive terms is not abolished, but preserved. Note that the trickster, which Agamben also evokes, is a highly contingent figure—indeed, a figure of contingency. In fact, any dialectic is a highly metaphorical operation, in that it has to presume the very metaphorical third that thesis and antithesis share in order to guarantee any sublation into a synthesis.

The trickster is thus emphatically *not* a dialectical sublation: It is able to bridge contingent truths without either dissolving the both/and into an either/or, and without establishing a metaphoric third. Indeed, if anything, the trickster is the "impure" metonymy at the heart of a metaphoric myth. And while myth, as Esposito claims with regard to Hobbes' analyses, might often have a murder in the family at its core,[22] this might pertain to the classical Greek myths—which already form a second stage of the development of myth—but hardly ever in early myth, where, even if siblings fight and kill each other, their contingent relationship with each other is upheld.

Moreover, it is quite striking that, in the face of an ever more contingent, globalizing world, rhetorical trickster figures seem to abound, in which mutually exclusive concepts are contiguous and, indeed, contingent upon each other: Vernacular (Bhabha) or rooted (Appiah) cosmopolitanisms, strategic essentialism (Spivak), particular universalisms, and other strange creatures and straight curves are peopling our globalized, discursive worlds, trying to describe the experience of our globalized communities, and in the process kissing any claim to syllogistic purity good-bye—which surprisingly no one seems to be too bothered with. The only difference from Lévi-Straussian myth is that, in some instances, the artful narrative mediation between the opposite poles that characterizes myth is not provided—or even attempted—anymore.

What I am arguing is that we might in fact have discursive models at our disposal, if we manage to unearth Lévi-Strauss's theory of myth from the layers of its Barthesian appropriation and abuse. Roland Barthes has definitely done us an utter disservice by completely mixing up the concepts of myth and ideology,[23] a conflation whose repercussions can still today be felt, for example, in the work of Jean-Luc Nancy, who considers myth a purely Western creation that "for others, for 'primitives,' for example . . . is quite aristocratic and ephemeral" (*The Inoperative Community*, 46). If anything, myth, as defined by Lévi-Strauss, admits and attests to the world's contingency; that, in my view, was indeed the main reason why Enlightened reason took such pains to disenchant—and discredit—it.

METONYMY AND CONTINGENCY

How difficult it is to achieve synthesis in the face of the contingency of modern life might be illustrated by another literary example which—although coming from a different theoretical angle—supports my point, as it is another instance of literary metonymy. One passage that Jacques Rancière frequently comes back to in order to exemplify what he calls the "aesthetic regime" is a scene at the beginning of Honoré de Balzac's novel *The Magic Skin* (also translated as *The Wild Ass's Skin*), which was first published in 1831. The passage is worth quoting in its entirety:

> At a first glance the place presented a confused picture in which every achievement, human and divine, was mingled. Crocodiles, monkeys, and serpents stuffed with straw grinned at glass from church windows, seemed to wish to bite sculptured heads, to chase lacquered work, or to scramble up chandeliers. A Sevres vase, bearing Napoleon's portrait by Mme. Jacotot, stood beside a sphinx dedicated to Sesostris. The beginnings of the world and the events of yesterday were mingled with grotesque cheerfulness. A kitchen jack leaned against a pyx, a republican sabre on a mediaeval hackbut. Mme. du Barry, with a star above her head, naked, and surrounded by a cloud, seemed to look longingly out of Latour's pastel at an Indian chibook, while she tried to guess the purpose of the spiral curves that wound toward her. Instruments of death, poniards, curious pistols, and disguised weapons had been flung down pell-mell among the paraphernalia of daily life; porcelain tureens, Dresden plates, translucent cups from china, old salt-cellars, comfit-boxes belonging to feudal times. A carved ivory ship sped full sail on the back of a motionless tortoise.
>
> The Emperor Augustus remained unmoved and imperial with an air-pump thrust into one eye. Portraits of French sheriffs and Dutch burgomasters, phlegmatic now as when in life, looked down pallid and unconcerned on the chaos of past ages below them.
>
> Every land of earth seemed to have contributed some stray fragment of its learning, some example of its art. Nothing seemed lacking to this philosophical kitchen-midden, from a redskin's calumet, a green and golden slipper from the seraglio, a Moorish yataghan, a Tartar idol, to the soldier's tobacco pouch, to the priest's ciborium, and the plumes that once adorned a throne. This extraordinary combination was rendered yet more bizarre by the accidents of lighting, by a multitude of confused reflections of various hues, by the sharp contrast of blacks and whites. Broken cries seemed to reach the ear, unfinished dramas seized upon the

> imagination, smothered lights caught the eye. A thin coating of inevitable dust covered all the multitudinous corners and convolutions of these objects of various shapes which gave highly picturesque effects.[24]

Note how close Balzac here comes to the panoramic view and list-like style of Whitman. For Rancière, hardly any other literary scene is as emblematic of the dehierachization that characterizes the aesthetic regime as this one. While the representative regime—which preceded the aesthetic one—based its genres, plots, and characters on the social hierarchies encountered in real life,[25] the aesthetic regime undoes this interconnection. *Sujets*—that is, both persons and things—that were formerly deemed unworthy of literary representation now could become objects of literature. In *The Politics of Aesthetics* Rancière comments upon this pivotal scene as follows:

> When Balzac . . . has his reader enter an antique dealer's shop, with the hero of *The Magic Skin*, where jumbled up together are objects both profane and sacred, uncivilized and cultured, antique and modern, that each sum up a world, when he makes Cuvier the true poet reconstructing a world from a fossil, he establishes a regime of equivalence between the signs of the new novel and those of the description or interpretation of the phenomena of a civilization. He forges this new rationality of the obvious and the obscure that goes against the grand Aristotelian arrangements and that would become the new rationality for the history of material life (which stands in opposition to the histories of great names and events). (37)

"In the topography of a plaza, the physiognomy of a facade, the pattern or wear of a piece of clothing, the chaos of a pile of merchandise or trash," according to Rancière, Balzac "recognizes the elements of a mythology. He makes the true history of a society, an age, or a people visible in the figures of this mythology, foreshadowing individual or collective destiny."[26] Here, however, I would venture to disagree: If anything, the objects collected in the shop window have, because of their contingent contiguity, lost all mythology that might formerly have pertained to them. The utter "democratization" of things high and low, sacred and profane, valuable and worthless, is emblematic of what Rancière considers to be at the heart of the political: contingency. In *Disagreement*, he defines this equality as "the equality of anyone at all with anyone else: in other words, in the final analysis, the absence of *arkhê*, the sheer contingency of any social order" (15). And a little later, he adds: "The problem is not the *always more* but the *anyone at all*, the sudden revelation of the ultimate *anarchy* on which any hierarchy rests. . . . The foundation of politics . . . is the lack of foundation, the sheer contingency" (16).

Contrary to the argument as developed, Rancière locates contingency at the root of any political order, any hierarchical social given, and not only in modernity. However, what the aesthetic regime, freed from Aristotelian mimesis—which, for Rancière, is indissolubly chained to those social hierarchies—enables us to see is exactly that: the anarchy/contingency/lack of foundation looming below the orderly surface. Thus, for Rancière, community is not a means to overcome contingency; it is, in fact, coextensive with manifestations of the latter:

> Equality and inequality are incommensurate with each other, and yet, when the egalitarian event and the invention of community connect, they do indeed become commensurable. The experience of this common measure is an extreme experience. Equality is an exception. Its necessity is governed by the contingency and the resolve which inscribe its presupposition in transgressive strokes lending themselves to the invention of community, to the invention of demonstrations of effective community. It is not hard, then, to understand the attraction, the continually renewed dream, of community as a body united by some principle of life (love, fraternity or work) having currency among the members of that body or serving as a yardstick in the distribution of functions within it. (*On the Shores of Politics*, 88)

However, this "continually renewed dream" cannot but be the attempt to narratively overcome the sheer contingency of equality as such. If the opening scene of *The Magic Skin* has any diagnostic virtue to it, it shows us that there is no possible synthesis anymore between the mythologies and the stories of either things or people. Needless to say, Balzac, we the readers, Cuvier, or anybody facing contingency will, almost instinctively, try to invent a story that in one way or another will help us overcome contingency. This is done by transforming metonymy into metaphor, fragments into a narrative, accident into "destiny." In so doing, however, we will also always lose something. Desperately trying to immunize us ourselves against contingency and the other by conceiving of it exclusively in terms of precariousness, danger, contamination, or incalculability might not only suffocate us within the same; it will also inevitably lead to mechanisms of exclusion that result from establishing the metaphoric third by which we nowadays define community.

A look at how an evolving community proceeds "tropologically" might also help us to realize what I consider a significant mistake as regards theories of figuration: In them, metonymy is very often reduced to synecdoche. I would argue, however, that synecdoche is much closer to metaphor than to metonymy. The evolution of the nation-state might serve to illustrate this: While, in a first phase, the citizens of a nation are usually contingent upon each other—there are significant differences between certain groups and communities—national myths are designed to forge a (usually highly fictive) "common history," which then turns a metonymic community into a metaphoric one sharing a third. Only once such a third is assumed, however, can we then enter the third phase of community building: the synecdochic one, in which every citizen of the nation can stand as a *pars pro toto* for the nation as such, as happens either in wars or, as can be seen nowadays, in huge sports competitions like the soccer World Cup or the Olympic Games. That is, a metaphoric community is the precondition for its members to arrive at a synecdochic relationship with it.

Those who are not a part—neither of the metaphoric third nor of the synecdochic whole—are those we tend to immunize ourselves against. As fugitives, immigrants, diasporic existences, they sometimes do not have "the right to have rights," as Hannah Arendt so succinctly put it. Do "having a right" and "having a cause" in some way or another interconnect?

At the end of *Communitas*, Esposito quotes Nancy, who poses the question of how to understand the "nothing itself. Either it is the void of truth or it is nothing other than the world itself, and the sense of being-toward-the-world" (149)—a state of affairs that nicely captures the contingent concepts with which we today describe our globalized world. What I have tried to show is that contingency might account for both: the void of truth and, as a consequence, our sense of being-in-the-world. If we manage to reappropriate those semantic fields that *immunitas* has monopolized, the contagious individualism of modernity might be reined in. Indeed, it might actually be an accident that Comte, whom Esposito quotes, co-angulates "Right"—a problematic term within the biopolitical discourse Esposito has so impressively unraveled—with the term "Cause":

> The word Right should be excluded from political language, as the word Cause from the language of philosophy. Both are theological and metaphysical conceptions; and the former is as immoral and subversive as the latter is unmeaning and sophistical.[27]

Maybe the inherent connection between "right" and "cause" is something still to be unearthed, especially since no right could possibly be claimed from a contingent root. But that would be material for another, probably rather lengthy essay.

NOTES

1. See Roberto Esposito, *Communitas: The Origin and Destiny of Community* and *Immunitas: The Protection and Negation of Life.*

2. Jock Young, *The Exclusive Society*, 164.

3. Cf. Pierre Bourdieu, "La précarité est aujourd'hui partout."

4. *Oxford Dictionary of Philosophy*, edited by Simon Blackburn (Oxford: Oxford University Press, 2005).

5. Cf. http://de.pons.com/%C3%BCbersetzung?q=contingo&l=dela&in=ac_la&lf=la. Last accessed December 15, 2014.

6. Cf. Thomas Claviez, *Aesthetics and Ethics*, 53–111.

7. Cf. Jacques Rancière, *On the Shores of Politics*, 27.

8. Cf. Jean-Luc Nancy, *The Inoperative Community*, 30.

9. That these were not as unforeseeable as Esposito claims them to be—that is, that the figure of the Jew is already outlined in *Being and Time*—is what I argue in my forthcoming essay "The Myth of the Early Heidegger."

10. This is also something that Philippe Lacoue-Labarthe points out in his essay "Transcendence Ends in Politics," 427.

11. Nor do we share, *qua* nation, a history. I cannot possibly share or have shared history with people that lived 100 or 500 years before me.

12. Cf. Thomas Claviez, "Traces of a Metonymic Society in American Literary History."

13. This, however, is not to say that there aren't renowned historical literary figures who also wrote in a metonymic style: The "ur-novel," Cervantes' *Don Quixote*, abounds in metonymies and contingencies; so does Rabelais' series of five novels spun around the story of Pantagruel and Gargantua that appeared already between 1532 and 1564. What I am arguing is that we see a clear increase of this style connected with modernity in general and modernism in particular.

14. Cf. Gilles Deleuze, *Essays Critical and Clinical*, 58.

15. Gilles Deleuze and Felix Guattari, *A Thousand Plateaus*, 240.

16. Cf. Slavoj Žižek, *Violence*, 183.

17. Frank Kafka, "The Cares of a Family Man," 29.

18. Cf. Slavoj Žižek, "Neighbors and Other Monsters: A Plea for Ethical Violence," 163–67.

19. Esposito, *Communitas*, 85.

20. Maurice Blanchot, *The Infinite Conversation*, 384.

21. Cf. Claude Lévi-Strauss, "The Structural Study of Myth," 212.

22. Esposito, *Terms of the Political*, 31.

23. Cf. Thomas Claviez, *Grenzfälle*, 135 ff.

24. Honoré de Balzac, *The Wild Ass's Skin*, 41.

25. This is a phenomenon already pointed out by Erich Auerbach in the second chapter of *Mimesis*, titled "Fortunata."

26. Jacques Rancière, *The Aesthetic Unconscious*, 35.

27. Auguste Comte, *System of Positive Polity*, 289–90.

POETICS OF ANXIETY AND SECURITY

The Problem of Speech and Action in Our Time

HOMI K. BHABHA

> But if the wind of thinking, which I shall now arouse in you, has roused you from your sleep and made you fully awake and alive, then you will see that you have nothing in your hand but perplexities, and the most we can do with them is share them with each other.
>
> —*PLATO'S SEVENTH LETTER* (SOCRATES)

It felt strange to keep our eyes so low and close in this city that measures its height only against the wide open sky and the endless ocean. Now, in the fallen city, close to the ground, you search deep in the dust for familiar fragments, signs of life, footsteps of the stranger or the neighbor. Your eye rises no higher than the wall, the fence, the notice board, the shop window, the empty door: Everywhere you see scribbled notes, torn photographs, Xeroxed images; the whole city a vestibule of the lost and found. These are not merely *cris du coeur*; they are fragments of a language of distress and dispossession, beginning to find a public voice. The archive of loss starts the work of mourning. You come to terms with the traumatism of the event, Jacques Derrida suggested, by touching the wound of the *what* and the *who* of 9/11; by "comprehend[ing], interpret[ing], describ[ing], speak[ing] of and nam[ing]."[1]

What's in a *name*? You may well ask this question of the War on Terror that so quickly reversed itself ethically, if asymmetrically, into the terror of war waged with the fury of trauma—civilian deaths, extraordinary rendition, violations of the Geneva Convention, the indeterminate holding of combatants at Guantánamo Bay. A few weeks after 9/11, Derrida reflected on the naming of the event with a perspicacity that rings true a decade later:

> The telegram of this metonymy [9/11]—a name, a number—points out the unqualifiable by recognizing that we do not recognize or even cognize, that we do not yet know how to qualify, that we do not know what we are talking about. . . . I believe always in the necessity of being attentive first of all to this phenomenon of language, naming and dating, to this repetition compulsion (at once rhetorical, magical, and poetic) . . . [n]ot in order to isolate ourselves in language . . . but on the contrary, in order to try to understand what is going on precisely *beyond* language. . . . [2]

The very naming of 9/11 has endowed the event with a *runic* character. The archaic etymology of "rune" captures both the symbolic and *affective* persistence of 9/11 as it circulates in the poetic and philosophical discourse of our times. A rune in Old Icelandic is a mark or a sign with secret, mysterious powers; but a rune in Old English also signifies something that runs or flows, like blood. This figurative inscription of 9/11 as *rune* designates a site of traumatic repetition that circulates a name and a knowledge that reach beyond the "event." Over time, across genres, between media, an iterative temporality sustains the *afterlife* of the event and burdens it with an anxious persistence of meaning and affect. For the repetition compulsion is surely nothing other than the continuation of traumatism by other means and in other times. It is, in particular, the *temporality* of terror/trauma as it has flowed rune-like through the decade, that has given 9/11 a symptomatic and symbolic reality far exceeding its own historicity. *Was 9/11 a major event?*

In responding to this question in the wake of the attack, Derrida identified the emergence of a historical temporality that would profoundly mark the political and psychic culture of a new decade of *mondialisation*. "Traumatism is produced by the *future*, by the *to come*, by the threat of the worst *to come*, rather than by an aggression that is 'over and done with.' . . . [F]or the future and for always, the threat that was indicated through these signs might be . . . worse even . . . than the threat that organized the so-called 'Cold War.'"[3] *Was 9/11 an event of the scale of the Cold War, we ask incredulously?* And in his response to our question, Derrida articulates the futurity of trauma with the "anonymous invisibility of the enemy" (both terrorist networks and the State) to suggest that the very language of scale—is this a quick, fleeting attack or a major event?—can be used as an autoimmunitary form of repression to "neutralize the effect of the traumatism." "For we now know," Derrida argues, "that repression in both its psychoanalytical sense and its political sense—whether it be through the police, the military, or the economy—ends up producing, reproducing, and regenerating the very thing it seeks to disarm."[4] The repression or neutralization of the awareness of the traumatic future—as a civilian and psychic temporality integral to the constitution of subjectivity and citizenship—leads to a *Realpolitik* of "unacknowledged" terror attacks, covert drone operations, and power games of Russian roulette played with the half-hidden card of "regional" nuclear proliferation.

A few years deeper into the decade, Jacques Rancière poses a question comparable in scale to Derrida's. *Does September 11 mark a symbolic rupture in our history?* he asks. If Derrida focuses on the deleterious, autoimmunitary effects of the repression of political trauma and its unconscious affects (fear, anxiety, ambivalence), Rancière considers "consensus" to be the derogation of the democratic duty to engage in *dissensus*. A symbolic rupture would reveal "a fissure in the relation of the real to the symbolic":[5] In such circumstances, the ideological and mythological textures of a society—its media, its image-archive, its discursive formation and institutions, its ethical practices and political rhetorics—break under the weight of an "event" that cannot be contained within the lifeworlds of existing hegemonic symbolic and semantic relations. A symbolic rupture interrogates the norms, customs, and existential values that enable a national or regional "population" to participate in "being-together." No symbolic rupture occurred after 9/11 because, according to Rancière, "[f]rom the beginning, the American government accepted, positing as its own axiom, the very principle of its attackers. It accepted to characterize the conflict in religious and ethnic terms as a combat between good and evil. . . ."[6] As a result, the "event" was integrated "within the framework in which it represents its relation to itself, to others and to the Other. . . . [T]here was no revelation of a gap between the real of American life and the symbolic of the American people."[7]

I want to extend some aspects of these important accounts by approaching traumatic time and symbolic rupture from a different angle. What does it mean to stare death in the face from the Other side? Recent work on *jihad* by Islamic scholars—Olivier Roy, Talal Asad, Faisal Devji, Maya Jayussi, and

Roxanne Euben, among others—has led me to think further about the structure of the anxious temporality of trauma as it manifests itself in a *future that is yet to come*, at once virtual and proleptic. Let me cite Euben at some length because her account of *jihad* emphasizes its temporal aspects, while her ethical interpretation of Islamism displays all the advantages of cultural translation:

> In the hands of contemporary fundamentalists (or "Islamists"), *jihad* is neither simply a blind and bloody-minded scrabble for temporal power nor solely a door through which to pass into the hereafter. Rather it is a form of political action in which to use Hannah Arendt's language, the pursuit of immortality is inextricably linked to a profoundly this-worldly endeavor—the founding or recreating of a just community on earth. . . . While the *mujahidin* may seek the ever-elusive rewards of the afterlife, *jihad* against modern *jahiliya* (moral savagery) entails the political struggle to realize the *umma* (the just community of Muslims) in a particular historical moment; in turn, it is the continued existence of the earthly *umma* that immortalizes their efforts. . . . [8]

It seems strange to have Hannah Arendt bear witness to immortality achieved through suicide bombing and acts of terrorism, when her stance "against violence" is as well known, as is her resolute belief that political "death" does not serve the human *inter-est*. I am, however, intrigued by Euben's account of the temporality of side-by-sideness that articulates, in the *jihadi* imagination, what is secular and chronological with what is sacred and anachronistic. "The immortality that those who engage in *jihad* seek is at once secular (of this world) and religious (of the next)"[9] is Talal Asad's neat summary of the argument. And as I take my stand on terror, constituted as it is *in between* the secular and the messianic, I find myself reflecting again on Derrida's fearful temporality of the *future*, of the trauma *to come*. Is his argument not too future-oriented? Does he not neglect, to a certain degree, the "return" of the proleptic, its logic of inversion?

The secular-messianic conjunction, when read not as confrontation but as the "open, undecided, indeterminable," may or may not be true of the *jihadi*, but it opens up for me a way of thinking about the "double and paradoxical" temporalities from which the witness to trauma—or the traumatized witness—speaks. "Is the moral witness a forward-looking creature even when his testimony is about the past?"[10] the philosopher Avishai Margalit once asked. If we think in terms of the side-by-sideness of "temporalities" (like the secular-messianic) rather than their sublation or sublimation, then it is possible to answer Margalit by saying that the temporality of witnessing presents us with a chiasmatic structure of inversions and reversals: of the present-as-future; of the past-as-future-present. If these chiasmatic time signatures inform the utterance of the witness, it is also because anxiety—the affect associated with the witnessing of trauma and the survival of terror—is itself a kind of chiasmatic experience: a structure of crossed symmetry; an affect placed cross-wise, while the anxious witness is caught in the crossroads of the "present," somewhere between the past continuous and the future anterior. My attempt to sketch an anxious temporality from which the witness speaks—a site of traumatic enunciation—is borne out by Freud's simile of "anxiety as a signal": perhaps a signal at the crossing of time and danger?

> The signal announces: "I am expecting a situation of helplessness to set in," or: "The present situation reminds me of one of the traumatic experiences I have had before. Therefore I will anticipate the trauma and behave as though it had already come, while there is yet time to turn aside." Anxiety is therefore on the one hand an expectation of a trauma, and on the other a repetition of it in a mitigated form. . . . But what is of decisive importance is the first displacement of the anxiety-reaction from its origin in the situation of helplessness to an expectation of that situation—that is, to the danger-situation.[11]

These remarks on the rune and the ruins of 9/11 have led us to the landscape of anxiety in our attempt to turn the traumatic moment of affect into a site of enunciation. To place the voice of the witness at the point of the "signal" of anxiety is indeed to suggest that anxiety is never simply overcome. Its chiasmatic structure opens up the side-by-sideness of disjunctive temporalities and territories which, through repetition, are prone to mitigation. There is here an important history lesson in the anachronistic uses of time as a form of consolation. It is with these thoughts in mind that I want to proceed with the repetition of W. H. Auden's poetry in the midst of 9/11 as I lay side by side the verses of Auden and the thoughts of Hannah Arendt. By bringing them together I will explore the anxiety of agency as it fibrillates between the public and the private—the What and the Who—in traumatic times.

Amidst the burnt offerings that poetry brought to the city of ashes on 9/11 was W. H. Auden's "September 1, 1939." In *The Times Literary Supplement*,

Daniel Swift commented on the symbolic capital of Auden's poetry,[12] "As New York explains the bombing to itself, Auden's words are everywhere." Paul Muldoon, Adrienne Rich, and other poets recited "September 1" at several memorial services, while newspapers, libraries, and radio stations across the country brought the poem to public attention.

I sit in one of the dives
On Fifty-second Street
Uncertain and afraid
As the clever hopes expire
Of a low dishonest decade:
Waves of anger and fear
Circulate over the bright
And darkened lands of the earth,
Obsessing our private lives;
The unmentionable odour of death
Offends the September night.

Accurate scholarship can
Unearth the whole offence
From Luther until now
That has driven a culture mad,
Find what occurred at Linz,
What huge imago made
A psychopathic god:
I and the public know
What all schoolchildren learn,
Those to whom evil is done
Do evil in return.

Exiled Thucydides knew
All that a speech can say
About Democracy,
And what dictators do,
The elderly rubbish they talk
To an apathetic grave;
Analysed all in his book,
The enlightenment driven away,

The habit-forming pain,
Mismanagement and grief:
We must suffer them all again.

Into this neutral air
Where blind skyscrapers use
Their full height to proclaim
The strength of Collective Man,
Each language pours its vain
Competitive excuse:
But who can live for long
In an euphoric dream;
Out of the mirror they stare,
Imperialism's face
And the international wrong.[13]

Written on the cusp of World War II, that September day in 1939 marks Hitler's invasion of Poland. In anxious anticipation of the impending war, the poem brings to the fore the collective guilt and shame of a "low dishonest decade":

Who, thinking of the last ten years,
Does not hear the howling in his ears
The Asiatic cry of pain,
The shots of executing Spain,
See stumbling through his outraged mind
The Abyssinian, blistered, blind,
. . .
The Jew wrecked in the German cell,
Flat Poland frozen into hell,
The silent dumps of unemployed
Whose *areté* has been destroyed.[14]

It was reassuring for New Yorkers to have the iconic gestures of their city—the Dizzy Club on West Fifty-Second Street, or "buildings groping the sky"—restored to them in a poem of such remarkable endurance. Auden's evocation of the "unmentionable odor of death / [that] offends the September night" was taken for nothing less than prophecy in the busy blogosphere. The unforgettable smell at ground zero—dioxins, asbestos, shattered glass, mercury, metal dust—has lingered ever since in memories of that time. Such sensory prefigurations of sense and situation turned Auden's poem into something of an urban myth in the wake of 9/11. Snatches of Auden, anxiously appropriated and quoted, gathered momentum, pivoting around the consolatory line—"we must love one another or die"—the very line that Auden retracted as being a lie.

More interesting, I think, than these cathartic emanations was Adam Gopnik's argument in the *New Yorker*. "What matters is the sound he makes," Gopnik writes. "Auden's emotional tone is our tone, even if his meanings are not always our meanings."[15] Tone is, of course, to a large extent a matter of metrics, prosody, rhetoric. But "emotional tone," while irreducible to "meaning," emanates from the *affect* that adheres to its rhetorical articulation. Auden's much travestied line "For Poetry makes nothing happen / It survives in the valley of its making" is not an affirmation of poetry's apathy; it is an argument for its endurance and survival in the public realm. As the concluding line of the verse makes clear—"*it survives, A way of happening, a mouth.*"[16]

Poetry does not rest in the realm of the "idea" or "emotion"; it survives through recitation, by being passed from mouth to mouth, in an embodied circulation. The *utterance of meaning* is the psychic and affective *happening* of the poem; and the "emotional tone" sets the note for this mnemonic iterability of meanings-in-performance. The *imminence* of poetry, the renewal and surprise that emerges in every recitation—makes something remarkable *happen*: It keeps redrawing the contingent boundary between what we represent as "public" and what we designate as "private."

The regular beat established by Auden's trimetric lines at the start of "September 1, 1939" maintains the poise and posture of the public voice—the voice of the Anglo-American journalist or reporter, as Joseph Brodsky imagines[17] the narrator to be:

> I sit in one of the dives
> On Fifty-second Street

But just beneath the surface of the barfly's *sangfroid* lies a more anxious private *pitch*:

> Waves of anger and fear
> Circulate over the bright

And darkened lands of the earth,
Obsessing our private lives . . .

How do these voices—public and private—connect with each other to compose an "emotional tone"? John Fuller, for instance, notices an "illusory casualness of argument"[18] that makes the poem's tone both laconic and urgent. Auden's playful answer, deadly serious in its intent, provides a surprising twist in the search for the truth:

. . . truth, like love and sleep, resents
Approaches that are too intense,
And often when the searcher stood
Before the Oracle, it would
Ignore his grown-up earnestness
But not the child of his distress.
For through the Janus of a joke
The candid psychopompos spoke.[19]

The oracular poet can only address the "truth" in an "emotional tone" that is indirect and oblique, no matter whether the poem deals with the articulation of public concerns and private confessions, or the intersections of reason and affect. The adult's earnest questions posed in a rationalized, normative discourse can only be answered by addressing the inchoate distress of the child *within*: those disavowed and disheveled infantile complexes that can only find expression in the language of symptom and transference. The oracular poet, like the Freudian joker, is a master of displacement and dissembling who opens up a "third" space of enunciation to unsettle the stable, symmetric alignments of binary subjects and polarized objects. The poet addresses *both* realms—the public interest and the private instinct—by refusing to answer either directly, face to face. It is by creating a displaced "third" discourse—the poem or the puzzle, the rebus or the riddle—that the poet reveals the asymmetry and anxiety invested in deciding where to draw the line between the obligations of the public voice and the interests of the private wish. For that line of difference and defense is also, paradoxically, the arch of affiliation.

O how the devil who controls
The moral asymmetric souls,
The either-ors, the mongrel halves
Who find truth in a mirror, laughs:[20]

> The public space where acts are done,
> In theory common to us all . . .
> The agora of work and news
> Where each one has the right to choose
> . . .
> The other is in the inner space
> Of private ownership, the place
> That each of us is forced to own,
> Like his own life from which it's grown.[21]

What stand does Auden's seeker take in relation to the truth? And from where is the reader or listener addressed by the poem's "emotional tone"? Both seeker and reader find themselves split (if that is possible) in a triangulation of desire: at one moment confronted by the imperatives of the public predicament; at another moment compelled by the drives and demands of private life; and then, in a "third" dimension, moving restlessly in this mediatory mongrel space in between what Auden calls the "public space of commonality" and the "inner space of private ownership," keeping both *eros* and *agape* in play.

The triangulation of voices that maps Auden's "emotional tone" raises the significant ethical issue of agency and individuation that is a recurrent concern for Auden's poetry. The struggle to reveal the individuated "agent" is a complex quest in a scenario in which the oracular poet dissembles his indirect Janus-faced discourse, and the "subject" is crafted with a "moral asymmetric soul." Can there be an agent when truth cannot be looked in the eye, and the split subjects of speech and action circulate anxiously, uncertainly, in the interstices between public space and inner space?

Our guide to this problem in Auden's poetry and beyond is a remarkable sentence from *The Human Condition* that you know only too well:

> [T]he stories, the results of action and speech reveal an agent, but this agent is not an author. . . . Somebody began it and is its subject in the two-fold sense of the word, namely, its actor and sufferer, but nobody is its author.[22]

The question of agency "in the absence of an author" is inscribed in the very form of "September 1, 1939." It takes shape in a partial or quasi-chiasmatic patterning of verses in which public space and inner space—the actor and the sufferer—cross paths, intersect with each other, but do not exactly exchange roles. In this meeting and parting of ways and means, is the author of what Arendt calls "the web of human relationships." There is a dialogue in this poem between the declarative, public voice and the inner diagnostic voice, but neither is given an unassailable or punctual authority. There are images of negative authority—historical, political, economic, and psychic—in conflict with positive, minoritarian or marginalized voices—poetic, spiritual, cultural—and in that contestation two things are revealed: first, that the struggle with hegemonic authority enables a viable "agent" of public and personal virtue to emerge. And second, the transformative agent emerges against a complex background of the chiaroscuro of negative and positive social conditions, the ambivalence of conflicts of interest and identification, the cross-references of belief and ideology. The chiasmus I am proposing as a way of understanding Auden's design of proximity within the polarized, or contingency in the midst of contradiction, is beautifully acknowledged by Walter Benjamin as "dialectical contrast":

> [O]n one side lies the "productive," "forward-looking," "lively," "positive" part of the epoch, and on the other side the abortive, retrograde, and obsolescent. The very contours of the positive element will appear distinctly only insofar as the element is set off against the negative. . . . [A] new partition [must] be applied to this initially excluded, negative component so that, by a displacement of the angle of vision . . . a positive element emerges anew in it too. . . . [23] (459)

Defenseless under the night
Our world in stupor lies;
Yet, dotted everywhere,
Ironic points of light
Flash out wherever the Just
Exchange their messages:
May I, composed like them
Of Eros and of dust,
Beleaguered by the same
Negation and despair,
Show an affirming flame.

In his extraordinary line-by-line reading of "September 1," Joseph Brodsky uses another measure to describe a contrastive scale of voices in the verse. He makes a distinction between meanings that are kept "low," close to the ground, and images and concepts that soar "upwards," proposing a kind of pedagogical or authoritative mastery that is brought down, toward the end, to a measure of the human condition. Where I see a chiasmatic proximity—a pattern of crossed paths and cross purposes—Brodsky proposes a complex form of connection that he describes as "blinding proximities." "It becomes your mode of cognition . . . for it is the principle of rhyme that enables one to sense that proximity between seemingly disparate entities."[24]

The windiest militant trash
Important Persons shout
Is not so crude as our wish:
What mad Nijinsky wrote
About Diaghilev
Is true of the normal heart;
For the error bred in the bone
Of each woman and each man
Craves what it cannot have,
Not universal love
But to be loved alone.

From the conservative dark
Into the ethical life
The dense commuters come,
Repeating their morning vow,
'I *will* be true to the wife,
I'll concentrate more on my work,'
And helpless governors wake
To resume their compulsory game:
Who can release them now,
Who can reach the deaf,
Who can speak for the dumb?

All I have is a voice
To undo the folded lie,
The romantic lie in the brain

Of the sensual man-in-the-street
And the lie of Authority
Whose buildings grope the sky:
There is no such thing as the State
And no one exists alone;
Hunger allows no choice
To the citizen or the police;
We must love one another or die.

The declarative, assertive opening of each verse represents the public domain of common knowledge, the realm of rights and freedoms, the witness and record of historical truth, the social and symbolic structures of urbanity, the politics of choice and recognition associated with public space. This is, indeed, the poetic space of the general type or character of personhood; a voice that establishes "a definition of *what* man is," Arendt writes, "of qualities he . . . could possibly share with other living beings. . . ."[25]

Roughly at the mid-point of the verse emerges a diagnostic reflection on *who* the person is, in all his quiddity and his specific difference, so that, as Arendt writes, "the distinct identity of the agent" may be disclosed in the act. The poetic "subject" inaugurates a mode of reflection more attuned to the dialogues of "*inner space*": the realm of affective or intuitive understanding, the obsessions of our psychic lives, the ethical or sentimental norms by which we live, or meditations on how we *ought* to live. "We must love one another or die."

Although the verses seem to divide halfway, the poem requires the *Who of the inner-space* and the *What of the public space* to be read as if they were held up against each other, as if they were "asymmetric souls" or "mongrel halves"—strangely *side by side* and abutting each other. Read in this way, there are, indeed, actors and sufferers in this "low dishonest decade," but it is difficult to discern an "author" or a single unifying "cause." Hitler—the psychopathic god of the poem—is, perhaps, the villain of the piece, but there are attendant cases and adjacent causes: "habit-forming pain / mismanagement and grief"; "Imperialism's face [and] the International wrong"; "error bred in the bone / of each woman and man / Not universal love / but to be loved alone"; "We must love one another or die."

In one of Arendt's most profound essays, "Thinking and Moral Considerations," dedicated to W. H. Auden, she reflects on the ontological and ethical condition of being "inevitably two-in-one." There are times when the "what" overlays the "who," and the language of human togetherness is reduced to an "objective" intercourse that obscures the agent-revealing capacity of speech and action. At other times, even the most "worldly" discourse is displaced and forced to take a tangential route to its end-oriented material object because the agent's unique and distinctive who-ness is struggling for the light. The subject lies "close" to the objects of material social practices; in fact, as Arendt says, it is integral to them. However, at the point at which the subject emerges as an *agent* to tell its own story, to give narrative texture to the intangibility of speech and action, a certain "strangeness" or alienation shadows its autonomy and affectivity. The web of human togetherness turns *close and strange*: "the physical, worldly in-between along with its interests is overlaid and, as it were, overgrown with an altogether different in-between which consists of deeds and words and owes its origin exclusively to men's acting and speaking directly *to* one another."[26] It is from these areas of overlay and overgrowth, where altogether different spheres of interest *almost* touch each other, that the agent emerges as a doubly wrought figure embodying an "original split" that aligns the "what" with the "who" at one moment, and estranges them at another. Such is the anxious fibrillation of agency in the living flux of action and speech.

"A difference is inserted into my Oneness," Arendt writes, "Everything that exists among a plurality of things is not simply what it is, in its identity, but it is also different from others; this being different belongs to its very nature. When we try to get hold of it in thought, wanting to define it, we must take this otherness (*alteritas*) or difference into account."[27]

Alterity incites a movement, *to and fro*, that turns the interiority of the self outward to face the world, while transforming external reality into an intimate relation, at once *close and strange*, within oneself, and with others. Such a double-edged movement activates an "original split"—"the soundless dialogue (*eme emautô*), between me and myself, the two-in-one . . . [of the who and the what] . . ."[28]—which is the basis of the agent's consciousness of "being together," of *seeing oneself as another.* And it is in that anxious moment of "turning," *to and fro*, within the web of human relationships, that the subject reveals, in the twofold sense of the word, a *regard* for the neighbor. It is by way of the turn and return of the human gaze that the subject bestows attention upon, and takes care of, the neighbor as, at once, strange and close—"an anachronous presence to consciousness."[29]

NOTES

1. Giovanna Borradori, *Philosophy in a Time of Terror: Dialogues with Jürgen Habermas and Jacques Derrida*, 93.

2. Ibid., 86–87.

3. Ibid., 97.

4. Ibid., 99.

5. Jacques Rancière, *Dissensus*, 97.

6. Ibid., 99.

7. Ibid., 99.

8. Quoted in Talal Asad, *On Suicide Bombing*, 57.

9. Ibid., 57

10. Avishai Margalit, *The Ethics of Memory*, 152–3.

11. Sigmund Freud, *Inhibitions, Symptoms and Anxiety*, 161.

12. Daniel Swift, "Letter from . . . New York," *The Times Literary Supplement* October 5, 2001: 17.

13. W. H. Auden, "September 1, 1939."

14. W. H. Auden, *New Year Letter*, 26 (emphasis added).

15. Adam Gopnik, "The Double Man," *The New Yorker* September 23, 2002. Web, September 29, 2014.

16. W. H. Auden, "In Memory of W. B. Yeats," 108.

17. Joseph Brodsky, "On 'September 1, 1939' by W. H. Auden," 306.

18. John Fuller, *W. H. Auden: A Commentary*, 267.

19. W. H. Auden, *New Year Letter*, 27.

20. Ibid., 103.

21. Ibid., 111.

22. Hannah Arendt, *The Human Condition*, 184.

23. Walter Benjamin, *The Arcades Project*, 459.

24. Joseph Brodsky, "On 'September 1, 1939' by W. H. Auden," 350.

25. Hannah Arendt, *The Human Condition*, 181.

26. Ibid., 182–83.

27. Hannah Arendt, "Thinking and Moral Considerations: A Lecture," 441.

28. Ibid., 442.

29. Emmanuel Levinas, *Collected Philosophical Papers*, 119.

LITERATURE, THE WORLD, AND YOU

DJELAL KADIR

> *Incipiamus igitur ab eo, qui cum frequentissimus est tum longe pulcherrimus, translatione dico, quae μεταφορά Graece vocatur. quae quidem cum ita est ab ipsa nobis concessa natura, ut indocti quoque ac non sentientes ea frequenter utantur, tum ita iucunda atque nitida, ut id oratione quamlibet clara proprio tamen lumine eluceat.*[1]
>
> [Let us begin, then, with the commonest and by far the most beautiful of *tropes*, namely, *metaphor*, the Greek term for our *translatio*. It is not merely so natural a turn of speech that it is often employed unconsciously or by uneducated persons, but it is in itself so attractive and elegant that however distinguished the language in which it is embedded it shines forth with a light that is all its own.][2]

We begin, then, where Quintilian would have us begin in this passage from the eighth book, sixth chapter, fourth part of his *Institutio Oratoria*, written at the end of the 1st century A.D., because the strongest claim I shall be making here is that literature is in your present (this is why we are taught to always refer to narrative events in the present tense); the world is in your time (etymologically, "world" means "man in time"); and theory is invariably localized and situated wherever you happen to be (since its origins in Greek antiquity, *theoría* means to witness for oneself and for one's own city-state the rituals of others). I deliberately situate these claims in your chronotopic immediacy, in your predicament, because the ultimate goal of this essay is to diagnose the stresses of a contestatory and, at times, antithetical situation that borders on an *aporia*—the tussle between poetics and community, or the paronomasia of anomalous construct, on the one hand, and normative structure on the other. This is the dialogical counterpoint between the uncommon and nonconformist *métier* of the poetic and the *koinos topos*, or commonplace, whose *nomos*, or law, defines community and its *sensus communis*. In terms of the tradition resonant in the Quintilian cited here, this is the counterpoint between Aristotle's *Poetics* and his *Nichomachean Ethics*, a counterpoint that is still operative in our present conjugation of poetics and community.

In the lines cited here, Quintilian gives us a demonstration of these commonplaces, even as he is illustrating the rhetorical and poetic protocols he describes through a self-conscious performative contradiction. And despite the fact that he spends some ink criticizing his older contemporary Seneca for his rhetorical performances aimed at manipulating his listeners rather than educating them, Quintilian's lines here are eminently performative, what he would call epideictic, rather than narrative or dialectical. In other words, he is showing us, as much as he might be telling us, something about certain figures of speech designed to optimize the effect of what he is performing—the drama of language, its vicissitudes, and the history of its predicament as literature. As we shall see presently, he performs what you are taught to perform as educated readers—to read and speak of literature in the contemporariness of its perpetually unfolding narrative, theorize its rituals, and historicize its worlds, which are also your world as you read and interpret what you are reading and interpreting. Let us see how Quintilian does it and what his performance might mean for our endeavors in theory and the contestatory operations of poetics and community two thousand years later.

The *Institutio Oratoria*, published in A.D. 95, about five years before Quintilian's death, is a classic example of what Edward Said identified as a work in the "late style." In discussing the late "Canonical Variations" of Johann Sebastian Bach and the last compositions of Ludwig van Beethoven, Said notes a consistent quality of work which "is extremely private, very concerned with the medium, really about the technique. . . . What you have, as you do in the last plays of [Henrik] Ibsen, is a sense of the artist turning inward and examining not only the medium of his art, but also his own work, and turning them inside out."[3] As a self-conscious rhetorician writing on the self-consciousness of public oratory, and doing so in the last decade of his life, Quintilian has left for posterity what became for centuries, and is for us still, a schoolbook on the protocols and ethics of performative intervention in the public sphere and in the polity of community. And, as I have already noted, he delivers his pedagogy by demonstration, as our epigraph from Book 8 of the *Institutio Oratoria* illustrates. The eighth book of the *Institutes*, as they are known in English, is devoted to what concerns us most. By "us" I mean those who study and teach the foundations of culture—its diverse languages, their intermediality, the critical metadiscourse of its theories, and the institutional place of these vocations in the world—actual, factual, and virtual. This is the book in which Quintilian defines the repertoire of tropes and figures available to the orator and poet, two vocations which Quintilian conflates when it comes to rhetoric and prosody. He knew about the first, rhetoric, from Aristotle's legacy, from his own older contemporary Seneca, and from his role as consul during the reign of Emperor Vespasian. And he had ample familiarity with prosody and poetics through his intimacy with the work of Horace, whose *Epistula ad Pisones* of 18 B.C. Quintilian renamed, alternately, *Liber de Arte Poetica* and *Ars Poetica*, with the latter title having endured in the annals of the Western tradition. What Quintilian learned from Horace and we from him is that practitioners of literature, and art in general, possess a craft and its mastery, have a systematic knowledge of that craft's technique and theory, and are capable of self-reflection and conscious self-criticism in their practice. And though neither Horace nor Quintilian were likely to have known the work of Aristotle directly, they were familiar with the legacy of Aristotle's Peripatetic School and, as such, they were deliberate in their acquittal of poetry and art from the indictment Plato had laid against them, especially in the tenth book of the *Republic*, as well as in the *Ion* and the *Phaedrus*. What Quintilian and all of these theorists/philosophers do share is an appreciation of the quandary the practitioner of language or of the visual arts, whether as poet or as theorist, has always had to countenance. Plato and Aristotle called this difficulty an *aporia*; Horace and Quintilian referred to it as *adequatio*, or being equal to the task. That competency is referred to as "*adequatio qua res ipsa loquitur*" when dealing in figures of language and the world, and "*adequatio intellectus et rei*" when dealing with figures of thought. On some other occasion I hope we can elaborate on these in turn. For now, suffice it to recall that we, in our time, call this difficult situation a predicament and, since poststructuralist deconstruction has become an integral part of our critical and theoretical toolkit, we have learned, like the poets did long ago, to value and optimize the liberatory potential of this aporetic dilemma, turning its difficulties into critical opportunity to countenance and contest the perils of unmitigated self-delusion and hegemonic totalization.

In other words, while not susceptible to mastery, the difficulty inherent in the practice of art and its theory is manageable, and Quintilian's *Institutio Oratoria* is a lesson in the management of this predicament. As such, the agency of the artist or theorist, and of the orator or rhetorician, Quintilian would add, is central to the process of managing difficulty. This, in fact, has been a parlous situation in which the best of poets, artists, and *theoroi* succeed in leveraging their aporias so as to optimize the acts and products of their *métier*. The result is that literature and its arts are always present in the time and world of their practitioners—whether composers, rhapsodes, or readers, including you, of course. And the example of Quintilian himself in the passage with which we began these remarks serves as an illustration of how one could manage this predicament.

This pivotal turn in the passage we have cited occurs when Quintilian says, "*translatione dico, quae μεταφορά Graece vocatur,*" ["namely, *metaphor*, the Greek term for our *translatio*"], a syntactical turn of phrase that, while speaking of the trope of *metaphor*, also demonstrates the figures of *hyperbaton* he discusses in the same passage (VIII.6.62–67), a reversal technically known as *anastrophe*, or *hysteron proteron*, which alters the logical order of sense and events and the etiological sequence of cause and effect. In this case, the reversal consists in switching what we refer to as source language and target language when we speak of translation, which is also called *translatio* in Latin, though here Quintilian uses the term to mean *metaforá*, which, he says, is "the Greek term for our *translatio*." The key reversal here is signaled in English by the preposition "for," which would have the original Greek be a translation of the current Latin of Quintilian's time. The etiological switch, or exchange of place of cause and effect, privileges Quintilian's temporal present, recursively rendering his Latin as precursive antecedent in the naming of what he defines as one of the most natural and most beautiful tropes ("*quae quidem cum ita est ab ipsa nobis concessa natura, ut indocti quoque ac non sentientes ea frequenter utantur, tum ita iucunda atque nitida, ut id oratione quamlibet clara proprio tamen lumine eluceat*"), a trope that naturally shines forth with a light all its own.

No doubt you will have noticed the performative contradiction here between the ruse, or stratagem, employed by Quintilian in his own self-consciously tactical gambit, and the spontaneity and naturalness that he attributes to that intricately wrought artifice called a metaphor, as if, as he says, such a poetic and rhetorical construct is a naturally occurring phenomenon that shines forth spontaneously of its own accord.

What, then, is the point of invoking the crafty and sempiternal revenant of Quintilian and the stratagems of language that lie at the foundation of poetic, theoretical, and public discourse, foundations that by now, after more than two millennia, are for the most part invisible to us and that most often operate imperceptibly, without our being aware of their indefatigable determinacies? The point I wish to be making is that literature and the artful uses of language, whether in poetry or in theoretical discourse, are always present; they are coeval with you and me, as long as we are together in community—though they might not be commensurate with us, or coterminous with themselves, as the aporetic performative contradictions and the anxieties of *adequatio*, or being equal to the task, emphatically demonstrate. The demonstration may be too subtle in Quintilian's Latin, but the predicament he illustrates has been regularly articulated in the history of theoretical discourse and essayistic self-examination, perhaps most comprehensibly for us because, closer to our time and modes of understanding, of writers such as the Czech gnomist Franz Kafka and one of his successors, Jorge Luis Borges of Buenos Aires, Argentina, in this life, and of Geneva, Switzerland, for eternity. In his 1951 text "Kafka y sus precursores," ("Kafka and His Precursors"[4]), Borges makes the highly Quintilianian observation that authors create their own precursors, an assertion that gives life, yet again, to the *anastrophe* Quintilian defined as a *hyperbaton*, or a reversal of the order of things, and which he demonstrates, as we have seen, by having the Greek *metaphorá* be a translation of the Latin *translatio*. It is my contention here that this is a procedure all of us engage in, often unawares, in an operation Jacques Derrida reasserted as *mondialisation*,[5] and that a year earlier I elaborated on in treating "worlding," or "to world," after Heidegger, as a transitive verb.[6] Apropos of world literature, especially as "new world literature," the procedure demonstrated by Quintilian and reiterated by Derrida is very much on point. Thus, just as Kafka, according to Borges, creates his own precursors each time he writes, we invent the world and its literature each time we read it, a process described by Martin Heidegger in his 1935 essay "The Origin of the Work of Art."[7]

It is in this context of what we might call the *poiesis* of theory that I wish to discuss the current critical discourse on world literature and its theoretical epiphenomena. In an essay entitled "The Scale of World Literature" that appeared in the volume *Immanuel Wallerstein and the Problem of the World: System, Scale, Culture*,[8] the Lebanese-Korean theorist and literary critic Nirvana Tanoukhi investigates the phenomenon of distance and the topic of scale in the current discourse of world literature. She begins with an epigraph that is as aporetic and as performatively ironic as Quintilian, only emphatically more so since the work she cites is, literally, a play, the 5th-century B.C. tragedy *Philoctetes* by the Greek playwright Sophocles, performed in 409 B.C., in the midst of the Peloponnesian War, to be exact. The epigraph reads, "This is his home; he can't be far away." Those of you who recall the play recognize the performative paradox, which is simultaneously a tautology and a self-contradiction: The place in question is indeed Philoctetes' cave-home, and he certainly can't be far away because, as you might recall, he is lame. At the same time, you will remember, he is a castaway on the desolate island of Lemnos far away from home. No doubt Professor Tanoukhi is fully cognizant of the resonant ironies in her epigraph, and her discussion of distance and scale as quotients of comparative-literature and world-literature discourse evinces this awareness. Within the language of distance and scale, and though she does not articulate it in these terms, the parameters of the discursive formations shift; and they keep on shifting. Thus, what would be a frame of reference and, after Derrida, professes to serve as a frame of deference, inexorably functions, in fact, as a frame of difference that cannot be reconciled. That implacable irreconcilability, which Derrida values as *phylacterion* against the threat of hegemony in his notion of *mondialisation*—a term he prefers to the totalizing Anglo-American lexis of "globalization"—resides in the performative contradictions at the heart of Sophocles' dramatic paradox and of Quintilian's aporetic *adequatio*. This is also the saving grace that finds its poetic and narrative dramatization in the plots of literature that simultaneously manifest the contradictory symptoms of a worldly ambition as they perpetually negotiate their place and global positioning as worlds of literature, as literatures *of* the world, and as literatures *in* the world community. Here, then, are some examples of this worlding by literary texts, texts whose worldliness often outdistances even the ambition of their authors, emerging, in the process, as perennially new world literatures, in good measure because of our ongoing acts of recognition as readers.

Now more overtly than at any other time, world literature is a critical discourse and an epistemological project. The focus of this project is trained on the relationship between the world and its literatures and, contrapuntally, between literature and its worlds. Our endeavors as comparatists, as I have been attempting to illustrate here, crosshatch this conversative mediation between literature and the world and the heterocosms these intersections engender. As a morphing episteme, as an institutional and aesthetic complex, world literature, then, not only designates a textual corpus and its poetics; it is also the name we give to this evolving complex and the way stations of its historical and institutional itinerary in the historical life world of our time.[9]

The history of world literature in our own time is marked, perforce, by the cultural and pragmatic *Realpolitik* that defines our era. Ours is an epoch characterized by a ghastly contestation between, on the one hand, what Jacques Derrida discerned as "the specters of Marx," and, on the other hand, what I shall call the vampires of capital. World literature circulates within this global *agon*, whose inexorable impetus moves through stages of recognition, commodification, consumption, and conversion—transformative processes that ultimately gravitate toward certain invariance or commonality in which exchange value becomes viable as an instrument that tends to consider the allophonic and the exoteric as enticing target and tempting novelty. What is deemed to be different in this process serves as exotic other that boosts the cultural self and intensifies self-identity. The endgame of this process in recent discourse points toward the world as a one-world planetarity the French call *mondialisation*, recently reconsecrated as "the World Republic of Letters."[10] The residual or symptomatic alter-effect of this process is an intriguing phenomenon dubbed *littérature-monde*. This mode of globalization is not an uncontested trajectory, by any means. In particular, it is the target of voices of postcolonial critique that still believe in the possibilities of difference as resistance, rather than as occasion for celebration of self and identity. The first are likely to see in difference a potential for relief from global hegemony, and they clamor admirably against the predations of inexorable neocolonialism. The latter, those given to view difference as occasion for celebration of self and of self-identity, are more likely to replicate the hegemonic impulse and either perpetuate, or be inadvertent accomplices to, neoimperial projects. My own aim here is to remind you how a close adherence to the textuality of literature itself and the (con)textualizing protocols we call poetics could well be our best antidote against this inexorable process. In an age of moribund but ravenous capital, whose predatory drones and zombie minions view all cultures as opportune targets, literature, like all other cultural productions subject to commodification, is considered in terms of its trans-local viability and circulatory market potential. And despite the fact that all signs clearly point to the bankruptcy of a neoliberal, market-driven world system, that phantom superstructure is no less voracious in its ghostly predatoriness.

Within this historical context, the poetics, the discursive formation, institutional idiom, critical categories, and epistemic modus operandi our own pursuits have helped engender as the current binomial of "world literature," entail a historical density that stands in some technical/structural relation to the multiple and diverse literatures of the world. This is by way of reiterating the truism that world literature is neither a given nor a spontaneously occurring phenomenon. As a historically specific and mutating human construct, world literature, like all human constructs, is, above all, self-validating and symptomatic of the particular cultural entailments invested in its construction. Beyond world literature's genesis in this commonplace, there remains the need for a dual discernment—what we might call a requisite literacy, on the one hand, and a worldliness, on the other, for the reading and understanding of world literature. This dual fact of poetics and polity consists in the recognition that (a) within literature itself dwell the precedents for literature's own worlding, and, simultaneously, (b) the world contains the potentiality for its own transformation into literary form. Thus, learning to read world literature makes one literate and worldly by turn. The success of our pedagogies may ultimately be the measure of achievement in enabling those we teach to exercise such dual discernment. Teaching to read literature is teaching to read the world and, once attained, our twofold literacy in these constantly morphing heterocosms enables us to discern the constitutive processes of poetics and politics that make the binomial "world literature" into a complex and contested historical reality with its own contextual attributes.

The most delightful and instructive illustrations of this dialectical relationship between what we construct as world literature and the literatures of the world are to be found in literary works we often read and teach. And this may well be part of what delights us as readers and teachers of literary worlds. In the remaining space of this essay, I would like to glance, however fleetingly, at three examples of literary works from very different epochs and geographies that illustrate this dialectical relationship we have been describing between the two terms under scrutiny—world and literature. The first is by the Chinese writer Lu Chi (his dates are A.D. 261–303); the second text is by the 17th-century English metaphysical poet Andrew Marvell (1621–1678); and the third is by the 20th-century Argentine author Jorge Luis Borges (1899–1986), who has already been mentioned. And although our performative mediation is certainly repercussive on the nature and history of world literature, I hope that the focus remains on literature and the world, rather than world literature as the isolated domain of our own particular poetic constructs.

The work of the 3rd-century Lu Chi teaches us that, much like the axe used to cut and shape an axe handle, the model for the object being constructed is not far off: "In making an axe handle by cutting wood with an axe, the model is indeed near at hand. But the adaptability of the hand to the ever-changing circumstances and impulses in the process of literary creation is such as words can hardly explain."[11] Our rituals of reading and our institutions of verbal literacy are far from being daunted by the difficulty so earnestly stated by Lu Chi. We perennially rise to the challenge of adapting to circumstances and explaining, in words, what Lu says "words can hardly explain," though he himself proceeds, incorrigibly, to give us a verbal explanation of this difficulty that, he says, cannot be explained in words. And, like the model for the maker of the axe handle, our models for making "world literature" are also close to hand, no matter how much we would distance ourselves in reading and theorizing them, as we have seen in the illustrative case of Quintilian, and as I shall continue to demonstrate here.

Like Lu Chi some thirteen centuries before him, the English poet Andrew Marvell performs for us, exemplarily, the conjugation of the literary subject with the object of the world. One of the metaphysical poets, Marvell gives the adjective "metaphysical" a most ironically suggestive resonance through his poem "To His Coy Mistress." In the conversative drama of Marvell's poem and in the urgency of its rhyming couplets, we find a model for the protocols we use in the construction of what we call world literature. We do so, as Marvell illustrates in his poem, by leveraging the differential relation between our metanarrative moves and the literary narratives we take as the object of our scholarly discourse and worldly intercourse. I shall remind us how this occurs momentarily. Here is the poem. First the strophe:

Had we but world enough, and time,
This coyness, lady, were no crime.
We would sit down and think which way
To walk, and pass our long love's day;
Thou by the Indian Ganges' side
Shouldst rubies find; I by the tide
Of Humber would complain. I would
Love you ten years before the Flood;
And you should, if you please, refuse
Till the conversion of the Jews.
My vegetable love should grow
Vaster than empires, and more slow.
An hundred years should go to praise
Thine eyes, and on thy forehead gaze;
Two hundred to adore each breast,
But thirty thousand to the rest;
An age at least to every part,
And the last age should show your heart.
For, lady, you deserve this state,
Nor would I love at lower rate.

And now, the antistrophe:

But at my back I always hear
Time's winged chariot hurrying near;
And yonder all before us lie
Deserts of vast eternity.
Thy beauty shall no more be found,
Nor, in thy marble vault, shall sound
My echoing song; then worms shall try
That long preserv'd virginity,
And your quaint honour turn to dust,

And into ashes all my lust.
The grave's a fine and private place,
But none I think do there embrace.

And, finally, the epode:

Now therefore, while the youthful hue
Sits on thy skin like morning dew,
And while thy willing soul transpires
At every pore with instant fires,
Now let us sport us while we may;
And now, like am'rous birds of prey,
Rather at once our time devour,
Than languish in his slow-chapp'd power.
Let us roll all our strength, and all
Our sweetness, up into one ball;
And tear our pleasures with rough strife
Through the iron gates of life.
Thus, though we cannot make our sun
Stand still, yet we will make him run.[12]

And run the poem does indeed, the impatient cadence of its trochaic tetrameters rushing headlong as tripartite syllogism of strophe, antistrophe, epode, whose logic would brook nothing but worldly consummation in a world and time precipitously waning. All too short of the world and time of otherworldliness and eternity, Marvell's poetic persona would neither defer to the amatory tradition of literary scripture and its amplitude "Vaster than Empires, and more slow," nor would he demur to the "Deserts of vast eternity." Like his model, the Horace of Ode I.11 who eschews the "Babylonian reckonings of Leuconoë" ("*nec Babylonios temptaris numeros*"), and who would, instead, "pluck the day" ("*carpe diem, quam minimum credula postero*"), Marvell's lover would foreshorten the proverbial *déférence* of poetic tradition and surrender, instead, to the urgency of worldly immediacy. Marvell forgoes literature's set poetic protocols as infinite deferral of the textual, opting for the here-and-now of the sexual and its signal "instant fires" of the moment.

Marvell's is an ironic performance by any measure, but irony is as much part of the world as it is of a literature that would constitute itself through the tactical negation of the literary and its discourse in favor of the worldly and its intercourse. While Marvell's erotic prosopopoeia would use the conditional tense in the enumeration, the poet, no doubt, knew full well that there is nothing conditional—of grammar or of eros—in the art of love; that, once loosed, love's invocations are themselves performative acts already clamoring for consummation. Marvell's poetic performance is no less ironic by virtue of likely having occurred at a historical period known as the Interregnum, a Puritan interruption in history whose time falls between the regicide of one monarch (Charles I in 1649) and the post-Cromwellian restoration (with Charles II in 1660). No less ironic in this poetic rehearsal in an apocalypse-tinged revolutionary moment out of normal time is the fact that Marvell's poem only saw the light of publication posthumously, that is, when his own time had already run out. Dispossessed of "world enough and time," "To His Coy Mistress"—the poem and its poetic persona—endures still as a resonant illustration of a literary text that would leave literature behind through a periphrastic juxtaposition of poetic tradition and worldly desire. What we inherit from Marvell, then, is not only an instance, but also an in-process instantiation of world literature in its worldly making.

In May of 1939 the poet Jorge Luis Borges published in the journal *Sur* of Buenos Aires the first literary text he had written in prose. It consists of an inventive *catalogue raisonné*, a genre most suited to the author's mishap and to the ensuing predicament that occasioned the text. Its composition was a test of the author's own reason. He had suffered a serious head lesion in a home accident the previous December, on Christmas Eve, 1938, that had caused fever, septicemia, and a period of loss of consciousness. A blatant instance of the use of literature to probe the reality of one's condition and sanity in the world, the piece has become one of Borges' most popular and oft-cited works precisely, perhaps, because it is a scene of enactment of the relationship between the lifeworld and the poetics of literature. This, of course, is a juncture where many of us often seek self-corroboration and the validation of our own reality and reason, especially since our lifeworld consists, for the most part, of literature. The text is entitled "Pierre Menard, autor del *Quijote*" ("Pierre Menard, Author of the *Quixote*").

Borges' text lends itself to a multiplicity of pedagogical and reading strategies. As a specimen for the teaching of world literature, my students and I view the text as an abyssed structure consisting of ten nested frames scripted in the narrative as its enfolding moves inward from the world to its own worldliness, starting with the seminar, and then the student, the professor, the reader, the translator, Borges, the narrator, Pierre Menard, Cervantes, and nucleating with Cervantes' *Don Quixote*, more accurately, with Pierre Menard's Cervantes' *Don Quijote*. The narrator tells us that the impossible achievement at the heart of this frame-up, part of the just-deceased "Pierre Menard's invisible" *oeuvre*, is his verbatim rewriting, more accurately, actual writing of Cervantes' 17th-century work. Though faithfully redacted, the written words resist the significance of the original because, as world literature, Menard's text is more literature of another world than the world of Cervantes. This is a clear instance of what I have described earlier as a frame of reference turning into a frame of difference, though the framed content may be verbatim. The parts of the *Quijote* Menard succeeded in writing, word for word, in his life-consuming endeavor are, not insignificantly, the ninth and thirty-eighth chapters and a fragment of Chapter 12 of Part I. Each of these deals with translation—the attribution of Cervantes' opus to an Arabic original from which it was rendered for Cervantes' authorial persona into Spanish—the treatment of the labyrinth; and, finally, the fragment, a tongue-in-cheek disquisition on the momentous realization by the hero that mirrors some of our own most stunning academic epiphanies, namely, that in Spanish the words yes and no, *sí y no*, consist of the same number of letters.

Though written in the original, Menard's Spanish is a foreign language, not only because of its different moment in history, but also because Menard is a French Symbolist poet from Nîmes. No doubt, you already begin to recognize the spectral echoes of Paul Valéry and Monsieur Teste as haunting revenants. Unlike the Castilian Cervantes' Spanish, Menard's is allophone, though identical word for word. Published seven decades ago, Borges' text, like the works of Lu Chi and Andrew Marvell, foreshadows some of the key issues in the epistemic complex we currently circulate as world literature.

In our construction of a knowledge field called world literature, as I hope to be illustrating, the examples of Lu Chi, Andrew Marvell, and Jorge Luis Borges had already complicated the more recent claim by our distinguished colleague Franco Moretti that the ambition to forge an epistemic epiphenomenon of literature called "world literature," in his words, "is now directly proportional *to the distance from the text*."[13] The three literary works alluded to here would seem to demonstrate the opposite, namely that the text already inscribes within itself, intimately and unavoidably, the analytical and epistemic protocols for its discursive and narrative permutation into theoretical complexity and critical field, most emphatically a field called world literature. Far from having to distance ourselves from the text through layers of analytical sedimentation in order to arrive at what Moretti, after Marc Bloch, whom he cites, calls "synthesis," the text itself often proffers, *avant la lettre*, a closeness that compromises us in worldly, and worlding, complicity. That proximity resonates declaratively, as in the case of the rhyming prose of Lu Chi's "Wen fu" ("Essay on Literature"), or urgently, as in the dramatic performance of worlding desire in Andrew Marvell's "To His Coy Mistress," or ironically, as in the textual self-ostentations of Jorge Luis Borges' "Pierre Menard." In these random exemplary cases, literature itself rehearses a performative function as projection from the realm of literature into the lifeworld, or a morphing *translatio* from the poetic to the pragmatic. In terms of prosody and poetics, we identify such moves as forms of *metalepsis*, or substitution by compounded metaphorical displacement and translocation. Thus, the axe handle held in the rhyming prose of Lu Chi's lines morphs from poetically created object to model for the creation of an axe handle by the artisan wielding an axe.

In Andrew Marvell, the performance of a passage from the counterfactual-poetic to the actual-noetic (from deed to knowing) is much more dramatically illustrated. Here, the metaphysical is breached in the enactment of a metaleptic glide from the otherworldly literariness into the literal worldliness of carnal knowledge, a slippage, we could say, from the epistemic to the epidermic. Far from the distant layering of sedimented syntheses, the closeness of Marvell's skin-on-skin concupiscence is a slippery propinquity that might leave our friend Moretti more than morose with envy. The world, Marvell demonstrates, is closer than one would think, and literature is the most efficient instrument for closing the distance between the poetically factual and the worldly actual. Marvell's poem maps this traversal through the poetic counterfactuality of a here-and-now that overtakes and subsumes into its world of intimacy the long literary tradition we call amatory, from which the poem itself emanates.

Borges, for his part, demonstrates how the literary text possesses "world enough and time" to foreshadow and romance our most advanced critical notions with trenchant irony. Our theories of historicity, intertextuality, translation, allophony, difference, and our fraught politics of cultural situatedness, originality, and authenticity are anticipated and presciently dramatized with wicked irony.

Our earnest labors would no doubt amuse all three of these predecessors, as they would charm Quintilian. The notional construct of world literature we now naturalize in the realm we are currently given to identify as a World Republic of Letters would appear to these writers to have something parochial about it, something that is highly localized to our disciplinary syndicate, even if its terms resonate around the planet, much to Derrida's chagrin, in global echo rather than in worldly interventions, what he might have called *interventions mondialissants*. There is a salutary reminder in reading or rereading these works, namely that just as the world has literatures, literature has worlds, and ours may well be one of them. Among these worlds, in other words, may well be one we inhabit as world literature. And a certain attentiveness to the etiology of our cosmogonies and to the genetic histories of worlds reminds us that in most human traditions some form of language utterance initially invented or created the world by articulating it into existence and then turned over to that world its own self-cultivation. This commission may well be the most elemental definition of culture, and the complex of language grammars and protocols we know as literature, or as orature, may well be integral to this cultivating task. Its particular jurisdiction that most concerns us we call literary culture. The risk in overlooking this legacy might be an oversight of what is meant by literacy and what the significance of "world" might consist in. Such negligence would likely put into question our worldliness and our viability as literate creatures, leaving us bereft of the ability to read and without the knowledge of what there might be to be read, not least the world itself. We would then be left with little more than what we ourselves construct under the rubric of "world literature" as discourses on, metanarratives to, and epiphenomena of the world and of literature. We in fact find ourselves on precarious ground under the regime of what now goes by the name of the "World Republic of Letters," with the middle term of the trinity—the republic—threatening to subsume the world before it and to spectralize letters into the aura of its own hauntological after-image. The best antidote to this danger and its ghosts might be an insurgent, critical, and worldly literacy. Like Lu Chi's model for the axe handle in hand while cutting a handle for an axe, this literacy is to be found in the literary texts themselves, as I hope to have demonstrated by the random examples of Quintilian, Lu Chi, Andrew

Marvell, and Jorge Luis Borges. The knowledge we attain from this experience translates us, as Quintilian would say, into the ethical horizon of critical theory and literary comparison.

In the first literary manifesto of the 21st century, these "spectropoetics" of self and community are eloquently manifest, more as inadvertent irony than as intentional paradox, in the proclamation of a distinguished coterie of Francophone writers with the declared goal of abolishing *Francophonie*.[14] That this manifesto, entitled *Pour une 'littérature-monde en français,'* should have appeared in a Paris newspaper called *Le Monde* creates a tautological reverberation between the "*monde*" in the title of the manifesto and the name of the Paris newspaper in which it was published. This echoic effect redoubles *mondialisation*, or the global worlding of literature, in ways that would unmistakably suggest *Francophonie* has never been considered to be either French, or properly Francophone. Rather, it seems to have always been, perhaps inadvertently for the signatories of the manifesto, a ghostly allophone—from elsewhere in its territorial genesis and linguistic origins. Dubbed "*littérature-monde*," between quotation marks at that, the new avatar of that literary corpus is finally declared to be "*en français*." In its self-declared soteriology and self-salvaging, the manifesto finally deems this literature to be "*littérature-monde*," having been rather *immonde* until its current cleansing and rebaptism for a renewed, some might say posthumous, form of incorporative exclusion. The collective political heft of the signatories, including a Nobel Laureate, in what used to be called *Francophonie* before this de-nomination is considerable—Maryse Condé, Ananda Devi, Edouard Glissant, Jean-Marie G. Le Clézio, Alain Mabanckou, Abdourahman Waberi. The declaration of this literature, some of the best of it created by the signatories themselves, as world literature, or "*littérature-monde*," now aligns it with its metropolitan French republicanism, bringing it in from the exoteric, allophonic, and non-worldly alterity of its genesis and making it integral to the true and universal Republic of Letters, where the differential and the allophonic are anointed on the common ground of "one-world" and its *heimlich* French foyer.

I read this event as symptomatic of the peculiar convergence of 21st-century *Realpolitik* and literary culture. There is clearly something ironic here that seems to be eluding the signatories of this manifesto, some of the most insightful masters of narrative irony among them: The decommissioning of the term *Francophonie* in the year 2007 in favor of "*littérature-monde en français*" reverts, as symptom of regression, to an originary primal scene. Such reversion resonates harmoniously with the invention of the term *Francophonie* in the 1880s by the French geographer and apologist for empire, Onésime Reclus (1837–1916),[15] for whom, in the best Roman Republican tradition of Horace and Quintilian, *lingua gentem facit*—language makes the people. Reclus himself, ironically named since there was nothing reclusive in his advocacy of imperial expansionism through language as empire's most efficacious instrument, modestly demurs on the ambition of "false universality," prognosticating in biblical and messianic declamation, instead, a world-language status for French extending from Indochina to Africa to both shores of the Mediterranean and both sides of the Atlantic:

> *Empire d'Afrique, Madagascar, Indo-Chine, semblent nous garantir la perpétuité, ce qui veut dire, humainement parlant, la longue continuité de notre idiome. Il cessera d'être la langue faussement dite universelle; mais, retiré dans son grand coin du monde, il deviendra le verbe de centaines de millions d'hommes de toute origine, fils de Japhet, de Sem, de Cham, de Gog et Magog et autres ancêtres inconnus. En dehors de l'île des Hovas et de la presqu'île des Annamites, il résonnera sur les deux rives de la Méditerranée, et aussi sur les deux bords de l'Atlantique.*[16]

The World Republic of Letters, with Paris as its doubly universal capital, "in belief and in reality," as Pascale Casanova would anoint it,[17] is already implicit in this planetary extension of *langue-monde*, now become *littérature-monde* through the first literary manifesto of the 21st century, declared by the progeny of those far-flung *départements d'outre-mer* of the global French commune. In attempting to supervene the paleo-imperial genesis of *Francophonie*, the distinguished signatories of the manifesto end by ushering in the spectral revenant of a neocolonial era, re-inscribing the proprietariness of empire by declaring themselves to be properly worldly and, finally, French.

I merely invoke this development as an articulate instance of what we might call fungible world literature in our age dominated by the specters of Marx and the ravenous revenants of capital. At the risk of troublesome redundancy, I reiterate that the best antidote to this ghastly predation might be an insurgent, critical, and worldly literacy. This literacy, I maintain, is to be found in the poetics of the literary texts themselves, as I hope to have demonstrated by the examples of Quintilian, Lu Chi, Andrew Marvell, and Jorge Luis Borges.

NOTES

1. Marcus Fabius Quintilianus, *Institutio Oratoria*, Liber VIII. Chap. 6. http://www.perseus.tufts.edu/hopper/text?doc=Perseus%3Atext%3A2007.01.0065%3Abook%3D8%3Achapter%3D6%3Asection%3D4

2. Quintilian, *Institutio Oratoria*. http://www.perseus.tufts.edu/hopper/text?doc=Perseus%3Atext%3A2007.01.0066%3Abook%3D8%3Achapter%3D6%3Asection%3D4

3. Edward Said, *Edward Said and the Work of the Critic: Speaking Truth to Power*, 14.

4. In *Other Inquisitions, 1937–1952*, 106–108.

5. Cf. Jacques Derrida, "What Does It Mean to Be a French Philosopher Today?"

6. Djelal Kadir, "To World, to Globalize: Comparative Literature's Crossroads."

7. In Martin Heidegger, *Basic Writings: From Being and Time (1927) to the Task of Thinking (1964)*, 137–212.

8. *Immanuel Wallerstein and the Problem of the World: System, Scale, Culture*, 78–98.

9. Some of the discussion that follows, especially the discussion of the proof texts for illustrating the claims of this essay, has appeared in modified form as part of my article "World Literature: The Allophone, the Differential, and the Common."

10. Pascale Casanova, *La république mondiale des lettres.*

11. Lu Chi, "Essay on Literature [Wen fu]." http://www.humanistictexts.org/luchi.htm

12. Andrew Marvell, "To His Coy Mistress." http://www.luminarium.org/sevenlit/marvell/coy.htm

13. Franco Moretti, "Conjectures on World Literature," 57 (emphasis in original).

14. For a vigorous debate on this development among a number of distinguished colleagues who specialize in French and Francophone studies, see the special issue of *Contemporary French and Francophone Studies* 14.1 (January 2010) devoted to this topic.

15. Onésime Reclus, *France, Algérie et colonies.*

16. Onésime Reclus, *Le plus beau royaume sous le ciel*, 842.

17. Pascale Casanova, *La République mondiale des Lettres*, 49–50.

The Politics of Aesthetics

LITERARY COMMUNITIES

JACQUES RANCIÈRE

I must make some preliminary remarks about my title. As I understand it, a literary community is not a community of writers. It is not a community of people who do, enjoy, or teach literature. Nor is it a community represented in literary works. It is a community framed by literature. This formulation in turn requires some clarifications regarding the two terms: community and literature. As I understand it, a community is not a reunion of persons sharing a common identity. It is a certain fabric made of things that individuals can perceive as constituting their lived world, of names under which they can identify them, of forms of identification of the situations, events, and meanings which make those individuals share a certain "common sense": a broadly shared sense of what is given and what is happening. A literary community is a form of construction of such a common sense. The point is not only about the characters that a literary plot gathers. It is about the weaving of a sensible common fabric within which characters can be individualized and relations between characters can be constructed. Weaving a common fabric does not mean simply inventing spaces and situations within which characters are interconnected. It means first inventing patterns of unity and multiplicity and, second, constructing forms of relation between two patterns of unity: the one which isolates units called "character" or "event," the other which links a multiplicity of characters, situations, and events to constitute the work as a whole.

The creation of such communities is made by words. In that sense, the notion of "literary community" goes far beyond the production of an art named "literature." A literary community exists whenever human beings are gathered by the power of certain words. A religious community (structured by obedience to the Word of God) or a political community (shaped by the power of words such as liberty or equality) are literary communities in that sense. And literature is an implementation—among others—of the broad literary capacity of the human animal. But, on the other hand, it is a specific form of that implementation. This is my second preliminary remark: Literature for me is not the whole made by all the works produced by the human art of writing. Literature is a historically determined regime of identification of this art, the genealogy of which I tried to sketch out in *Mute Speech* and *The Politics of Literature*. Therefore, when I speak of "literary communities" in the narrow sense of the word, I speak of the forms of construction of the common that are specific to literature as a historical form of the art of writing, in opposition to other forms. Now, it should also be clear that the historicity of literature is not simply the historicity of an art. It is the historicity of a form of implementation of the "literary capacity" of the "human animal." The practice of literature sets to work a regime of presentation of facts, connection of events, and production of significations, a sense of the individual and the totality, in short a whole regime of perception and interpretation of experience which exceeds the limits of a specific art. This means that the communities constructed by literary practice do also reveal something about the ways common worlds work in social life and political practice. This is the wider scope of my investigation, though its immediate object is to examine some problems regarding the forms of construction of the common that characterize literature as a historical regime of the art of writing.

As a matter of fact, the novelty of literature as a new regime of writing is not something that has been proclaimed by historical manifestoes. Instead, it has been perceived in a restricted way, mainly through the criticism of critics who only saw its characteristics as the peculiar shortcomings of individual writers or specific literary schools. In *The Politics of Literature* I tried to show how the critique leveled against the "realist" school targeted some features that actually characterized the novelty of literature as such. Now, the interesting point is that such criticism specifically aimed at two main "shortcomings," which in fact concern the two fundamental characteristics that define a fictional community: the community of characters that constitutes the space of fiction and the relation among events that defines its form of rationality. This is notably the case with the criticism leveled in the 1850s and 1860s against the writer who was considered the champion of the so-called "realist" school. Flaubert was blamed first for his incapacity to construct his fictions as a whole, then for his incapacity to select his characters. Reviewing *Sentimental Education*, his colleague Barbey d'Aurevilly found fault with the novelist's incapacity to construct a whole. Flaubert, he said, is a materialist who only knows material events as they are perceived by the senses. Consequently, he cannot build a plot that is an intellectual connection of events. He has only composed pictures and nailed them together. As Barbey puts it:

> . . . [T]here is no book there; there is not this thing, this creation, this work of art constituted by a book with an organized development. . . . He goes without a plan, pushing ahead, without a preconceived overview, not being aware that life, under the diversity and the apparent disorder of its vagaries has its logical and inflexible laws . . . it is a loitering among the insignificant, the vulgar and the abject for the sole pleasure of the walking. . . . [1]

The new novelist was thus blamed for his inability to construct a community of events. Some years before, another critic, Armand de Pontmartin, had given a political interpretation of this incapacity to link events in a whole as he reviewed *Madame Bovary*. It was for him an effect of the invasion of democracy in literature: too many people and things, he said, and, what's worse, too many insignificant people, people who clutter up the space of fiction and hinder the deployment of outstanding feelings and actions. He counterposed this overpopulation to the selection of characters and situations that characterized the fiction of aristocratic times. In the latter, he said,

> . . . the characters embodying all the refinements of birth, education and the heart left no room for secondary figures, still less for material objects. This exquisite society saw ordinary people only through the doors of its carriages and the countryside only through the windows of its palaces. This left wide and fertile scope for the analysis of the finest sentiments, which are always more complicated and harder to decipher in the souls of the elite than amongst the lower classes.[2]

On the contrary, the new "realistic" novel, epitomized by *Madame Bovary*, has no walls separating the inside from the outside, which means that it has no principle of hierarchy. Everybody and everything has equal importance:

> All characters are equal, the farmhand, the groom, the beggar, the kitchen maid, the chemist's assistant, the gravedigger, the tramp, the dishwasher take up a huge space; naturally, the things around them become as important as them. Only the soul could make the difference, but, in this literature, the soul does not exist.[3]

Those criticisms thus make a strict connection between two shortcomings. The "new" literary school is unable to give a novel the unity of a whole because it is unable to select the individualities that are the basic components in the fabrication of this whole. My point is that what is at issue here is not the opposition of two "literary schools." It is an opposition between two ideas of the singular and the whole, two ideas about what an individual and an event are, two regimes of the art of writing which are two regimes of interpretation of experience and of construction of a common sense. What those critiques testify to is not only bourgeois anxiety in the face of the so-called egalitarianism sweeping across society and literature. They epitomize the opposition between the logic of the representative regime of the arts, to which the old practice of the *belles-lettres* belonged, and the logic of literature. *Sentimental Education* is *not* a book, Barbey says, because it does not obey the idea of the whole that makes a "work of art."

The idea of the whole that sustains this judgment dates back, in fact, to Aristotle's *Poetics*. What makes a poem, Aristotle said, is the construction of a fiction. A fiction is an arrangement of actions according to necessity or verisimilitude. This linkage according to necessity or verisimilitude makes the poetic plot a whole—in Greek, a *καθολον*. This is what opposes poetry to history, which only tells events as they happen in their particularity, or, in Greek, *καθ' εκαστον*, one thing after the other. From this opposition Aristotle drew a conclusion: What is important, what constitutes the fabric of the novel, is the arrangement of events that makes a *καθολον*. The words and attitudes of the characters are defined by this arrangement, not by their own personality. But this privilege of action over characters has a correlate: Such actions can only concern individuals who live at the level of the whole, individuals who are able to conceive of great ends and try to reach them, at the risk of facing the strokes of Fortune. They cannot concern people who live in the universe of the *καθ' εκαστον*, people to whom events just happen, one after the other. The distinction between poetic causality and historical succession is also a distinction between two forms of life and two classes of human beings. The wholeness of the work is linked with a certain configuration of the community, a certain distribution of forms of life, separating two kinds of human beings. This is why, in 17th-century France, the Aristotelian hierarchy between events and characters that could be subverted as action was redefined as a conflict of passions—those passions that could only be felt by "the souls of the elite"—in short, by persons of a high rank. This does not mean that ordinary people were excluded from the universe of fiction. They were not excluded, but they were given specific places and roles, or they were included in specific genres—low genres—of fiction. The fictional community was a hierarchical community, defining what individuals could feel, say, and do, according to their place and their identity.

It is this connection between a formal principle of linkage (a causal link of necessity or verisimilitude) and a substantial hierarchy of forms of life that defined the representative community. And it is what was shattered by the emergence of literature as such. The critics denounced this as democratic subversion. Now, it is worth determining what this subversion means exactly. Democracy for them meant that everything and everybody was given the same importance. But this is obviously not the case. All characters are not equal in *Madame Bovary*: Emma Bovary is the character around which all things and all bodies revolve. What is important, then, is the kind of individuality she embodies and the kind of "revolution" of things and bodies linked to that individuality. I shall examine these two points in turn.

First, Emma is not simply the figure of the "anybody" who has the same importance as anybody else. She is the figure of the "anybody" who affirms her capacity to experience any form of life, or, more precisely, to experience the form of life which was reserved to the "souls of the elite," to the "exquisite society," feeling and expressing the refinements of ideal passion. Now, this affirmation is itself the embodiment of a certain "literary" power, the power of words that provoke a split within the existence of those people who were destined to lead the repetitive life of the everyday. Something has happened to her, something that she sums up herself in a few words—such as *felicity*, *passion*, and *ecstasy*—that she has read in novels that were not destined for persons of her condition but for the "souls of the elite." Her individuality, then, is the individuality of the child of the book, who dedicates his/her life to the embodiment of some words. The form of equality that she represents is not the indifferent leveling down described by the critics. It is much more a disruption, the disruption of a normal distribution of forms of life. And this is why her individuality is singled out.

Now comes the second point: How is she singled out? How is that singularity articulated in the common fabric of the novel? What form of linkage of individuals and events does this singling out entail? To answer these questions, I propose that we look at the most famous episode in the book, an episode that has become emblematic of a new mode of construction of fiction, the episode that tells the birth of the love of Emma for Rodolphe amidst the agitation of the agricultural meeting. Rodolphe, the seducer, displays a whole arsenal of words and attitudes, obeying a classical logic of ends and means. But it is not this causal construction that makes him succeed. The birth of Emma's love is a result of a chain of sensory events that occur *καθ' εκαστον*—one after the other—without their aggregation being the effect of any design: the heat of a summer afternoon, the voices of orators filling the air, the murmur of a crowd, the bellowing of the oxen, the bleating of the lambs, small golden lines radiating from black pupils, a perfume of vanilla and citron, a long trail of dust dragged by a stage coach, the memories of a waltz and of old desires whirling like grains of sand under a gust of wind, whose last consequence is that a hand lets itself be seized by another hand. The individual love is born as the consequence of a multiplicity of microsensory events that are carried into a broader flood made up of words read in books, images seen on plates, colored vignettes in prayer books or on keepsakes, perfumes of the altar, or rhythms of sentimental ballads.

In other terms, the disruptive egalitarian individuality is reconstructed by the writer as the manifestation of a new form of common sense. If anybody can set out to live any form of life, and notably to feel the "fine sentiments" of felicity and passion which had previously been reserved to the "souls of the elite," it is because neither the "fine sentiments" nor life itself are any more what they used to be. They are no longer the dispositions of individual souls, but the crystallizations of an impersonal life of sensations that goes through them. What structures the new "literary" community is a new form of common sense. This common sense is made of a whirlwind of impersonal sensory events, a "life of the soul" that has nothing to do anymore with the "souls of the elites" invoked by the champions of the representative universe, since it is an impersonal community of events: a perpetual movement randomly assembling an infinity of atoms that get intertwined, part with one another, and get interlaced again in a perpetual vibration. It is from such a random combination of impersonal events that the "individuality" of an individual is composed. Or, rather, this individuality itself is the conjunction of two processes. On the one hand, it is this combination of sensory events; on the other, it is an identity defined by some narrative functions that fit social forms of identification: being a member of a social class, an inhabitant of a little country town, a daughter, a wife, a lover, and so on. Therefore the story of the "anyone" trying to live the life of ideals and passions formerly reserved to "the souls of the elite" is the story of an individuality participating in two forms of common sense: the common sense constituted by the impersonal dance of the atoms and the common sense defined by the distribution of social identities and proprieties. The character is defined at the junction of those two worlds. But it is also defined by the impossibility of perceiving that duality. Emma is unable to single out the impersonal tissue of events that makes "her" love. She reinterprets this random combination of impersonal events in terms of identity and causality, by making them the manifestations of her personal love for another person. This is why she falls prey to the social logic.

The writer thus retains the power of the impersonal. He retains it as the power of writing, the power of unfurling the life of the impersonal itself by constructing a specific form of egalitarian community: the equality of the sentences, each of which conveys the power of the whole, the egalitarian power of the common breath within which all sensory events are carried.

The literary community is thus constructed as the articulation of two forms of common sense: the common sense of the plot as an arrangement of actions determined by a set of relations between social identities, and the common sense of the sentences conveying a flood of perceptions animated by the breath of the impersonal. Such an articulation raises two kinds of problems. The first concerns the status of the literary unit; the second concerns the status of the literary link. The first problem can be set up as the problem of the relation between the anonymous as a political figure and the anonymous as a literary power. The new novel is made possible by a certain figure of the anonymous: the anonymous as a figure of the literary animal. The peasant's daughter who wants to change her life by experiencing the truth of some words drawn from books destined for the "souls of the elite" belongs to the same family as the emancipated workers who rethink the everyday constraints of their work out of the words describing the pains of the romantic heroes who have "no place in society" or the revolutionaries who appropriate for their struggle the tropes of ancient rhetoric and the emblems of the Roman Republic. Her story is part of a wider form of disruption of the distribution of places, competences, and aspirations that framed a social order. It belongs to a wider affirmation of the capacity of the anonymous, or, in my words, of the power of "taking part," belonging to those who have no part. This power works through operations of disidentification: Individuals who were identified as occupying a certain place in the social whole, and destined to a certain form of life, break away from that identity. The power of the anonymous is the power of disidentification through which individuals break away from the universe of invisible, repetitive life to which they were destined by setting to work capacities that do not fit their "identity."

The revolution through which literature destroys the old fictional hierarchies and proprieties is made possible by those forms of disidentification that disrupt the "normal" relations between identities and capacities. Now, the literary revolution performs a very specific operation in relation to those subversive manifestations of the power of the anonymous. It separates that power of disidentification from the agents who implemented it. Thus, the power of the anonymous is no longer located in the affirmation of those who want to live a life that is not "their" life. It is located in the flood of the micro-events that produce those affirmations as singular forms of crystallization of the Impersonal. Literature turns the power of disidentification into the power of writing itself, the power of dissolving, for its own sake, the rigid forms of social identity and relationships to produce its own events in the breath of the sentences, while leaving its characters on the "bad side" of individuality, the side which entraps them in the universe of stereotyped sentiments and social conventions.

But this repartition of competences between the writer—who takes hold of the power of the anonymous—and the character—who must deal with the order of identities—results in a division of the literary power of constructing the common. This problem can be formulated out of the distinctions made by a writer of the following century who stages in her own way the "politics" of the literary community. In her essay on "Modern Fiction," Virginia Woolf made the conflict of the two forms of common sense explicit as she overturned the opposition expressed by the critics of Flaubert between materialism and spiritualism. In her view, the materialist writers are those who stick to the social, tyrannical logic of the plot with its arrangements of actions and norms of verisimilitude. Those writers, she says, seem constrained by some "unscrupulous tyrant"

> to provide a plot, to provide comedy, tragedy, love interest, and an air of probability embalming the whole so impeccably that if all his figures were to come to life they would find themselves dressed down to the last button of their coats in the fashion of the hour.[4]

To this social/representative distribution of characters and arrangement of events she opposes the truth of life: Life is "a luminous halo, a semi-transparent envelope surrounding us from the beginning of consciousness to the end."[5] It consists of an incessant shower of innumerable atoms that come from all sides. And the task of new fiction is to "record the atoms as they fall upon the mind in the order in which they fall."[6] The representative whole, conceived of as an organic body, is a lie. What is true, what is the truth of life, is the *καθ' εκαστον*. It is the community of the atoms, the patterns that they draw under the name of individual feelings. From this point of view, the construction of the Flaubertian novel looks like a compromise. It tries to reconcile the singularity of the *καθ' εκαστον* with the necessity of making the fiction a whole. Flaubert was the first to raise the main problem of modern fiction: What kind of common fabric of persons and events can be weaved once the old hierarchical distribution of forms of life which circumscribed the space of fiction has been shattered? How can the luminous halo of life be reconciled with the organic link of fiction with a beginning, a development, and an end, which also means a story of wills, actions, successes, and failures? Flaubert proposed a solution that became canonical for "modern fiction": There is no solution at the level of the whole. The solution has to come from the *καθ' εκαστον*: not only at its level, but through it. The solution is to give a twofold function to the thread of narration. It must also serve as a bridge between two worlds: As it links one sentence with another sentence and one narrative event with another, it must also bridge the gap between the logic of the impersonal connections of life and the logic of action, which is a logic of personalization and of causal relation between individual wills and acts. The logic of succession and the logic of action must slide imperceptibly on each other. The writer inserts the vibration of the "power of the anonymous" in the interstices of the plot of love and money. That vibration produces the imperceptible deviation that changes, from the inside, the mode of production of the narrative "action." But we can also put it the other way around: The expression of the luminous halo is incorporated into the inner vibration of the phrases in order to be more easily enslaved to the tyranny of the plot—the chronicle of the everyday, village intrigues, imaginary love stories, and real money worries.

The absorption of the power of disidentification in the respiration of the sentence results in a new subordination to the power of the plot-tyrant. Is it possible then to imagine a form of literary community free from the power of the "tyrant"? And what form of inclusion of the power of the anonymous is implied by that form of community? That question is at the core of Woolf's essay: How to articulate the life of the halo, the construction of singularities, and the construction of the work with a beginning, a middle, and an end, without sacrificing the power of the anonymous, either by absorbing this power in the respiration of the sentence or by submitting the democracy of the manifestations of anonymous life to the tyranny of the plot?

Virginia Woolf's work explores the paradoxes raised by this problem in two directions. On the one hand, the short story "An Unwritten Novel" sets out to draw the whole of a story from the face of an anonymous woman met on a train. As the storyteller is struck by the expression of unhappiness on her face and her vain attempts to rub a stain on the window pane, she sets out to *read* that face, to decipher its secret: the negligence that made the young woman cause the death of a child as she was lingering in a draper's shop, fascinated by trays of colored ribbons; the humiliations suffered at her brother's home; the cruelty of a sister-in-law, and so on. As the story is completed, the train reaches its terminus. At this moment it turns out that the poor lonely creature is a mother that her son welcomes at the station. The lesson of the story is not about the opposition between reality and imagination. It is about the way in which the anonymous can be individualized and work as the principle of construction of a whole of narrative events. The lesson is that the presence of the anonymous in the literary fabric cannot be the revelation of its secret. The will to *read* the face of the anonymous reestablishes the tyranny of the plot. The face must be present, but there must be a mediation between the singularity of the unknown face and the whole of the community of literary events: a mediation working as both a passage and a separation.

In the opposite direction, there is the attempt at constructing the whole as made of singularities that are mere sensory events. The second section of

To the Lighthouse offers an example of this strategy. It describes the life of a house during the long absence of its inhabitants, a life which is, finally, entirely impersonal: the wind blowing, or the trails of dust now standing up as narrative events of their own, instead of becoming the sensations of a woman; the only characters playing in the house are little airs venturing indoors, toying with flapping wallpaper, creaking wood, or tarnished and cracked china; the only events are a board springing on the landing, the fold of a shawl swinging to and fro, a thistle thrusting itself between the tiles, and so on. The events of that impersonal life of airs, dusts, or reflections in pools on the beach are explicitly contrasted with the events that mark the life of human beings and that are the ordinary matter of plots—notably stories of marriage and death—which are irregularly sprinkled in by the narrator in three lines inside square brackets. Those square brackets emblematize the full separation between the life of the Impersonal, which is the stuff of modern fiction, and the events of personal life, which were the stuff of the old one. But they emblematize as well the artifice of that separation. Loneliness and solitude reign in the empty house, but this very solitude presupposes a look seeing it at a far distance, as one perceives a pond in the sunset "from a train window."[7] The community of sensory events cannot have full autonomy. The events of the novel must be micro-sensory events happening to characters who, at the same time, live the normal lives of individuals making plans to achieve their ends: a marriage or a divorce, a degree course at the university, a performance, or a party. Again, some kind of window, both transparent and opaque, must be set up between the "domestic" chain of events and the dispersion of anonymous life.

The construction of the literary community thus appears as the articulation of three terms: the individual, the multiple, and the whole. To understand the problem, we can go back to the episode of the agricultural meeting in *Madame Bovary*. The episode was constructed from the point of view of a spectator able to embrace the three spheres that constituted the scene: first, the couple of individuals standing at the foreground; next, the circle of social types surrounding them; and, finally, the sphere of the impersonal and inhuman chorus spreading around it, including the blows of wind and the trails of dust as well as the bleating and bellowing of the beasts answering one another at street corners. The Impersonal thus was captured inside a whole made of concentric spaces. On that stage, the effect of the crystallization of small perceptions interiorizing the song of the infinite could coincide with the effect of the strategy of the seducer and the logic of construction of the plot. The open universe of sensations was condensed in one point—the individuality of the character—and the effect of this condensation was left to the tyrannical power of the plot.

To avoid that capture, the relation of the individual to the multiple must be constructed as a two-way movement in a decentered space. This two-way movement can be exemplified by the street scenes in Woolf's *Mrs. Dalloway*. At first sight, those scenes are constructed from a solipsistic point of view. Instead of an objective narration of the coexistence of persons and things, we see the characters and events in the street through the perceptions of one individual whose present sensations are blended with old memories. We see them as episodes in the narration of one day in the life of an upper-class woman who goes out in the morning to buy flowers for the party she will give in the evening. But things must be seen the other way around. The decision to buy flowers herself, which determines Clarissa's walk, means the reduction of the acts of will—which determined characters and relations between characters according to the tyranny of the plot in the representative logic—to their most simple expression. Thereby the condensation of sensory events determined by her walk will not become her possession. On the contrary, it will work as a principle of decentering. In *Madame Bovary* the trail of dust dragged by the stagecoach was absorbed in Emma's subjectivity along with the power of the anonymous. It is just the contrary with the sound of an explosion and the rings of smoke traced by a plane during Clarissa's walk. They allow the narration to move from the consciousness of the main character to anonymous lives, on which Clarissa exerts no power and that she does not even know, but which, for a while, get a name and a story—the passers-by who decipher the letters of the advertisement written by the smoke in the sky: Mrs. Bletchey who reads the smoke words as "Kreemo," Mrs. Coates who reads "Glaxo," or Mr. Bowley who thinks it's toffee; the young Maisie Johnson who is just arriving from Edinburgh to work in London, the old Mrs. Dempster who remembers in a flash her hard life, the unemployed truth seeker on the steps of Saint Paul's cathedral with his leather bag stuffed with pamphlets that nobody reads, or the quivering shape, looking like a rusted pump or wind-beaten tree, whose frail voice with no age or sex bubbles up a song without beginning or end and deprived of any human meaning. In the same way, the evening walk of Clarissa's former wooer, Peter Walsh, reveals a virtual community, half hidden, half appearing through uncurtained windows: "parties sitting over tables, young people slowly circling, conversations between men and women, maids idly looking out, stockings drying on top ledges."[8] An infinite richness of anonymous life, which also appears as the upsetting of a social order to the old man rediscovering the city he had left long ago and "suspecting from the words of a girl, from a housemaid's laughter—intangible things you couldn't lay your hands on—that shift in the whole pyramidal accumulation which in his youth had seemed immovable."[9]

The windows through which the walker perceives this infinite democracy of life now work in a way strictly opposite to the windows of the palaces or carriages through which the elites invoked by the 19th-century critic saw ordinary people from afar to preserve the wide space of interaction of their refined feelings. Like the sound of the explosion or the rings of smoke of the plane, they organize the two-way relation through which the determinate life of the characters and the indeterminate life of the anonymous passers-by or the figures behind the windows are reflected into one another. The walk of the upper-class woman who prepares for her party can weave a democratic fabric of community to the extent that it includes those indeterminate lives without absorbing them. The faces seen in a glimpse, in the street or through windows, contain unwritten novels, but those novels must remain unwritten. The possibility must remain a possibility, a virtual opening that puts the "characters" of the novel out of themselves and prevents them from becoming predatory identities. The agenda of Clarissa Dalloway must lose itself in the indeterminate circulation drawn by the spectacles of the street, the loops of a plane, or the echoes of a song. The literary community is made of the intertwining of definite subjective identities and indefinite possibilities of subjectification. The space of interaction of fictional characters must be opened, exceeded by this space of virtual subjectification. That intertwining defines a sphere of coexistence released from the tyrannical constraint of the plot. The literary community exists to the extent that it puts the fictional community out of itself. The lesson of the "unwritten novel" is that the literary fiction cannot be self-contained. It is a milieu without a beginning or an end.

It is, or rather it should be. Like any novel, *Mrs. Dalloway* still must constitute a whole and get to an end. Now it is worth seeing how it can do so. The fact is that, in describing the circulation of the impersonal between Clarissa Dalloway's or Peter Walsh's perceptions and the anonymous figures in the streets or behind the windows, I deliberately skipped over a subjective figure which is central in *Mrs. Dalloway*: the figure of Septimus Smith, the madman who—in a sense—plays the same role as Emma Bovary as he interprets the impersonal succession of sensory events in a personal way. For him, the leaves quivering in the rush of air, the sun dazzling them with soft gold, the sparrows rising and falling in jagged fountains, the swallows flinging themselves round and round, the chime tinkling on grass-stalls, or the gold glow produced by the reflection of light on an omnibus are signs revealing a new religion of love and beauty. He deprives the sensory events of their impersonality and turns them into signs announcing the new religion to the chosen One. Thereby the chosen One becomes the prey of the tyrants: the doctors, who are the social regulators of the right relationships between the personal and the impersonal. As is well known, Septimus can only escape the tyrants by throwing himself through the window. With Septimus's "madness," the happy relation between the walk of the individual characters and the indeterminate sphere of the anonymous around them is broken. The tyranny of the plot is back in the novel. But it is that tyranny that makes the fiction a whole, determined by the opposition of two modes of subjectification: that of the healthy Clarissa and that of the mad Septimus.

Now, there is something more about the inclusion/exclusion of the "mad man." As a fictional figure, Septimus is not only the young man whose brain has been disturbed by the trauma of the war. He is also, the author tells us, "one of those half-educated, self-educated men whose education is all learnt from books borrowed from public libraries, read in the evening after the day's work, on the advice of well-known authors consulted by letter."[10] He is another incarnation of the child of the book: the child of the lower classes who wants to live another life than "his" life; the autodidact who has made a random education for himself and left his obscure provincial town seeking poetic glory in the big city, where he has been swallowed along with millions of other young men called Smith. This new capability of ordinary men and women is what allows "modern fiction" to part with the old logic of action and find its "proper stuff" in any insignificant event. But it is also what modern fiction must send back to its place in order to separate the luminous halo of impersonal life from the personal aspirations of the "half-educated, self-educated" children of the people. Once again, the power of anonymity is separated from its subject—the literary subject, the "anyone" seized by the power of words—so that literature can construct its own power of disidentification and give to the child of the book the role of the wrong interpreter of that power. Emma Bovary, who weaves a personal love story out of perfumes, breaths of air, plumes of dust, little rays of gold around pupils, or reflections of light on rippling water, has to be sacrificed to draw the line of separation between the impersonality of art and the petty bourgeois aspirations to romance, noble feelings, and artistic environment. Septimus, who reads personal messages sent to him by God in the quivering leaves, the dazzling sun, or the rise and fall of the sparrows, must be sacrificed to create the gap preventing the luminous halo of life from identifying with the domestic agenda of a housewife. Their subjective power is absorbed in the power of the sentences before being left to the tyranny of the plot. They are like hostages in the negotiation between the literary community of life and the fictional order of action.

One could say that, through these operations, literature makes itself the hostage of the old tyrant. Literature had absorbed the power of the anonymous and sacrificed the child of the book to its own dream of self-containment. But there is no self-containment of literature. The tyrannical function of the plot must be called for help in order to complete the book. As the "sacrificed" character is also the agent of this return, we could see here something like a return of the repressed. But it is worth looking at another aspect of this impossible self-containment. Literature cannot be self-contained because it has itself blurred the borders that the representative order had drawn between the realm of fiction and that of ordinary experience. This impossibility of self-containment also means that literature, instead of constructing its "own" fabric by absorbing the power of the anonymous, can migrate out of itself and call into question the existing distribution of the roles that puts fiction on one side and reality on the other. Some hasty minds have interpreted this power as an ominous tendency to erase the criteria distinguishing real facts from fictional events that leads notably to the revisionist falsification of history. I think this deduction is off target. The point is not about the existence or nonexistence of reality. It is about its modality. As literature deconstructs the patterns of causality that structured the fictional community, it does not "deny" reality. It calls into question the modes of presentation of facts and the forms of causal linkage that enclose it in the logic of necessity or verisimilitude—a logic which ends up making verisimilitude and necessity equivalent. Now, the point is that this "equivalence" of verisimilitude and necessity is what structures the order of domination itself. It is what is called "consensus." Consensus is not the peaceful agreement of polite interlocutors. It is the form of common sense—or the form of distribution of the sensible—that puts everything and everybody in its place by imposing modes of presentation of facts and modes of articulation of their meaning which preclude the possibility of perceiving other "facts" or giving them another meaning. In that sense, the consensual construction of "our" reality, as it is implemented every day by our governments and our media, is in line with the principles of Aristotle's poetics. Reality is constructed as a certain construction of the possible, a certain arrangement of perceptual facts and significations normally associated with those facts. More precisely, it is constructed as a certain set of relations between the individual and the whole, between the markers of individual reality and the signifiers of statistical generality. It is this articulation that works every day in the dominant discourse and turns rhetorical verisimilitude into historical necessity. And it is also this articulation that literature has the power to break in order to undo the consensual order and give back its power to anonymous life on condition of getting out of itself.

I will briefly examine two examples of such a "sortie." I will first evoke the way in which the young reporter James Agee subverted the practice of documentary reporting that was supposed to give the readers of *Fortune* a general impression of the way in which Alabama sharecroppers lived the hard times of the Great Depression. Agee disrupts the journalistic construction of the real as a likely/necessary set of relations between the markers of individuality and the signifiers of generality. His inventory of all the items stored in all the drawers of the house, his attempt at capturing the light or the smell of the oil lamp, the grain, and the scent of the pine planks of the walls and the breath of the sleeping bodies, his description of the innumerable patches that make the overalls of the sharecropper look "as intricate and fragile . . . as the feather mantle of a Toltec prince,"[11] push to the extreme the "democracy"—the impossibility of selecting—which Flaubert was already accused of. He refuses to select in the décor of the destitute sharecroppers the marks and signs that would make their lives available for the readers/consumers. Instead, his writing emphasizes the absolute singularity of the existence to which this décor belongs, which also means that it connects those lives with the infinity of all the connections in space and time contained in a single minute of the world, with that inexhaustible totality of every instant that literature, in the age of Proust and Virginia Woolf, had opposed to the journalistic selection of marks and signs that frame consensus. The consequence of this choice, of course, is that the journalistic report was turned into a poetic book which no longer had any identity and had, literally speaking, no beginning and no end.

In a different way, Winfried Georg Sebald sought to construct a literary community including all those who have disappeared, who have been exiled or have lost their identity because of historical violence, notably of the Nazi genocide. This attempt demanded a mode of narration able to shift from the diary of the traveler, writing down what he sees while walking at random in the country, to the construction of fictional characters and events, such as the character of Austerlitz in the eponymous novel. This circulation on the border between documentary inquiry and fictional invention is also a circulation between literature and its outside, between the power of the sentence which creates a community of sensory events and the power of the photograph which singles out a person, a face, or a place. The book that tells the story of Jacques Austerlitz combines three elements: first, a fictional relation between two persons that loosely reproduces the social dispositif of the relation of the interviewer and the interviewee; next, a narration condensing a multiplicity of forgotten individual destinies in the story of a single individual; and, finally, a series of photographs scattered all over the narration. The relation between the last two elements is worth commenting on. Those photographs, in fact, play on the indeterminacy of the relation between two characteristics of photography. A photograph is both a marker of singularity and a marker of identity. Now the two aspects can be dissociated and the relation can be left indeterminate. This is the case with the photograph of the young Austerlitz, aged 5, dressed up as a page for a masked ball. This portrait is the photograph of an anonymous young boy, one of those postcards that anybody can buy at a flea market. The duplicity of the photograph reproduces the literary tension between the fictional characters and the indefinite possibilities of subjectification. The pseudo-inquiry—or the pseudo-novel—breaks the consensual distribution of genres of writing. It constructs the life of an individual and weaves around it a community of the living and the dead. It does so by playing on the relation between two forms of anonymity: the anonymity of all those who have been violently deprived of their life or of their identity, and that of all the ordinary lives, those "births" that "have sunk into anonymity," evoked by Mallarmé in the prose poem "Conflict."[12]

The community constructed by literature then appears to be an unstable community. In a first sense, it is the expression of a new "literary community" in the broad sense of the word. It expresses the paradoxical identity of a new social and political figure, the anonymous, that breaks away from the identity allotted to him or her in the old hierarchical order. Literature tried to construct its own fabric by absorbing that power. But it never succeeded in enclosing it inside a steady set of relations between the individual, the multiple, and the whole. It thus made the power of the anonymous travel between two poles: the pole where it is dissolved in the tissue of impersonal life and the pole where it is subdued again to the forms of definition of individualities and the forms of construction of the whole, framed by the representative tradition. But literature can also migrate outside itself and use that power of dissolution of identities and links to question the consensual distribution of the genres of discourse and of the forms of identification of individuals and events which reproduces, in the conditions of the present, the old hierarchical distribution of the forms of life.

NOTES

1. Barbey d'Aurevilly, "L'Éducation sentimentale" (my translation).
2. Armand de Pontmartin, "Le Roman bourgeois et le roman démocratique. MM. Edmond About et Gustave Flaubert," 322 (my translation).
3. Ibid., 322–23 (my translation).
4. Virginia Woolf, *Modern Fiction: The Essays of Virginia Woolf*, 160.
5. Ibid.
6. Ibid.
7. Virginia Woolf, *To the Lighthouse*, 176.
8. Virginia Woolf, *Mrs. Dalloway*, 118.
9. Ibid.
10. Ibid., 109.
11. James Agee, *Let Us Now Praise Famous Men*, 268.
12. Stéphane Mallarmé, "Conflit," 360 (my translation).

ANTIRACISM AND (RE)HUMANIZATION

PAUL GILROY

> Atheism, being the supersession of God, is the advent of theoretical humanism, and communism, as the supersession of private property, is the vindication of real human life as man's possession and thus the advent of practical humanism. Or, atheism is humanism mediated with itself through the supersession of religion, whilst communism is humanism mediated with itself through the supersession of private property. Only through the supersession of this mediation—which is itself, however, a necessary premise—does positively self-deriving humanism, *positive* humanism, come into being.
>
> —KARL MARX, *CRITIQUE OF HEGEL'S PHILOSOPHY IN GENERAL*

Fanon's advocacy of revolutionary change was distinguished by his preparedness to speak from the torrid zone in humanity's name, yet the commitment to a new humanism that runs through his writing has proved to be a tricky subject for contemporary commentators. As a result, his humanism is rarely discussed. However, the claims to novelty and distinctiveness that frame it are ripe for reassessment. He makes a series of arguments which move toward what, following the South African psychologist and TRC commissioner Pumla Gobodo-Madikizela, we might venture to call a "reparative" humanism.[1] This tantalizing prospect can help to clarify a number of problems that characterize the embittered workings of our *post-colonial* world.

The reparation involved in this new humanism is neither straightforwardly financial nor moral. Fanon had a variety of ontological reparations in mind and they were rooted in the specific task of undoing the damage that had resulted from the violent institutionalization of racial orders. The need for those repairs raised a second important possibility: We may need to begin to become human outside of (as well as in opposition to) racial-corporeal schemas and the epidermalized worlds that they generate and secure.

Fanon's humanism was configured by a larger anticolonial project: the *revolutionary* overcoming of racial orders stemming from colonial conquest as well as those that gave rise to colonial rule. The pressing need for a new humanism emerged in tandem with active pursuit of national liberation, a goal that Fanon qualified by introducing an equally novel and emphatically postcolonial world consciousness that exceeded the abstract formalities of previous kinds of internationalism. These universal hopes had been formed by World War II and the wars of decolonization that followed, as well as by his conviction that an authentic existence, celebrated in human desire, could remain uncorrupted by the sociogenesis of racialism. Additionally, a distinctive cosmopolitanism was signaled by Fanon's insistence that Europe's colonial crimes and errors should not be repeated by newly independent, postcolonial states—a historic determination that resonated loudly with his choice of a cosmic rhetoric that it would be wrong to write off as mere juvenilia. As Ato Sekyi-Otu has suggested, an affirmative conception of the human was introduced by seeing the human being as "a yes that vibrates to cosmic harmonies."[2] It bears repetition that Fanon's idiosyncratic response can be seen to have been shaped by the need to respond to the exclusionary power of racism which specified blacks and other natives as infrahuman.

Pumla Gobodo-Madikizela has augmented Fanon's unfashionable commitment to a new humanism by connecting it with an unlikely argument about the transformative power of empathy which has been created from the project of undoing apartheid in South Africa. Her suggestion is deeply unsettling to the closed system of contemporary scholastic theory. She presents the post-traumatic restoration of amputated and alienated humanity as a central component in a shared process. Through their empathy which generates acts of forgiveness, the victims of apartheid—and by extension, of colonial terror in general—acquire the dignity that racism denies them and are freed from the grip of trauma. Simultaneously, and more controversially, the criminal perpetrators of white supremacist brutality may also gain access to the humanity they have neglected or destroyed through their cruelty and violence. She describes this element as their rehumanization, though humanization might be a more appropriate name for it. This double change can only be accomplished if the latter group is prepared to open itself to the difficult, healing potency of telling the truth. The significance of that evasive possibility increases in the South African case when it is undertaken in the shadow of palingenetic, nonracial justice.

Taken together, these developments can contribute to a distinctive figure of the human. Their confluence illuminates some of the difficult issues pending far away from the reformed precincts of apartheid: in the crisis of Europe's postcolonial multicultures and the ongoing battle against the racial ordering of the world that has recently been recast in civilizationist language as a global counterinsurgency.

In Europe's postcolonial countries, a distinctive political agenda has recently emerged from the pursuit of a habitable multiculturalism and the related need to appreciate and perhaps also cultivate exposure to alterity as something beyond mere plurality and something apart from loss, anxiety, and risk.[3] Those struggles have helped to shape responses to the belligerence that has lately come to define Europe's geopolitical predicament and cement the corrosive conviction that cultural diversity cannot coexist with either democratic fraternity or social solidarity.

HISTORY

Understanding Fanon's approach to the human can only be enriched by intimate familiarity with the French intellectual and political scene in which his intervention first took shape. However, the enduring currency of *The Wretched of the Earth* shows that the significance of the issues he raised extends far beyond that original setting.[4] I cannot reconstruct those debates in their entirety here, but we should note that they involved a mixture of political and philosophical argument. His contributions to a range of debates—over phenomenology, corporeality, subjectivity, and temporality—were conditioned by the aftermath of the war against the Nazis, which had left the French polity deeply fractured. It is harder, but no less important, to appreciate that those discussions were also addressed to the new context emerging from the war against the Vietminh. The conflict over decolonization was reignited in 1945, just after French forces moved into Sétif, Guelma, Kherrata, and other Algerian towns to extinguish the pro-independence sentiment evident among soldiers returning from Europe's battlefields.

In that context, Fanon was not just indicting previous humanisms for being too readily reconciled with racial hierarchy; he was also taking aim at the complacent brand of antihumanism that had been catalyzed by the effects of war. Indeed, the need to establish a connection between the ethics and politics of anti-Nazi resistance and the moral momentum of anticolonial struggles provided the trigger for his reflections on the pitfalls that resulted from racializing humanity. His thoughts were framed by an antiracist disposition that could not have been more broadly defined. The social habits required by humanity's epidermalization presented Fanon with a particular target, and he placed his analysis of them in a world-historic setting:

> In reality, the national flow, the emergence of new states, prepare and precipitate the inevitable ebb of the international colonialist cohort. The advent of peoples, unknown only yesterday, onto the stage of history, their determination to participate in the building of a civilization that has its place in the world of today give to the contemporary period a decisive importance in the world process of humanization.[5]

Other aspects of Fanon's call for a new humanism prove equally perplexing to a contemporary readership. His non-immanent critique of race cuts through conventional approaches at an oblique angle. The idea of race is presented and then dismissed as a symptomatic feature of modern political ontology which had been marked indelibly by Europe's colonial contacts and conflicts. This distinctive stance amplified Fanon's vociferous attachment to the idea that the variety of humanism he proposed was entirely novel. His determination that implacable opposition to racialism made this different from other humanisms resonates with his earlier identification of what he had termed the "real dialectic between my body and the world."[6]

The original formulation of that rare dialectical possibility arose in a difficult passage from *Black Skin, White Masks* in which Fanon was at his closest to both Merleau-Ponty and Césaire. It still repays careful study.[7] A racialized—and therefore, in his terms, an alienated—modality of being in the world, "the corporeal-racial schema," is contrasted negatively with the altogether different kind of existence evident in the ordinary operations of bodily schemata outside of, or more accurately, both prior to and after, the sociogenesis of a racialized world born from bloody conquest and reproduced by brutal colonial administration. This race-producing aberration from the normal mechanisms that assemble human subjects provides an additional stimulus for the embodied curiosity which Fanon invested with revolutionary force. His approach involved a view of selfhood being composed slowly as different human bodies move—with varying degrees of difficulty—through time and space.

In conjunction with colonial domination, Manichaeism both creates and supports racial orders—mutually reinforcing ensembles that are essentially unstable. The tropical para-politics formalized in governmental instruments like the British dual mandate[8] constitute what we can call pseudo-polities—formations that disrupt historical and social processes among the conquered and colonized. The damage that results from them is manifest in a deep estrangement from the human that is always transacted under the ontological architecture of race. Here we are obliged to acknowledge that Fanon's approach to alienation differs substantially from Hegelian and Marxist understanding of that concept. In an example of what it meant practically to stretch Marxian analysis until it became adequate to colonial settings, his emphasis does not fall, as is usual, upon the interrelated dynamics of domination and mystification with recognition, but on two adjacent problems: first, the issue of systematic misrecognition, and second, the need for a sharpened sense of mutual relation which will, we are told, pave the way to "the reciprocal relativism of different cultures, once the colonial status is irreversibly excluded."[9]

Fanon's presentation of a profound, deeply racialized variety of alienation shares something with the disturbing work undertaken on the same topic by of one of his key African American influences: Richard Wright. The novelist had steered similar paths through the analytical problems presented by interwar Marxism and the relationship between racism and Fascism. Wright had tried to theorize these problems during the 1940s while still fighting his way out of communist orthodoxy.[10] Both thinkers acknowledged the metaphysics of race that was inscribed in a sequence that involved several stages. Initially, one sees oneself being misrecognized. Then one experiences the effect of being coerced into becoming reconciled with the dismal, infrahuman object with which one has become confused: the

Negro, nigger, or *negre*. Finally, the habitual, social character of the whole destructive process becomes apparent through appreciation of its ubiquity.

> The word "Negro," the term by which . . . we black folk in the United States are usually designated, is not really a name at all nor a description, but a psychological island whose objective form is the most unanimous fiat in all American history; a fiat buttressed by popular and national tradition . . . which artificially and arbitrarily defines, regulates, and limits in scope of meaning the vital contours of our lives, and the lives of our children and our children's children.
>
> This island, within whose confines we live, is anchored in the feelings of millions of people, and is situated in the midst of the sea of white faces we meet each day; and, by and large, as three hundred years of time has borne our nation into the twentieth century, its rocky boundaries have remained unyielding to the waves of our hope that dash against it.[11]

Whether or not they are specifically colonial, all racial orders reveal how the damage to humanity accumulates. Wherever they are, eventually those formations initiate something like a habitual culture of their own. For Fanon, their undoing can only commence once the liberating refusal to "accept the present as definitive" becomes shared and the door of every consciousness is opened by "the real *leap*" that introduces "invention into existence."[12] That huge transformation involves decisionistic acts of freedom-seeking which confidently refuse the diminished, in Fanon's terms the "amputated" or "mutilated," humanity offered by alienated Europe's "constant denial of man" and its symptomatic accompaniment: an "avalanche of murders."[13] *The Wretched of the Earth* sets out what these transformative aspirations involved in the context of national liberation.

POSTCOLONIAL EUROPE

The postcolonial settlers who, like Fanon, made their way to Europe as its empires were being painfully renounced, have now created a substantial archive in many languages that extends his projects and shows their significance at both ends of the no-longer imperial chain. Today, European readers can turn to the fruits of a multilingual, antiracist tradition which, like Sven Lindqvist's exemplary *The Skull Measurer's Mistake*, explores how the perennially unfashionable commitment to a world without racism might specify a division of labor for transformative endeavors even when they are conducted inside the fortifications of postimperial and neocolonial countries.

Analysis of Anders Brevik's murderous, civilizationist assault on multiculturalism in Norway—his response to the rise of Islam in Europe—is likely to bring renewed urgency to this task. It is impossible to understand his islamophobic actions or the misoxenist justification he provided for them without paying close attention to the histories of European raciology. The examination of his crimes conducted so far has not only generated a political geography that encompasses the virtual world but also shows how successive layers of respectable racism and ultranationalism have organized the relationship between fringe and mainstream strands of political opinion.[14] The complexities of the trans-local formation that sustained his murderous ideology are still evolving, but they exhibit the general features of the racism that endorses it. Its hatred, like its libertarian credentials, is framed by appeals to racial rationality.[15]

Lest the immediate significance of Fanon's stubborn humanism be made to appear too self-evident in this setting, we should also note that the warm and cold currents of structuralist and poststructuralist thought converged around the idea that any humanism was, at best, an anachronism. In different ways, Fanon's earnest, and today firmly disreputable, commitment to an *antiracist* humanism, fell afoul of the founding presuppositions of 20th-century scholastic theory. Following the viral circulation of the UN Declaration of Human Rights and its various vernacular recordings by antiracist and anticolonial struggles, the cold war–era politics of humanism developed in antinomic patterns that still haunt our own situation. As a result, the pressure to reformulate the human in both human rights and humanitarian intervention has initiated deeper conflicts than Fanon was able to anticipate.

I do not want my plea for a return to Fanon's humanism to be misunderstood. This is not a moment in which to indulge the facile idea that interpretation of the postcolonial world can or should proceed easily from the proposition that there is a unitary human essence—as simple as it is universal—which gets somehow lodged in every individual subject. However, it is unrealistic to imagine that the power of that proposition can be answered simply by pretending that we can easily dispose of it and its extensive institutional consequences. What can be termed tactical use of that idea has been made repeatedly. It has appeared in the political claims made by movements for democracy, national liberation, and emancipation from the effects of racial hierarchy. It has recurred in the pursuit of civil and political rights which have long been intertwined with the thwarted aspiration to win recognition as fully human—an enterprise that now stains the post- and neocolonial world just as it once marked the colonial era.

The argument below follows Fanon in making a much more specific demand: the damage done by racism, raciology, racialism, and racial hierarchy requires particular forms of acknowledgment. They must involve not only political and juridical gestures but also philosophical ones. They must amount to significantly more than a vague admission that people are doomed always to do bad, hurtful things to each other—perhaps because their self-hatreds and resentments consistently interact with and usually corrupt their relationship to alterity.

Several historical and conceptual problems become evident here.[16] Addressing them demands a much larger inventory of the toll that race-thinking has taken from the age of European universalism than is currently conventional even on the left. The political ontology of races necessitates a revision of modernity understood as epistemology, *techne*, and aesthetics as well as the historic union of capitalism with democracy. In an insightful and provocative piece on racism, Cornelius Castoriadis linked the vitality and ubiquity of misoxeny and racial hatred to the "natural inclinations" that underpin human sociality as well as the self-creation and self-loathing that distinguish modern society and ipseity. We do not have to travel the full distance with him in order to see that the unsettling path he has identified may lead us away from the idea that European racism has unique features and the belief that confronting it is an important task of political struggle.

The Jamaican American philosopher Sylvia Wynter has suggested that the pursuit of these aims can be strengthened if it is articulated together with Fanon's view of racism's sociogenesis and his plan for the destruction of its psycho-existential complexes. In the longer term, those battles may be able to contribute to what she describes as humanism's "re-enchantment," a creative and joyful process that, in Jamaica, had been dominated by the subversive Ethiopianist reworkings of UNESCO's blank poetics by insubordinate roots reggae artists like The Abyssinians, The Heptones, and Burning Spear, all of whom authored anthems on the theme of humanity and human rights which have endured, while the vindicationism, Pan-Africanism, and Garveyism from which they grew have ebbed away.

THE COSTS OF ANTIHUMANISM

The 20th-century antihumanists who first authored the dubious positions that still warrant today's campus common sense have enabled unsympathetic interpretations of Fanon that masquerade as critiques of his perspective delivered from the left. His daring hopes are represented as naïve or incompletely thought-through responses that—their supposedly enthusiastic view of violence aside—spill over into empty, compromised humanisms of the liberal and UNESCO varieties. From this angle, Fanon is judged to have remained too fixated on Europe's oblique redemption rather than its systematic provincialization. So far, that absurd verdict—which involves a grave misreading of his arguments about the necessity of *and* the costs involved in colonialism's violent overthrow—has not been tested.

During the phase of decolonization, it was not only dissenting fragments of the colonial elite who observed that discussion of the integrity (and the boundaries) of the human was being conditioned by the aftermath of the struggle against Hitlerism. Then, as now, it was neither respectable nor polite to focus on the constitutive power of racism as populism or to analyze Nazi statecraft as the governmental implementation of a racial hygiene directly connected to the genocidal history of colonial rule conducted both inside and beyond Europe. Old 20th-century rules still prevail in the rarified world of scholastic antihumanism. The vestigial disciplinary force mustered by fascism's philosophical apologists does not sanction any uncomfortable considerations of their own relationship to the political ontology of race that was celebrated and affirmed by the likes of Heidegger, Schmitt, and the other Nazi colossi of contemporary theory. However, the influence of those figures helps to make Fanon's reparative, antiracist humanism, like his politics of national liberation, appear facile. If Nazism was, after all, not radical evil but rather a catastrophic trace of metaphysical humanism that reveals the problems with all forms of humanism, few brave souls will be prepared to subscribe to the grand folly of humanism's reconstruction.

The Marxian philosophical anthropology, with which Fanon's project had been enmeshed, moved in different directions under the impact of Foucault's work. At the same time, a variety of feminist pronouncements raised questions about the relationship of gendered categories to humanity and citizenship as well as to the prospects of trans- and posthumanity after the end of our species' natural evolution. Donna Haraway's classic pronouncements on this theme resolved it by collapsing the agency of the military cyborg into the posthuman affinities of California's women of color. In her later work, Haraway's disaggregation of the human seems to have required her to displace the challenges of alterity and interdependency on to inter- rather than intraspecies relations. The distinctive U.S. conditions in which she operates specify that racialized interactions should continue as long as they are purged of hierarchy as far as practicable. She transmits a sense of her priorities in this passage:

> The discursive tie between the colonized, the enslaved, the noncitizen, and the animal—all reduced to type, all Others to rational man, and all essential to his bright constitution—is at the heart of racism and flourishes, lethally, in the entrails of humanism.[17]

Rather than making humanism responsible for the development of racism, Fanon, who does not share Haraway's apparent interest in reifying racial identity, approaches racism as a cause of the corruption of humanism that is evident in the history of colonial rule. In other words, he sees humanism as a factor in undoing Haraway's "discursive tie." Additionally, he provides us with an incentive to imagine a new humanism that has been contoured specifically by the denaturing of race and the repudiation of racial orders.

Before we can proceed further, we must reckon with the fact that in the name of science, the proper name "humanist" has lately been hijacked and monopolized by the zealous secularism of Richard Dawkins and his ilk. They represent a proud formation that is studiously indifferent to the postcolonial reconfiguration of the world and significantly refuses to make even the smallest gesture that might compromise its view of Islam as what the great scientist recently termed "an unmitigated evil."[18] How debates over the human and its limits became linked to the political ontology of races and the resulting struggle against racial hierarchy is scarcely of interest to their belligerent, scientistic civilizationism. Whatever Defoe and Diderot, Montesquieu and Mary Shelley had to say on the subject of human selves and human others, their subtleties do not detain today's ethnocentric caricatures of Enlightenment.

To follow Fanon's lead, then, we must accomplish what brittle, formulaic humanisms refuse to do and reorient ourselves precisely by developing an intimate familiarity with Europe's continuing colonial crimes and the raciology and xenology that sanction them. Then we may start to ask how a refiguration of humanism inspired by, but moving beyond, Fanon's own might help rectify Europe's inability to acknowledge its postcolonial predicament.

We must therefore address the question of how to remake and improve Europe's relationships with its unwanted settler-migrants, refugees, denizens, and illegals: all those racial and civilizational inferiors judged infrahuman, whose lives are accorded a diminished value even when they fall inside the elastic bounds of the law. That belated adjustment is now an urgent matter. The problems associated with it have only been augmented by the way that the imperative of security saturates fading political institutions which are inadequately sustained by their supposed humanitarian commitments.

While new further humanitarian military interventions are being planned in the name of our civilization and its supposedly distinguishing values, we cannot turn away from the full impact of this unfortunate alignment of forces. And yet neither can we deny that debates over the ethical underpinning of our species' life have a long, important, and, I would submit, an unfinished history. Edward Said pointed to some of the relevant ground in his book *Beginnings*, where, as part of a bigger argument over the implications of a recurrent pattern in which "humanism thus engenders its own opposite,"[19] for a tantalizing moment he dared to place the legacies of Vico and Fanon in a provocative counterpoint:

> When Vico speaks of a mental language common to all nations, he is, therefore, asserting the verbal community binding men together at the expense of their immediate existential presence to one another. Such common language—which in modern writing has appeared as Freud's unconscious, as Orwell's newspeak, as Lévi-Strauss's savage mind, as Foucault's épistémè, as Fanon's doctrine of imperialism—defers the human center or *cogito* in the (sometimes tyrannical) interest of universal, systematic relationships. Participation in these relationships is scarcely voluntary, only intermittently perceptible as participation in any egalitarian sense, and hardly amenable to human scrutiny.

The formulations that Said lists emerge from what could be identified as a succession of "strategic" universalisms. Typically, their architects have attempted to liberate the human, and indeed humanism, from the strictly bounded Cartesian space enclosed neatly on one side by a relationship with animal nature and on the other by an evolving account of ourselves defined by the most advanced or prosthetic technologies. Digitalia is a long way from clockwork, but Said is right to identify this difficult, challenging agenda as a spine supporting the weight of Fanon's emancipatory, anticolonial projects. In other words, he was right to place Fanon's cold war scheme in that distinguished company.

If the challenge to humanism implied here is to endure into the era of genomics and biometrics, molecularization and humanitarianization, depoliticization and neoliberalization, it will have to be updated. We will be required to relocate the desire to reassemble humanism so that it can appear in conjunction with a renewed analysis of the alienated modes of social interaction that still derive from the racialization of the world and the Manichaean specifications that underpin it.

Fanon's demand for a new humanism is, as I have said, a key aspect of his non-immanent critique of racialized modalities of being-in-the-world. His historical ontology and his humanism should therefore be approached as vehicles for the reconstruction of social orders that manifest their enduring pathology via the attachment to race and the characteristic forms of alienation that raciologies transmit and amplify. Fanon's humanism is neither a residue of, nor a throwback to, debates over philosophical anthropology that preceded the emergence of a scientific anatomization of capitalist domination and its human cost. That essential but also limited agenda was surpassed when he dared to place racial hierarchy, racial epistemology, and the political ontology of races at the center of a self-consciously anticolonial yet firmly cosmopolitan analysis. At this point, we can begin to appreciate that the new humanism, as Fanon imagines it, is asking us to consider problems that previous humanisms have been reluctant to entertain.

The 20th century saw the racial *nomos* that had been established in the process of European imperial expansion steadily being overthrown. The persistence of racism in postcolonial and multicultural societies renews the obligation to re-engage with—and, as Sylvia Wynter suggested, hopefully to re-enchant—humanism. The antiracist and reparative humanism that results is only warranted by its detailed, critical grasp of the damage done to ethics, truth, and democracy by racial discourses that would not be undone even by the therapeutic grotesqueries of "identity politics" that Fanon swiftly dismissed elsewhere as "the Fraud of a black world."[20]

HUMAN TERRAIN: WAR AND HUMAN RIGHTS

The decolonization process is still incomplete. However, the terms of its legitimization have been redefined by the effects of human rights discourse, by the newfound power of humanitarian political rhetoric that has been employed to justify a sequence of neoimperial conflicts over scarce resources: energy, water, minerals, and so on—and, in particular, by changes in communications technology. The way that racism can be articulated has also been altered, initially by a shift away from biology and hierarchy toward cultural difference and plurality, and then by a further change which saw race projected and enacted on the molecular scale. Thus reconfigured, biology and political anatomy have returned with a vengeance in the "neuro" and the "nano."

Despite the postcolonial and neoliberal framings imbued in them through the corporate multiculturalism celebrated by an emergent global elite, these developments support the tacit racialization of the world which is being pronounced emphatically elsewhere in culturalist and civilizationist terms. The old fantasy of linear progress is retained but can be offered in two new flavors: secular enlightened and postsecular Christian. They share a common foundation from which monolithic, medieval, and despotic Islam can be repeatedly counterposed to attractive images of Europe and the West. The racialization process is cemented by the invocation of an absolute ethnicity that is usually signaled in religious terms: a pattern that circulates through the conflicts it feeds, consolidating and monopolizing the human in heavily culture-coded forms where issues of gender and generation are primary.[21]

The resilience of this system can be explained both by its Manichaean character and by the fact that postcolonial relations, including global counterinsurgency struggles and civilizationist wars, are no longer confined exclusively to obviously postimperial states.[22] NATO's expansive role, like that of ISAF at war in Afghanistan, makes all the participating military forces it includes into postcolonial actors whether or not they see themselves as having previously been beneficiaries of colonialism. More than that, there is a high degree of historical and geographical continuity between the wars of imperial decolonization and the global campaign that is currently underway.

These apparently interminable conflicts, which have developed far beyond the contested airwaves that had attracted Fanon's keen and curious ears, now feature the full repertoire of "smart power." The informational aspects of the war encompass all the digital mechanisms which Bob Zoelick, then president of the World Bank, termed "Facebook diplomacy" in 2008. Before he had helped to find that proper name for them, something like the same idea had already been taken up, instrumentalized, and refined as a strategic instrument by a number of key thinkers in the U.S. State Department, the U.S. military, and their various corporate counterparts. This was long before 2011's "Arab Spring" brought infowars and social media tools into mainstream geopolitical view.

The most vocal and prominent of these governmental figures was Jared Cohen, who had served under both Bush and Obama administrations as a member of the secretary of state's Policy Planning Staff charged with the development of 21st-century statecraft. Cohen, who recently left U.S. government employment to become the director of Google Ideas, had been centrally involved with the task of diverting young Muslims from the "radicalization track." His wide-ranging analysis presented social media, youth, and consumer cultures as key resources for organizing U.S. interests in the Middle East. Drawing inspiration from events in the Philippines and Latin America, Cohen viewed the distinctive demography of the Middle East as an additional inducement to address the experience of the disenchanted young and to turn their frustrations into a novel political movement from which they might emerge, de facto, as vanguard parties of opposition to despotic regimes:

> . . . [I]n Colombia, young people used Facebook to put 12 million people into the streets against the FARC, a 40-year-old terrorist organization. As a result of what new technology offers, the current generation of youth can act one way at home and in their community, while having the option of taking greater risks online. More prescriptively, they have unprecedented tools for empowerment at their disposal.[23]

Waging an effective infowar requires exercising control over social media and cultural habits. The young are therefore to be influenced or steered remotely through the autopoietic, technological infrastructure of their own ludic personal "empowerment." Cultural and indeed military diplomacy aspire to employ all the techniques of propaganda and public relations in conjunction with new digital tools in order to engineer the imagination. We must therefore concede the growing inadequacy of critical approaches based upon a too-simple view of digital communications technologies as neutral or transparent.

The trajectory of Jared Cohen's career supplies an indication that the relationship between private and governmental actors in this emergent field of power and statecraft has not yet solidified. Further clues as to the impact of that blurring can be deduced from the fact that the work of global securitocracy has been partially outsourced and contracted to secret and shady entities like Xe Services—now blandly rebranded as "Academi." This kind of war is often conducted from an invulnerable distance by remote devices such as drones.[24]

The latest sequence of doomed military adventures, which is novel only in being warranted by the liberal goal of enforcing gender equality, introduced what was called the "Human-Terrain System."[25] It ensured that anthropologists were embedded alongside kinetic and infowarriors in a total military effort that could engage directly with the problems of cultural difference, relation, and translation.

These schemes presented the human as a contested object on an expanded battlefield. They dovetailed with an expanded definition of humanitarian intervention—a term that specifies that uniquely vulnerable groups—LGBT, women, children—must be protected from the cavalcade of medieval barbarity that is Islam. This will be done surgically through all the advanced killing equipment of a uniquely clean war: UAV drones, cluster bombs, depleted uranium shells. Kinetic warfare must be supplemented by softer and subtler technologies. In Afghanistan, for example, there has been an innovative system of corruption-reducing, capacity-building banking based on mobile phones that will conveniently also double as cameras and screens for photographing oneself and one's loved ones rather than circulating unhelpful video clips of the latest war crimes and collateral damage.[26]

The same digital technology has other battlefield applications which not only help to identify exactly where the porous boundaries around vulnerable humanity are going to fall but also help to demonstrate how particular technologies assemble and project the human. The U.S. military has recently invested in a new set of biometric devices that will, no doubt, eventually find broader applications in the fields of security and law enforcement at home and abroad. These methods were pioneered in the battle of Fallujah.[27] A dispatch from the Afghan frontline captured their place in the unfolding of what one theorist of global counterinsurgency has called "armed social work":[28]

> Things reached a chaotic peak when soldiers spotted a young man with a neatly trimmed goatee, apparently snapping photos with a cellphone camera. They stopped him, made sure the pictures were deleted from his phone and digitally scanned his irises and fingerprints with a BATS (Biometric Automated Tool Set) scanner. The young man was not detained, but now he was in the system.[29]

MAN AS USUAL: BETWEEN ANIMALITY AND TECHNOLOGY

The proliferation of biometric technology requires that we acknowledge the emergence of a biometric humanity as something of a successor to the withered contours of the epidermalized infrahuman. Even when it operates in the service of securitocracy and civilizationist warfare, biometric control specifies a degree of "somatic individualism"[30] and therefore points in a different direction from approaches to security that can be straightforwardly premised upon the logics of racial type and group profile.

If the boundary with technology has supplied one traditional axis of inductive investigations into human finitude, the other principal frame for those operations has been provided by imagined relationships with animal nature. The history of racism directs the latter interface to the problem of pain and its varieties which preoccupied so many early explorers of political anatomy.[31] Today, the themes of human dignity and rights cannot be disassociated from debating cruelty and torture and their recurrent utility in fighting the desperate kinds of conflict that respecify legality and statecraft in the antique cultures of impunity that thrive when emergency becomes the rule.[32] The torturer may be targeted as "*hostis humani generis*," but torture is simultaneously rebranded and routinized, spun and banalized in the densely networked patterns of a military diplomacy that we cannot escape. This development should also be linked to the growing role of privately commissioned special forces and remotely operated weaponry in prosecuting what we are told is a new paradigm of global warcraft.

The "Arab Spring" of 2011 highlighted how the old colonial double standards rooted in Victorian racial theory were still in evidence. The unsustainable repression in Libya and then Syria was, for example, sharply distinguished from the bloody events simultaneously under way in Bahrain, where U.S. and British strategic interests summoned a different geopolitical ethics. The securitocracy of that Gulf state had been designed and implemented by a highly decorated British police officer, Ian Henderson, who has been repeatedly and consistently accused of being a brutal torturer, both during the Kenyan emergency, where he won his security policeman's spurs, as well as in Bahrain, where he acquired the nickname "Butcher of Bahrain" for the steel and energy with which he organized the government's response to the 1990s revolt.[33]

The revolting crimes of which Henderson has been accused were played down, justified, euphemized, and garlanded with flowers in a self-serving memoir he penned in 1958 with the assistance of the Conservative politician Philip Goodhart. What Henderson's career as a hammer of subversion and national liberation in Africa and the Gulf tells us now about the political geography of Europe's postcolonial statecraft cannot be adjudicated here. However, his text has other uses, not the least of which is its figuration of the ambiguities intrinsic to the relationship between races and species. Henderson describes what he takes to be the characteristic feature of his many encounters with Mau Mau prisoners captured during Kenya's emergency while hunting for the Kikuyu leader Dedan Kimathi. Kimathi, like Fanon, had served in a European army fighting against the Axis powers until 1945. Here is Henderson:

> I often saw terrorists a few moments after their capture. Some would stand there wide-eyed, completely speechless, and shivering violently from shock and cold. They would think of the moment of death, and that moment seemed very near. Others would be past the stage of thinking at all. Mad with shock, they would shout and struggle or froth at the mouth and bite at the earth.
>
> Under these circumstances it was not easy to remember that they were fanatics who had enjoyed killing children and slitting open the stomachs of pregnant women. They were savage, vicious, unpredictable as a rabid dog, but because they were now cornered, muzzled, powerless, and terrified, one felt like giving them a reassuring pat.[34]

There is much to say about this passage and the text from which it has been extracted. Its presentation of the captured insurgent native as savage, primitive, and effectively infrahuman belongs to the moral prescriptions associated with systems of racial classification in general. I have addressed those issues before.[35] Now my attention is caught by Henderson's hint that the enemy's reduction to animal status creates a confusing range of different obligations and moral pressures in the mind of the capturer *cum* torturer.

Similar material can be found in the records of Africans and Caribbean islanders captured on European battlefields by the Nazis or shot down and incarcerated by them in POW camps, where their fellow prisoners sometimes exceeded the guards in seeking the comforts of racial hierarchy and segregation as partial compensation for their loss of freedom.[36] For all the self-evident character of race as natural difference, the boundaries between human and infrahuman, human and animal, human subject and object are not in the least bit obvious. Even, or perhaps especially, those who monopolize violence have to specify and determine that very boundary in a difficult psychological setting where torture, castration, and other highly sexual acts of brutality had to compete with "a reassuring pat" as the most appropriate outcome.

Though Henderson's impunity had been sanctioned repeatedly by several different sovereign powers, a complex and multi-sited sequence of litigation arose from the Kenyan case as a result of applying the contemporary legal standards defined indirectly by the language of human rights and the concept of crimes against humanity. That intervention was resolved into a scheme for financial compensation in the upper reaches of postcolonial Britain's judicial system. Apart from the effects those cases have on the litigants and governmental actors involved, it is clear that they can also impact the nation's understanding of its colonial history and, deeper still, the idea that British people have of themselves as a political body imbued with the civilized values they have been told remain at stake in today's conflict with terror. David Anderson, a professor of African politics who specializes in the Kenyan "emergency," recently told the BBC that an extensive new batch of previously secret files released by the government as a result of the continuing court action would prove to be of "enormous significance." He continued:

> These are a set of selected documents withheld for their sensitivity. We will learn things the British government of the time didn't want us to know. They are likely to change our view of some key places. . . . [Their release] will clarify the last days of Empire in ways that will be shocking for some people in Britain.[37]

According to a damning internal review carried out by Anthony Cary for the Foreign Office, these documents were regarded by bureaucrats as a "guilty secret" and simply hidden.[38] How they came to be secret and how they acquired the capacity to shock people to this rare extent raises a number of questions that deserve detailed historical answers beyond those I offered in *After Empire*. Here, too, part of what is really shocking is the way that disturbing instances of brutality can generate a painful acknowledgment of where the boundaries of the human should fall—the same lesson that is not being learned in managing refugees and others seeking entry to Europe.[39]

Following the classical contours of debate with regard to the boundaries of humanity, a further instance of how the human is being contested in post- and neocolonial varieties of political and juridical conflict can be helpful. This final example relates to the future rather than the past. Fanon's sense of how colonial conflict discovers and exports new definitions and boundaries for the human can be applied to the emergent technological, legal, and moral environments involved in the deployment of robotic military systems.

Here the pattern has not developed as Donna Haraway might have predicted, that is, by sublation of the human into a post- or transhuman cyborg figure. Automated and autonomous weapon systems will operate without immediate human control in changing circumstances deemed too complex and rapid to be amenable to human decisions—a change that does not remove us from the human, but returns us to it.[40] Peter Singer's book *Wired for War* provides an excellent introduction to this topic.[41]

Britain's Ministry of Defence emphasizes that it "currently has no intention to develop systems that operate without human intervention in the weapon command and control chain."[42] Nonetheless, they chose recently to spell out relevant legal and ethical issues in an extensive briefing note, *The UK Approach to Unmanned Aircraft Systems*, which was prepared for senior officers in all branches of the services by the MoD's "thinktank," the

Development, Concepts and Doctrine Centre (DCDC).[43] This needs to be quoted at length:

> There is . . . an increasing body of discussion that suggests that the increasing speed, confusion and information overload of modern war may make human response inadequate and that the environment will be '*too complex for a human to direct*'.
>
> If the role of the human in the loop has, before now, been a legal requirement which we now see being eroded, what is the role of the human from a moral and ethical standpoint in automatic systems? Most work on this area focuses on the unique (at the moment) ability of a human being to bring empathy and morality to complex decision-making. To a robotic system, a school bus and a tank are the same—merely algorithms in a programme—and the engagement of a target is a singular action; the robot has no sense of ends, ways and means, no need to know why it is engaging a target. There is no recourse to human judgment in an engagement, no sense of a higher purpose on which to make decisions, and no ability to imagine (and therefore take responsibility for) repercussions of action taken. This raises a number of questions that will need to be addressed before fully autonomous armed systems are fielded. The other side of the autonomy argument is more positive. Robots cannot be emotive, cannot hate. A target is a series of ones and zeros, and once the decision is made, by whatever means, that the target is legitimate, then prosecution of that target is made mechanically. The robot does not care that the target is human or inanimate, terrorist or freedom fighter, savage or barbarian. A robot cannot be driven by anger to carry out illegal actions such as those at My Lai.

This view of technology has been commonplace in the development of ever more sophisticated means of killing.[44] It reacquaints us with the fact that both of humanity's conventional boundaries, on one side with the animal and on the other with the machine, are being divined through events in the spaces of colonial statecraft. Seen historically, this observation necessitates a fundamental adjustment. Raciology may suggest otherwise, but the colonial space and the conflicts that arise there do not belong in the past. Encountering the native or colonized person is not, as common sense once dictated, a form of time travel. The challenge presented by exposure to alterity as something other than loss or jeopardy is being able to dwell in the same present as the others whose difference we deploy in order to represent our past. That achievement alone provides access to the portal through which belated entry into a universal, disalienated history can be obtained.

Achille Mbembe has approached these dilemmas through a meditation on what appears to be their animating political theology. It has assembled new forms of theologico-political criticism and turned to the ethico-juridical in order to answer the unsettling effects of a "radical uncertainty" prompted less by civilizational conflict and technological transformation than the steady reordering of the world that has been consequent upon its continuing decolonization:

> . . . [W]e no longer have ready-made answers to such fundamental questions as: Who is my neighbour? What to do with my enemy? How to treat the stranger or the prisoner? Can I forgive the unforgivable? What is the relationship between truth, justice, and freedom? Is there anything that can be considered to be so priceless as to be immune from sacrifice?[45]

It is difficult to see how the history of race as political ontology, aesthetics, and *techne*, of racism and its racial orders, can be made to count as part of how this crisis is to be answered. However, I am certain that Fanon can help us with that task. Indeed, his approach to the human and, in particular, his final alignment of self and humanity in the transcendence (though not the redemption) of Europe remains suggestive. Perhaps it is best to say that approaching the human outside of the alienated and alienating configurations demanded by Manichaeism delirium and the racial-corporeal schema can contribute both to its re-enchantment and to what might be called the elusive, reparative element in Fanon's thinking.

That proposal, which would be easy to dismiss as utopian, has, in one form or another, been a goal common to every major political thinker of decolonization and racial democracy. All of them turned in that direction seeking ways to enforce modes of human dignity and recognition that had been consistently denied and thwarted by the invocation of race. Fanon's is only the loudest, clearest voice in that unhappy congregation for precisely the reasons that irritate the unassailable conventions of "identity politics" and its sophist tribunes.

NOTES

1. Pumla Gobodo-Madikizela, "Alternatives to Revenge: Building a Vocabulary of Reconciliation Through Political Pardon."

2. Ato Sekyi-Out, *Frantz Fanon's Dialectic of Experience.*

3. Charles Taylor, *Multiculturalism and the "Politics of Recognition"*; Stuart Hall, "The Multicultural Question."

4. James D. Le Sueur, *Uncivil War: Intellectuals and Identity Politics during the Decolonization of Algeria.*

5. Frantz Fanon, *Toward the African Revolution* (*TTAR*), 146.

6. Frantz Fanon, *Black Skin, White Masks*, 83.

7. Ato Sekyi-Out, *Frantz Fanon's Dialectic of Experience*, 95.

8. Frederick John Dealtry Lugard, *The Dual Mandate in British Tropical Africa.*

9. Frantz Fanon, "Racism and Culture," *TTAR*, 50.

10. Ibid., 41. "Exploitation, tortures, raids, racism, collective liquidations, rational oppression take turns at different levels in order literally to make of the native an object in the hands of the occupying nation. This object man, without means of existing, without a *raison d'être*, is broken in the very depth of his substance. The desire to live, to continue, becomes more and more indecisive, more and more phantom-like. It is at this stage that the well-known guilt complex appears. In his first novels, Wright gives a very detailed description of it."

11. Richard Wright and Edwin Roskam, *12 Million Black Voices: A Folk History of the Negro in the United States*, 30.

12. Frantz Fanon, *Black Skin, White Masks*, 179.

13. Frantz Fanon, *The Wretched of the Earth*, 236.

14. Niall Ferguson, "We Must Understand Why Racist Belief Systems Persist," *The Guardian*, July 11, 2006. http://www.guardian.co.uk/commentisfree/2006/jul/11/comment.race?INTCMP=SRCH

15. Sindre Bangstad, "Norway: Terror and Islamophobia in the Mirror." http://www.opendemocracy.net/sindre-bangstad/norway-terror-and-islamophobia-in-mirror

16. Cornelius Castoriadis, "Reflections on Racism." "The idea that to me seems central is that racism participates in something much more universal than one usually wants in fact to admit. Racism is an offspring, or a particularly acute and exacerbated avatar—I would even be tempted to say: a monstrous specification—of what, empirically, is an almost universal trait of human societies. What is at issue is the apparent incapacity to constitute oneself as oneself without excluding the other, coupled with the apparent inability to exclude the other without devaluing and, ultimately, hating them" (4).

17. Donna Haraway, *When Species Meet*, 18.

18. http://richarddawkins.net/discussions/624093-support-christian-missions-in-africa-no-but. Accessed March 27, 2012.

19. Edward Said, *Beginnings*, 373.

20. Frantz Fanon, *Black Skin, White Masks*, 179.

> "One duty alone: That of not renouncing my freedom through my choices.
>
> I have no wish to be the victim of the *Fraud* of a black world.
>
> My life should not be devoted to drawing up the balance sheet of Negro values.
>
> There is no white world, there is no white ethic, any more than there is a white intelligence.
>
> There are in every part of the world men who search.
>
> I am not a prisoner of history. I should not seek there for the meaning of my destiny.
>
> I should constantly remind myself that the real *leap* consists in introducing invention into existence.
>
> In the world through which I travel, I am endlessly creating myself.
> I am a part of Being to the degree that I go beyond it."

21. Vron Ware, "Infowar and the Politics of Feminist Curiosity."

22. See Mattias Gardell on the meaning of Anders Breivik's crimes: "The roots of Breivik's ideology: where does the romantic male warrior ideal come from today?" http://www.opendemocracy.net/mattias-gardell/roots-of-breiviks-ideology-where-does-romantic-male-warrior-ideal-come-from-today

23. http://www.huffingtonpost.com/jared-cohen/digital-age-has-ushered-i_b_151698.html

24. http://www.washingtonpost.com/wp-dyn/content/article/2010/06/03/AR2010060304965_pf.html

25. http://humanterrainsystem.army.mil/

26. http://www.telegraph.co.uk/technology/mobile-phones/8002755/Afghanistan-shows-the-UK-how-mobile-banking-should-be-done.html, http://www.bloomberg.com/news/2011-04-13/afghan-police-now-paid-by-phone-to-cut-graft-in-anti-taliban-war.html

27. http://www.wired.com/dangerroom/2007/08/fallujah-pics/

28. David Kilcullen, "Twenty-Eight Articles Fundamentals of Company-Level Counterinsurgency," May 2006. http://www.au.af.mil/info-ops/iosphere/iosphere_summer06_kilcullen.pdf

29. http://www.wired.com/dangerroom/2009/08/danger-room-in-afghanistan-the-perils-of-armed-social-work/

30. I am thinking here of the work of Nikolas Rose. See his *Politics of Life Itself.*

31. Immanuel Kant, "On the Different Races of Man."

32. Gareth Pierce, *Dispatches from the Dark Side: On Torture and the Death of Justice.*

33. http://www.guardian.co.uk/politics/2002/jun/30/uk.world, http://www.youtube.com/watch?v=ETMiHa8cdgg

34. Ian Henderson with Philip Goodhart, *Man Hunt in Kenya*, 149.

35. The distinct order of "racial" differentiation is marked by its unique label, by the peculiar slippage between "real relations" and "phenomenal forms" to which it always corresponds, and by a special (a)moral and (anti)political stance. It has involved not only confining "nonwhite" people to the status of animals or things, but also reducing European people to the intermediate status of that lowly order of being somewhere between human and animal that can be abused without the intrusions of bad conscience. Paul Gilroy, *Between Camps*, 301.

36. Cy Grant, *A Member of the RAF of Indeterminate Race: WW2 Experiences of a Former RAF Navigator and POW.*

37. http://www.bbc.co.uk/news/uk-13317076, http://www.guardian.co.uk/commentisfree/2011/jul/25/kenya-empire-mau-mau-britain?INTCMP=SRCH, http://www.guardian.co.uk/world/2011/jul/21/mau-mau-torture-kenyans-compensation?INTCMP=SRCH, http://www.guardian.co.uk/world/2011/apr/11/mau-mau-high-court-foreign-office-documents?INTCMP=SRCH

38. Ben MacIntyre. *Times*, May 6, 2011, 20. http://www.historyworkshop.org.uk/britains-secret-colonial-files/

39. http://www.guardian.co.uk/world/2011/may/08/nato-ship-libyan-migrants

40. See also Peter W. Singer's essay "Robots at War: The New Battlefield." http://www.wilsonquarterly.com/printarticle.cfm?aid=1313

41. Peter W. Singer, *Wired for War: The Robotics Revolution and Conflict in the 21st Century.*

42. http://www.guardian.co.uk/world/2011/apr/17/terminators-drone-strikes-mod-ethics?INTCMP=SRCH

"The US-manufactured General Atomics Reaper is currently the RAF's only armed unmanned aircraft. It can carry up to four Hellfire missiles, two 230kg (500lb) bombs, and 12 Paveway II guided bombs. It can fly for more than 18 hours, has a range of 3,600 miles, and can operate at up to 15,000 metres (50,000ft).

"The Reaper is operated by RAF personnel based at Creech in Nevada. It is controlled via a satellite datalink. Earlier this year, David Cameron promised to increase the number of RAF Reapers in Afghanistan from four to nine, at an estimated cost of £135m.

"The MoD is also funding the development by BAE Systems of a long-range unmanned aircraft, called Taranis, designed to fly at 'jet speeds' between continents while controlled from anywhere in the world using satellite communications." Richard Norton-Taylor and Rob Evans, *Observer Sunday*, April 17, 2011.

43. http://www.mod.uk/NR/rdonlyres/F9335CB2-73FC-4761-A428-DB7DF4BEC02C/0/20110505 JDN_211_UAS_v2U.pdf

44. Sven Lindqvist, *A History of Bombing*.

45. Personal communication.

Sociological Reflections

CAN SOCIETY BE COMMODITIES ALL THE WAY DOWN?

Post-Polanyian Reflections on Capitalist Crisis

NANCY FRASER

A CRISIS IN THREE DIMENSIONS

We are presently living through a crisis of great severity and great complexity. Yet we lack a conceptual framework with which to interpret it, let alone one that could help us resolve it in an emancipatory way. Evidently, today's crisis is multidimensional, encompassing not only economy and finance, but also ecology, society, and politics. Of these dimensions, I want to single out three as especially salient. There is, first, the ecological strand of crisis, reflected in the depletion of the earth's nonrenewable resources and in the progressive destruction of the biosphere, as witnessed first and foremost in global warming. There is, second, the financialization strand of crisis, reflected in the creation, seemingly out of thin air, of an entire shadow economy of paper values, insubstantial yet able to devastate the "real" economy and to endanger the livelihoods of billions of people. Finally, there is the strand pertaining to social reproduction, reflected in the growing strain, under neoliberalism, of what some call "care" or "affective labor," but what I understand more broadly as the human capacities available to create and maintain social bonds, which includes the work of socializing the young, building communities, and of reproducing the shared meanings, affective dispositions, and horizons of value that underpin social cooperation. Taken singly, each of these strands of crisis is scary enough. Put them together, and you have a constellation that is truly alarming. It is the convergence of these three strands—the ecological, the financial, and the social—that constitutes the distinctive character, and special severity, of the present crisis.[1]

Under these conditions, one conclusion is axiomatic. A critical theory for our time must encompass all three of these crisis dimensions. To be sure, it must disclose the specificity of each. But it should also clarify the ways in which the ecological strand of crisis, the financialization strand of crisis, and the social reproduction strand of crisis are intertwined. Finally, it should explore the possibility that all three derive from a common source in the deep structure of our society and that all three share a common grammar.

Today, however, we lack such a critical theory. Our received understandings of crisis tend to focus on a single aspect, typically the economic or the ecological, which they isolate from, and privilege over, the others. For the most part, ecological theorists isolate the crisis of nature from that of finance, while most critics of political economy fail to bring that domain into relation to ecology. And neither camp pays much attention to the crisis of social reproduction, which has become the province of gender studies and feminist theory, and which therefore remains ghettoized.[2]

Nowadays, such "critical separatism" is counterproductive. In the present context, when crisis is patently tridimensional, we need a broader, integrated approach that connects the ecological, the economic, and the social. Eschewing economism on the one hand, and what I shall call "ecologism" on the other, we need to revive the project of large-scale social theorizing that tries to encompass all three dimensions of crisis and to clarify the relations among them. In elucidating the nature and roots of crisis, such a perspective would also seek to reveal prospects for an emancipatory resolution.

The thought of Karl Polanyi affords a promising starting point for such theorizing. His 1944 classic, *The Great Transformation*, elaborates an account of an earlier crisis that connects ecology, political economy, and social reproduction. The book conceives crisis as a multifaceted historical process that began with the rise of economic liberalism in 19th-century Britain and proceeded, over the course of a century and a half, to envelop the entire world, bringing with it intensified imperial subjection, periodic economic depressions, and cataclysmic wars. For Polanyi, moreover, this crisis was less about economic breakdown in the narrow sense than about disintegrated communities, destroyed livelihoods, and despoiled nature. Its roots lay less in intra-economic contradictions than in a momentous shift in the place of the economy vis-à-vis society. Overturning the heretofore universal relation, in which markets were embedded in social institutions and subject to moral and ethical norms and to political regulation, proponents of the "self-regulating market" sought to build a world in which society, morals, ethics, and politics were subordinated to, even modeled on, markets. Conceiving labor, land, and money as "factors of production," they treated those fundamental bases of social life as if they were ordinary commodities and subjected them to market exchange. The effects of this "fictitious commodification," as Polanyi called it, were so destructive of habitats, livelihoods, and communities as to spark an ongoing counter-movement for the "protection of society." The result was a distinctive pattern of social conflict, which he called "the double movement": a spiraling conflict between free marketeers on the one hand, and social protectionists on the other, which led to political stalemate and, ultimately, to fascism and the Second World War.[3]

Here, then, is an account of crisis that avoids at least two forms of critical separatism. Eschewing both economism and ecologism, *The Great Transformation* interweaves an account of financial breakdown and economic collapse with accounts of natural despoliation and social disintegration, all subtended by intractable political conflicts that failed to resolve, indeed exacerbated, the crisis. Refusing to limit himself either to the economic on the one hand, or to the ecological on the other, Polanyi elaborated a conception of crisis that encompasses both dimensions, as well as the dimension of social reproduction. By incorporating the latter, moreover, his framework is capable, at least in principle, of embracing many feminist concerns and, indeed, of connecting them to the concerns of political ecologists and political economists. This point alone would qualify Polanyi as a promising resource for those who seek to understand the crisis of the 21st century. But there are other, more specific reasons for turning to him today. The story told in *The Great Transformation* has strong echoes in current developments. There is at least a *prima facie* case for the view that the present crisis was triggered by recent efforts to disencumber markets from the governance regimes (both national and international) established in the aftermath of World War II. What we today call "*neo*liberalism" is little more than the second coming of the very same 19th-century faith in the "self-regulating market" that unleashed the crisis Polanyi chronicled. Now, as then, attempts to implement that creed are spurring efforts to commodify nature, labor, and money: Witness the burgeoning markets in carbon emissions and biotechnology; in child care, schooling, and the care of the old; and in financial derivatives. Now, as then, the effect is to despoil nature, rupture communities, and destroy livelihoods. Today, moreover, as in Polanyi's time, counter-movements are mobilizing to protect society and nature from the ravages of the market. Now, as then, struggles over nature, social reproduction, and global finance constitute the central nodes and flashpoints of crisis. On its face, then, today's crisis is plausibly viewed as a second great transformation, a great transformation redux.

For many reasons, then, Polanyi's perspective holds considerable promise for theorizing today. Yet we should not rush to embrace it uncritically. Even as it overcomes economism and ecologism, *The Great Transformation* turns out, on closer inspection, to be deeply flawed. Focused single-mindedly on the destructive effects of "self-regulating markets," the book overlooks harms originating elsewhere, in the surrounding "society." Preoccupied exclusively with the corrosive effects of commodification *upon* communities, it neglects injustices *within* communities, including injustices such as slavery, feudalism, and patriarchy that depend on social constructions of labor, land, and money precisely as *non*-commodities. Demonizing marketization, the book tends to idealize social protection, as it fails to note that protections have often served to entrench hierarchies and exclusions. Counterposing a "bad economy" to a "good society," *The Great Transformation* flirts with communitarianism and is insufficiently sensitive to domination.[4]

What is needed, then, is a revision of Polanyi's framework. The goal should be a new, post-Polanyian perspective that not only overcomes economism and ecologism but also avoids romanticizing and reifying "society" and thereby whitewashing domination. That is precisely the aim of the present essay. Seeking to develop a critique that comprehends "society" as well as "economy," I propose to examine one of Polanyi's signature concepts, namely the fictitious commodity. I shall argue that while this idea affords a promising basis for an integrated structural analysis of the present crisis, it needs to be reconstructed in a form that is sensitive to, and critical of, domination.

FICTITIOUS COMMODIFICATION IN *THE GREAT TRANSFORMATION*

Let me begin by sketching Polanyi's idea of fictitious commodification. He contended, as I already noted, that 19th-century industrial capitalism inaugurated a historically unprecedented relation between "economy" and "society." Previously, markets had been "mere accessories" of economic life, and no such thing as a separate "economy" had ever existed. Production and distribution were organized by what we could call "non-economic" institutions (for example, kinship, community, and state) and subject to non-economic norms (for example, religious, communal, and legal), which limited what could be bought and sold, by whom, and on what terms. The idea of a "self-regulating market," subject only to supply and demand, was virtually unthinkable (*TGT*, 46–58).

All that changed, however, with the invention of the utterly novel idea of a "market economy." Decisively rejecting all previous understandings, proponents of this idea envisioned a separate economic system, institutionally differentiated from the rest of society and entirely directed and controlled by market mechanisms. In this system, all production would be organized for sale on price-setting markets, which would be governed immanently by supply and demand. Not just luxury goods, not just ordinary goods, but *all the inputs of production*, including human labor, raw materials, and money credit, would be traded on such "self-regulating markets." Thus, the necessary conditions for commodity production would themselves become commodities. But that meant introducing the logic of market relations into virtually every aspect of social life.

What was originally envisioned as a separate economy would inevitably colonize the surrounding society, remaking the latter in the image of the former. A "market economy" could only exist in a "market society" (*TGT*, 71–74).

For Polanyi, however, this idea of a "market economy-cum-market society" is inherently unrealizable. To posit that labor, land, and money can be traded like ordinary commodities is to suppose that society can be commodities all the way down. But this assumption, Polanyi claimed, is "entirely fictitious," and attempts to implement it are bound to backfire. In reality, labor, land, and money have a special, foundational status. Constitutive of the very fabric of social life, they also supply the necessary background conditions for commodity production. To treat them as ordinary objects of market exchange is thus to attack at once the "substance" of society and the indispensable presuppositions of a capitalist economy (*TGT*, 75–79, 133–137). The result could only be a crisis of society on the one hand, and a crisis of economy on the other. Society, in Polanyi's view, cannot be commodities all the way down. He writes:

> To allow the market mechanism to be the sole director of the fate of human beings and their natural environment, indeed, even of the amount and use of purchasing power, would result in the demolition of society. For the alleged commodity "labor power" cannot be shoved about, used indiscriminately, or even left unused without affecting also the human individual who happens to be the bearer of this peculiar commodity. In disposing of a man's labor power the system would, incidentally, dispose of the physical, psychological, and moral entity "man" attached to that tag. Robbed of the protective covering of cultural institutions, human beings would perish from the effects of social exposure [and] social dislocation. . . . Nature would be reduced to its elements, neighborhoods and landscapes defiled, rivers polluted, military safety jeopardized, the power to produce food and raw materials destroyed. Finally, the market administration of purchasing power would periodically liquidate business enterprise, for shortages and surfeits of money would prove as disastrous to business as floods and droughts were in primitive society. Undoubtedly, labor, land and money *are* essential to a market economy. But no society could stand the effects of such a system of crude fictions even for the shortest stretch of time unless its human and natural substance as well as its business organization was protected against the ravages of this satanic mill. (*TGT*, 76–77)

As we shall see, this passage can be interpreted in more than one way. Nevertheless, its central point is beyond dispute: Efforts to create a "market society," composed of commodities all the way down, necessarily trigger crisis. Destabilizing nature, finance, and social reproduction, such efforts are bound to undermine both the constitutive elements of social life and the presuppositions of commodity production and exchange. They are also bound to provoke resistance.

The Great Transformation recounts the process by which 19th-century British commercial interests sought to commodify labor, land, and money.

In Polanyi's account, their actions set in motion a far-reaching crisis in three dimensions. First, the attempt to create a "self-regulating market" in "labor power" did indeed demoralize "the human individual who happen[ed] to be the bearer of this peculiar commodity" (*TGT*, 76). Fracturing communities, splintering families, and fraying social bonds, it disturbed the processes of social reproduction on which markets rely (*TGT*, 136). Second, land enclosures, free trade in corn, and the importation of cheap foodstuffs upended agriculture and sapped the lifeblood of rural communities, even as industry pillaged the world and gouged the earth in pursuit of "raw materials," while polluting the air and water. Thus, the new economic regime did indeed "reduce nature to its elements" and "defile neighborhoods and landscapes," endangering both the ecological conditions of production and the living conditions of human beings. Finally, unbridled speculation in currency and credit instruments destabilized the money supply, causing the value of money to fluctuate wildly, wiping out savings, discouraging investment, and depriving producers and consumers alike of their ability to plan for the future. Thus, the commodification of money undermined the temporal preconditions for social and ontological security, as well as the financial preconditions for capital accumulation (*TGT*, 136–38, 201–9). For Polanyi, then, the result of fictitious commodification was crisis. Simultaneously social, ecological, and economic, this was a crisis for nature and society as well as for capital.

COMMODIFICATION, DOMINATION, AND EMANCIPATION

Polanyi's idea of fictitious commodification is remarkably prescient. Whatever its merits for the period he chronicled, his identification of nature, labor, and money as central nodes of crisis is highly pertinent to the 21st century. Equally important, his conception relates those three flashpoints of crisis to a common dynamic. Thus, the notion of fictitious commodification affords the prospect of an integrated crisis theory that encompasses in one fell swoop the concerns of ecologists, feminist theorists, and political economists. Capable of connecting those bodies of thought, it promises to overcome the separatisms that currently divide, and weaken, critical theorizing. In effect, this concept locates all three strands of critique as interconnected moments of a broader critique of capitalism.

As usually interpreted, however, Polanyi's account of fictitious commodification rests on some dubious underpinnings. These stem from the claim, made repeatedly in *The Great Transformation*, that a commodity is a good (or service) produced for sale (*TGT*, 75). Basing his argument on this definition, Polanyi contends that labor, land, and money cannot be genuine commodities because not one was produced for sale. Neither labor nor land is produced at all, he claims; and although money is a human creation, it has the status of a social convention, akin to language, not that of an object produced for sale (*TGT*, 75, 137, 204–5). When traded, therefore, none of the three behaves like a true commodity. In each case, an original condition of not having been produced for sale destabilizes the process of marketization. Absent the proper origins, the would-be commodities can only be "fictitious."

Let us call this the "ontological interpretation" of fictitious commodification. It is problematic, I think, because it is essentialist, ahistorical, and insensitive to domination. Appealing to an original condition, the condition of not having been produced for sale, the ontological interpretation posits that to commodify labor, land, and money is to violate their inherent nature. As a result, it obscures their historicity—covering over the fact that none of the three is ever encountered pure, but only in forms that have already been shaped by human activity and relations of power. This interpretation fails to register, too, that long before they were marketized, social constructions of labor, land, and money typically encoded relations of domination—witness feudalism, slavery, and patriarchy, all of which, as I noted before, cast those three constitutive elements of social life as *non*-commodities. Then, too, the ontological reading orients the critique of commodification overwhelmingly to its disintegrative effects on social communities, focusing on its tendency to destroy existing solidarities and social bonds, which it implicitly assumes to have value and to be worth preserving. Associating change exclusively with decay and decline, it overlooks the possibility, noted by Marx, that marketization can generate emancipatory effects by dissolving modes of domination external to the market and creating the basis for new, more inclusive and egalitarian solidarities. Conversely, the ontological reading occults the fact that struggles to protect nature and society from the market are often aimed at entrenching privilege and excluding "outsiders." Ignoring hierarchy and exclusion, it lends itself to a defensive project: protecting extant constructions of labor, land, and money, along with the domination inhering in them, from marketization. Precluding consideration of trade-offs, it discourages efforts to reckon the pluses and minuses of such complex historical developments as the introduction of markets into authoritarian command economies or the opening of labor markets to women and former slaves. All told, the ontological reading inflects the critique of crisis with a defensive, conservative thrust that is at best insensitive to, and at worst complicit with, forms of domination that are not grounded in market mechanisms.

What is needed, then, is another interpretation of fictitious commodification, one that is historicized, non-defensive, and sensitive to domination. A useful model, I suggest, is Hegel's argument in *The Philosophy of Right* as to why society cannot be contract all the way down. In that work, Hegel argued that a sphere of contractual relations is possible only on the basis of a background of noncontractual social relations; efforts to universalize contract necessarily undermine it by destroying the noncontractual basis on which it depends.[5] Adapting Hegel's argument, we might define fictitious commodification as the attempt to commodify the market's conditions of possibility. Understood in this way, attempts to fully commodify labor, land, and money are conceptually incoherent and inherently self-undermining, akin to a tiger that bites its own tail. For structural reasons, therefore, society cannot be commodities all the way down. Let us call this the "structural" interpretation of fictitious commodification. Unlike the ontological interpretation, this one does not suppose an original condition of labor, nature, and money that inherently resists commodification. It directs attention, rather, to the tendency of unregulated markets to destroy their own conditions of possibility. It construes those conditions, moreover, as socially constructed and historically specific, and hence as potentially intertwined with domination and as subject to contestation. It reminds us, accordingly, that what commodification erodes is not always worth defending, and that marketization can actually foster emancipation by weakening traditional supports for domination. Freed from the communitarian bias of the ontological reading, the structural interpretation makes possible a more complex critique of capitalist crisis. Sensitive not only to desolidarization, but also to domination, it enhances the critical force of the concept of fictitious commodification.

To elaborate further, the structural reading of fictitious commodification foregrounds the inherently self-contradictory character of free-market capitalism. It is analogous in that respect to Marx's idea of the tendency of the rate of profit to fall.[6] But unlike Marx, Polanyi identifies not one, but three contradictions of capitalism—the ecological, the social, and the financial—each of which underpins a dimension of crisis. For Polanyi, moreover, each of the three contradictions unfolds by way of a common logic: Each pertains to a necessary condition of production, which capitalism simultaneously needs and tends to erode. In the case of the ecological condition of production, what is at stake are the natural processes that sustain life and provide the material inputs for social provisioning. In the case of social reproduction, what is at stake are the sociocultural processes that supply the solidary relations, affective dispositions, and value horizons that underpin social cooperation, while also furnishing the appropriately socialized and skilled human beings who constitute "labor." In the case of the monetary condition of production, what is at stake is the ability to conduct exchange across distance and to store value for the future, hence the capacity to interact broadly in space and in time. What is at stake in each case is sustainability: the sustainability of capitalism on the one hand, and that of society and nature on the other.[7]

In principle, then, each strand of crisis lends itself to a structural critique, focused on sustainability. And indeed, as a matter of fact, three different variants of such critique are presently circulating. An ecological variant claims that neoliberalism's increasingly invasive subsumption of nature as a fictitious commodity today is irreparably eroding the natural basis that sustains life and supplies the material inputs for commodity production.[8] A feminist variant holds that the increasing commodification of women's labor on the one hand, and of "care" on the other is depleting the capacities for social reproduction on which the supply of "labor power" and society as such depend.[9] Marxian and Keynesian variants claim that financialization is destroying the monetary presuppositions for capital accumulation, as well as the possibility of politically organized social protection and public provision of social welfare.[10]

Each of these critiques is powerful and deserving of further development. But each captures only one strand of a larger totality, and each needs to be connected to the others. Far from being neatly separated from one another, the three dimensions of crisis are inextricably interwoven in the deep grammar of capitalist society. Let me suggest how they might be connected via Polanyi's notion of fictitious commodification. By reading this notion structurally, I want to show how we might decouple his three-dimensional critique of capitalism's unsustainability from the communitarian ethos to which he unwittingly joined it, and how we might link it instead to a critique of domination.

FICTITIOUS COMMODIFICATION IN THE 21ST CENTURY

I begin with the commodification of labor. Here, Polanyi was surely prescient, laying the basis in 1944 for a feminist critique of capitalism, albeit one that he himself did not develop. Not confining himself to criticizing exploitation, he situated labor's commodification in a broader perspective, the perspective of social reproduction, which concerns maintenance of the social bonds that are indispensable both to society in general and to market exchange in particular. Adopting this perspective, Polanyi understood that proletarianization is as much about ruptured communities and frayed solidarities as about exploitation and immiseration. He understood, therefore, that unbridled commodification of labor threatens the universe of meanings, affective dispositions, and value horizons that underpin society and economy, while also jeopardizing the supply of appropriately skilled and socialized "labor power" that capital requires. He understood, finally, that under conditions of rampant proletarianization, social reproduction is bound to be a flashpoint of crisis and a site of struggle (*TGT*, 39, 83, 133). As Polanyi saw it, the result could only be an epochal battle between two social forces: on one side, the party of free-market liberalism, bent on ripping labor out of its lifeworldly context and turning it into a "factor of production" in the service of profit; on the other side, the party of social protection, set on defending the lifeworlds, families, and communities that have always enveloped labor and suffused it with social meaning.

But for all its insight, Polanyi's perspective also harbors a major blind spot. What he failed to note was that the construction of "labor power" as a fictitious commodity rested on the simultaneous co-construction of "care" as a non-commodity. The unwaged labor of social reproduction supplied wage labor's necessary conditions of possibility; the latter could not exist, after all, in the absence of housework, child-raising, schooling, affective care, and a host of other activities that maintain social bonds and shared understandings. But the division between paid "productive" labor and unpaid "reproductive" labor was overwhelmingly a gendered division, which underpinned modern capitalist forms of women's subordination. Missing this deep-seated structure of gender domination, Polanyi risked inscribing the ideal of the "family wage" at the heart of his understanding of "social protection." In that case, what would be protected was less "society" as such than arrangements premised on gender hierarchy.[11]

The effect was to skew Polanyi's understanding of the grammar of social conflict. Neglecting the history of feminist struggles against "protection," which included demands for women's right to employment, among other things, he failed to see that struggles around labor's commodification were actually three-sided: They included not just free marketeers and proponents of protection, but also partisans of "emancipation," whose primary aim was neither to promote marketization nor to protect society from it, but rather to free themselves from domination.[12] Emancipation's ranks have included feminists, to be sure, but also the billions of slaves, serfs, peasants, racialized peoples, and inhabitants of slums and shantytowns for whom a wage promised liberation from slavery, feudal subjection, racial subordination, social exclusion, and imperial domination, as well as from sexism and patriarchy. Such actors vigorously opposed the oppressive protections that prevented them from selling their labor power. But they did not on that account become proponents of free-market liberalism. Rather, their struggles constituted a third pole of social movement, above and beyond the two poles identified by Polanyi: not just marketization and social protection, but also emancipation. Hence not a double movement, but what I've elsewhere called a "triple movement."[13]

This revision enables a better understanding of the "labor" dimension of the current crisis. By introducing the problematic of (male) domination and (women's) emancipation, we can grasp crucial aspects of the present constellation that are occulted in more orthodox Polanyian accounts. It is true, of course, as these accounts suggest, that wage labor is everywhere in crisis as a result of neoliberal globalization—witness astronomical rates of unemployment, attacks on unions, and the involuntary exclusion of roughly two-thirds of the world's population from official labor markets. But that is not all. In a further turn of the screw, much of the formerly unwaged activity of social reproduction is now being commodified—witness the burgeoning global markets in adoptions, child care, babies, sexual services, elder care, and bodily organs. Now add to this the fact that it is increasingly women who are being recruited today into waged work. Thus, neoliberalism is proletarianizing those who still do the lion's share of the unwaged work of social reproduction. And it is doing so at the very moment when it is also insisting on reduced public provision of social welfare and curtailed state provision of social infrastructure. The overall result is a deficit of care. To fill the gap, global capitalism imports migrant workers from poorer to richer countries. Typically, it is racialized and/or rural women from poor regions who take on reproductive and caring labor previously performed by wealthier women. But to do this, the migrants must transfer their own familial and community responsibilities to other, still poorer caregivers, who must in turn do the same—and on and on, in ever longer "global care chains." Far from filling the care gap, the net effect is to displace it—from richer to poorer families, from the Global North to the Global South.[14]

Here we see a new, intensified form of fictitious commodification. Activities that once formed the uncommodified background that made commodified labor possible are now themselves being commodified. The result can only be intensified crisis as the tiger bites ever more deeply into its tail.

No wonder, then, that struggles over the social construction of "family and work" have exploded in recent years—witness the rise of feminist movements and women's movements of various stripes; of grass-roots community movements seeking to defend entitlements to housing, health care, job training, and income support; of movements for the rights of migrants, domestic workers, public employees, and of those who perform social service work in for-profit nursing homes, hospitals, and child care centers. But these struggles do not take the form of a double movement. They are better grasped, rather, as three-sided struggles, encompassing not only neoliberals and social protectionists, but also proponents of emancipation, including those for whom exploitation represents an advance.

Consider, next, the commodification of nature. Here, too, Polanyi was prescient, laying the basis in 1944 for an ecological critique of capitalism *avant la lettre*. He understood that nature is an indispensable precondition both for social life in general and for commodity production in particular. He understood, too, that unbridled commodification of nature is unsustainable, bound to impair both society and economy. He understood, finally, that, reduced to a factor of production and subjected to unregulated market exchange, nature is destined to become a node of crisis (*TGT*, 136–37). Such treatment is bound, moreover, to provoke resistance, sparking movements to protect nature and human habitats from the market's ravages. Here, too, Polanyi envisioned a "double movement," a two-sided battle between environmentalists and free marketeers.

Without question, this perspective is pertinent today. In the 21st century, commodification of nature has proceeded far beyond anything Polanyi imagined—witness the privatization of water, the bioengineering of sterile seeds, and the patenting of DNA. Such developments are far more intrusive, and destabilizing, than the land enclosures and free trade in corn he wrote about. Far from simply trading already existing natural objects, these forms of commodification generate new ones; probing deep into nature, they alter its internal grammar, much as the assembly line altered the grammar of human labor.[15] Adapting terminology used by Marx, one could say that such new forms of fictitious commodification effect not just the "formal subsumption," but the "real subsumption," of nature into capitalism.[16] Hence, nature truly is now produced for sale. In addition, the depletion of the earth's nonrenewable resources is far more advanced today than in Polanyi's time—so advanced, indeed, as to raise the prospect of full-scale ecological collapse. Finally, the neoliberal cure for the ills of markets in nature is more market—markets in strange new entities, such as carbon emissions permits and offsets, and in even stranger meta-entities derived from them, "environmental derivatives," such as carbon emissions "tranches," modeled after the mortgage-backed CDOs that nearly crashed the global financial order in 2008 and are now being briskly traded by Goldman Sachs.[17]

No wonder, then, that struggles over nature have exploded in recent years—witness the rise of environmental and indigenous movements, locked in battles with corporate interests and proponents of "development" on the one hand, and with workers and would-be workers who fear the loss of jobs on the other hand. If there was ever a time when nature was a flashpoint of crisis, it is today. But these conflicts, like those surrounding labor and care, do not take the form of a simple two-sided struggle between neoliberals and environmentalists. Like labor, nature is now a site of conflict for a complex array of social forces, which also include labor unions and indigenous peoples, ecofeminists and ecosocialists, and opponents of environmental racism. Here, too, in other words, not a double, but a triple movement. Also encompassing movements for emancipation, such struggles belie romantic ecofundamentalist perspectives that would flat-out prohibit commodification of nature, just as the feminist critique of patriarchal protection belied romantic communitarian approaches that would ban commodification of the labor of care. In this case, too, accordingly, what is needed is a structural critique, divested of all nostalgia and linked to the critique of domination.

Consider, finally, the commodification of money. In this case, too, Polanyi was remarkably prescient. In the 21st century, financialization has achieved new heights of dizziness, far beyond anything he could have imagined. With the invention of derivatives, and their metastasization, the commodification of money has floated so free of the materiality of social life as to take on a life of its own. Untethered from reality and out of control, "securitization" has unleashed a tsunami of insecurity, nearly crashing the world economy, bringing down governments, devastating communities, flooding neighborhoods with underwater mortgages, and destroying the jobs and livelihoods of billions of people. As I write, moreover, financialization is threatening to destroy the euro, the European Union, and any pretense of democracy, as bankers routinely overrule parliaments and install governments that will do their bidding. Is it any wonder, then, that politics is everywhere in turmoil, as movements on both the left and the right mobilize to seek protective cover? More perhaps even than in Polanyi's time, finance is at the center of capitalist crisis.

Here, too, however, Polanyi's perspective harbors a major blind spot. He identified the modern territorial state as the principal arena and agent of social protection. Granted, he appreciated that the regulatory capacities of states depend importantly on international arrangements. Thus, he criticized the early-20th-century free trade regimes for depriving European states of control over their money supplies and preventing them from adopting policies of full employment and deficit spending (*TGT*, 142–43, 227–36). But the implied solution was a new international regime that would reinstate national currency controls, thereby facilitating protective policies at the national level. What Polanyi did not anticipate was that the "Embedded Liberalism" established after the war would serve some states far better than others.[18] In that era of decolonization, imperialism took on a new, indirect, "non-political" form, based on unequal exchange between newly independent ex-colonies and their erstwhile masters. As a result of this exchange, the wealthy states of the core could continue to finance their domestic welfare systems on the backs of their former colonial subjects. The disparity was exacerbated in the neoliberal era, moreover, by the policies of structural adjustment, as international agencies like the IMF used the weapon of debt to further undercut the protective capacities of postcolonial states, compelling them to divest their assets, open their markets, and slash social spending. Historically, therefore, international arrangements have entrenched disparities in the capacities of states to protect their populations from the vagaries of international markets. Effectively *misframing* social protection, they have shielded the citizens of the core, but not those of the periphery.[19] In fact, the national social protection envisioned by Polanyi was never universalizable to the entire world; its viability in the Global North always depended on value siphoned off from the Global South. Thus, even the most internally egalitarian variants of postwar social democracy rested on external neoimperial predation.

Today, moreover, as many on the left have long warned, and as Greeks have discovered to their dismay, the construction of Europe as an economic and monetary union, without corresponding political and fiscal integration, simply disables the protective capacities of member states without creating broader, European-level protective capacities to take up the slack. But that is not all. Absent global financial regulation, even very wealthy, free-standing countries find their efforts at national social protection under pressure from global market forces, which institute a "race to the bottom." The globalization of finance requires a new, post-Westphalian way of imagining the arenas and agents of social protection. It requires arenas in which the circle of those entitled to protection matches the circle of those subject to risk; and it requires agents whose protective capacities and regulatory powers are sufficiently robust and broad to effectively rein in transnational private powers and to pacify global finance.[20]

No wonder, then, that present-day struggles over finance do not conform to the schema of the double movement. Alongside the neoliberals and national protectionists that Polanyi foregrounded, we also find alterglobalization movements, movements for global or transnational democracy, and those who seek to transform finance from a profit-making enterprise into a public utility that can be used to guide investment, create jobs, promote ecologically sustainable development, and support social reproduction, while also combating entrenched forms of domination. Such actors represent a new configuration, which aims to integrate social protection with emancipation.

What all of this shows, I believe, is that Polanyi was right to identify labor, land, and money as central nodes and flashpoints of crisis. But if we are to exploit his insights today, we must complicate his perspective, connecting a structural critique of fictitious commodification to a critique of domination.

CONCLUSION

Let me close, however, by returning to a point I stressed at the outset. The purpose of centering our understanding of crisis on nature, social reproduction, and finance is not to treat these three dimensions separately. It is rather to overcome critical separatism by developing a single comprehensive framework, able to encompass all three of them and thus to connect the concerns of ecologists, feminist theorists, and political economists.

Far from being neatly separated from one another, the three strands of capitalist crisis are inextricably interwoven, as are the three corresponding processes of fictitious commodification. I have already noted that neoliberals are pressing governments everywhere to reduce deficits by slashing social spending, thereby jeopardizing the capacity of families and communities to care for their members and to maintain social bonds; thus, their response to financial crisis is undermining social reproduction. Likewise, I have mentioned the new speculation in environmental derivatives. What such "green finance" portends is not only economic breakdown, but also ecological meltdown, as the promise of quick speculative super-profits draws capital away from the long-term, large-scale investment that is needed to develop renewable energy and to transform unsustainable modes of production and forms of life that are premised on fossil fuels.[21] The resulting environmental destruction is bound to further disturb processes of social reproduction and will likely produce some nasty effects—including zero-sum conflicts over oil, water, air, and arable land, conflicts in which broader solidarities give way to "lifeboat ethics," to scapegoating and militarism, and perhaps again to fascism and world war. In any case, we do not need to rely on such predictions to see that finance, ecology, and social reproduction are not neatly separated from one another, but are deeply and inextricably intertwined.

This sort of analysis illustrates four major conceptual points that have been central to my argument and that I would like to restate now in closing. First, a critical theory for the 21st century must be integrative, oriented to understanding the present crisis as a whole. We make a good start at developing such a perspective by adopting Polanyi's idea of fictitious commodification, so as to connect three major dimensions of crisis, the ecological, the social-reproductive, and the financial, all conceived as constitutive moments of a crisis of *capitalism*. Second, 21st-century critical theory must go beyond Polanyi by connecting the critique of commodification to the critique of domination. We make a good start here by rejecting the standard ontological reading of fictitious commodification, with its defensive communitarian overtones, in favor a structural reading, which is sensitive not only to desolidarization but also to domination. Third, a critical theory for the 21st century must develop a conception of the grammar of social struggle that goes beyond Polanyi's idea of a double movement. Factoring in struggles for emancipation alongside those for marketization and social protection, indeed cutting across them, it must analyze the struggles of our time in terms of a triple movement, in which those three political projects combine and collide. Finally, to mention a point only hinted at here, a critical theory of contemporary crisis needs a complex normative perspective that integrates the leading values of each pole of the triple movement. Such a perspective should integrate the legitimate interests in solidarity and social security that motivate social protectionists with the fundamental interest in non-domination that is paramount for emancipation movements, without neglecting the valid concern for negative liberty that animates the most principled and consistent free-market liberals. Embracing a broad, integrative understanding of social justice, such a project would serve at once to honor Polanyi's insights and to remedy his blind spots.

NOTES

1. For helpful comments, I am grateful to Leila Brannstrom, Andries Gouws, Steven Lukes, Adrian Parr, Hartmut Rosa, Bill Scheuerman, and Ines Valdez. For research support, I thank the Stellenbosch Institute for Advanced Study and the Humanitas Visiting Professor Scheme at Cambridge University. For research assistance, I thank Blair Taylor.

2. An exception is: Adelheid Biesecker and Sabine Hofmeister, "(Re)productivity: Sustainable Relations Both Between Society and Nature and Between the Genders."

3. Karl Polanyi, *The Great Transformation*. Hereafter cited as *TGT*.

4. Cf. Don Robotham, "Afterword: Learning from Polanyi," 280–81.

5. Cf. G. W. F. Hegel, *The Philosophy of Right*. I read this work as arguing, contra social contract theory, that society cannot be contract all the way down, and as invoking that argument to establish the necessity of embedding "Abstract Right" within the broader context of "Ethical Life." For a detailed interpretation along these lines, see Michel Rosenfeld, "Hegel and the Dialectics of Contract."

6. Cf. Karl Marx, *Capital*, Vol. 3, especially 317–38.

7. Cf. James O'Connor, "Capitalism, Nature, Socialism: A Theoretical Introduction."

8. See, for example, James O'Connor, "Capitalism, Nature, Socialism: A Theoretical Introduction" and "On the Misadventures of Capitalist Nature"; Larry Lohmann, "Neoliberalism and the Calculable World: The Rise of Carbon Trading" (online at http://mayflybooks.org/?page_id=21); Vandana Shiva, "Life Inc: Biotechnology and the Expansion of Capitalist Markets"; Neil Smith, "Nature as Accumulation Strategy."

9. See, for example, Isabella Bakker and Steven Gill, *Power, Production and Social Reproduction*; Arlie Hochschild, *The Commercialization of Intimate Life: Notes from Home and Work*; Catherine Hoskyns and Shirin Rai, "Recasting the Global Political Economy: Counting Women's Unpaid Work"; Silvia Federici, *Revolution at Point Zero: Housework, Reproduction, and Feminist Struggle*.

10. For neo-Keynesian critiques, see Paul Krugman, *The Return of Depression Economics and the Crisis of 2008* and Robert Skidelsky, *Keynes: The Return of the Master*. For neo-Marxian critiques, see David Harvey, *The Enigma of Capital* and Greg Albo, Sam Gindin, and Leo Panitch (eds.), *In and Out of Crisis*.

11. Gender hierarchy was in fact built into virtually all the regimes of social protection established by post–World War II welfare states. I assess the implications of this fact for Polanyian critique in Nancy Fraser, *Fortunes of Feminism: From State-Managed Capitalism to Neoliberal Crisis*, especially Chapter 10, "Between Marketization and Social Protection: Feminist Ambivalences in the Context of Capitalist Crisis."

12. For a fuller account of "emancipation" as a third pole of social aspiration not reducible to protection or marketization, see Nancy Fraser, "Marketization, Social Protection, Emancipation: Toward a Neo-Polanyian Conception of Capitalist Crisis." For an analysis of feminist politics in these terms, see Fraser, "Between Marketization and Social Protection: Feminist Ambivalences in the Context of Capitalist Crisis" in *Fortunes of Feminism*.

13. I have elaborated the concept of a triple movement (comprising marketization, social protection, and emancipation) in Fraser, "Marketization, Social Protection, Emancipation: Toward a Neo-Polanyian Conception of Capitalist Crisis." I have applied it to gender politics in Fraser, "Between Marketization and Social Protection: Feminist Ambivalences in the Context of Capitalist Crisis."

14. Cf. Nancy Folbre, *The Invisible Heart: Economics and Family Values*; Arlie Hochschild, "Love and Gold"; Diane Elson, "Gender Justice, Human Rights, and Neo-Liberal Economic Policies"; Shirin Rai, *Gender and Political Economy of Development: From Nationalism to Globalization*.

15. Cf. Vandana Shiva, "Life Inc: Biotechnology and the Expansion of Capitalist Markets"; Brian Tokar, *Redesigning Life* and *Earth for Sale*; Joel Kovel, *The Enemy of Nature*.

16. Cf. Martin O'Connor, "On the Misadventures of Capitalist Nature" and Neil Smith, "Nature as Accumulation Strategy."

17. Cf. Larry Lohmann, "Neoliberalism and the Calculable World: The Rise of Carbon Trading" (online at http://mayflybooks.org/?page_id=21).

18. The phrase "Embedded Liberalism" is from John G. Ruggie, "International Regimes, Transactions, and Change: Embedded Liberalism in the Postwar Economic Order."

19. For a fuller discussion of the "misframing" of social protections, and indeed of colonialism as a protection racket, see Fraser, "Marketization, Social Protection, Emancipation."

20. Cf. Nancy Fraser, *Scales of Justice: Reimagining Political Space in a Globalizing World.*

21. Cf. Lohmann, "Neoliberalism and the Calculable World: The Rise of Carbon Trading."

TWO EXAMPLES OF RECENT AESTHETICO-POLITICAL FORMS OF COMMUNITY

Occupy and Sharing Economy

DIETMAR WETZEL

INTRODUCTION

Do new aesthetico-political forms of community exist? And if so, can they be found, in whole or in part, in the social reality of the present? Can the sociophilosophical discourse around community/communities or, more precisely, can aspects of that discourse of the past twenty years be empirically observed in more recent social movements? Is it possible to determine criteria that will help distinguish newer forms of community from traditional ones? This essay will systematically address these and similar questions. Classical or traditional communities have always been distinguished by the greatest possible degree of social integration of their members, which has led to the ethno-politically problematic exclusion of nonmembers with or without explanation. By comparison, on the societal level, a low degree of social integration has been found among members of a society, who might not only support a position of non-difference but even encourage it. Contrary to the old underlying separation of community and society,[1] later also identified as systems and lifeworlds (*Lebenswelt*),[2] new tendencies and currents in social philosophy and social theory appear to be suggesting a different relationship between community and society. If anything, a different concept (or a different ontology) may be necessary to adequately describe the phenomena of newer social and/or political movements/currents in terms of communalization (*Vergemeinschaftung*)/socialization (*Vergesellschaftung*) (which makes the discussion around community and society more complicated and more difficult). In order to properly illustrate this (hypothetically assumed) need and the underlying problematic, this essay is divided into a three-step argument.

It was (and is) primarily French poststructuralist thinkers, above all Jacques Derrida, Jean-Luc Nancy, and Jacques Rancière, who have generated new momentum in the debate around poetic-aesthetic community forms. For that reason, after outlining significant background information about the sociological debate so that the resulting disengagement can be more easily comprehended (section 1), the first step will be to address some of the important innovations, namely "Alterity and Society" (2.1), "Politics and Policies of Community" (2.2), and the issue of "Metonymic Communities" (2.3) (section 2). In the ensuing second step, I will attempt to investigate these concepts by applying the ideas of aesthetico-political as well as metonymic community thinking. These reflections will culminate in a third step that questions whether there are in fact any new social forms in the empirical reality of the 21st century and, if so, how they can be recognized (section 3). For that purpose, I will look more closely at two social movements that I consider to be (at least partly) based on such new ideas of community. They are the global *Occupy* movement (3.1) and conceptions of a *sharing economy* (3.2). The considerations that come into play will lead to a conclusion that neatly summarizes the most important results of the theoretico-empirical reflections in four points (section 4).

POINT OF DEPARTURE AND THESIS

The present text will embark on a socio-theoretical as well as an empirically oriented search for new, aesthetico-political forms of community in the 21st century. It will do so against a background of apprehension toward traditional forms of thinking about community as it was generally established by the end of the 20th century (including but not exclusively in sociology).[3] Regarded empirically, an asynchrony arises in the simultaneity of completely distinct forms of community that more or (usually) less peacefully coexist alongside one another. However, what I am interested in is not taking stock but focusing on ostensibly new forms of aesthetico-political community. My thesis, which takes up two positions, is: (a) There is a need for a new, plural conception of community/communalization that partly breaks away from the traditional conception in order to be able to grasp the transition of empirically identifiable forms of community into the form of social movements; and (b) the new social (protest) movement Occupy and the sharing economy movement are exemplary representations of such new forms of community. I would like to make these two initial theses plausible by mounting incremental arguments. An additional goal will be to pull possible criteria for aesthetico-political community formations from theoretical as well as empirically oriented discussions.

1. Community and/or Society

The concept of community has been a challenge not only for sociology since its establishment in the mid-19th century but for all (post)industrial societies. Nonetheless, that is where the moral foundations of any society as well as issues concerning (dis)integration, or rather inclusion and exclusion, are debated.[4] Community and society often have an antagonistic and detached relationship with one another, not least because community is perceived as a "warm" and emotionally charged form as contrasted with a "cold" society that values distance. According to the concomitant apprehension, society appears in lieu of community, bringing with it social coldness and relationships that are regulated (largely impersonally) via the market.[5] In this regard, the following distinction has been established: While community aims to integrate its members as completely as possible, society is ruled by a form of benevolent indifference—or rather non-difference—with respect to its members' dealings with one another. Accordingly, its members tend to be incompletely integrated (because integration is unnecessary).[6] To the extent that it refers to *communalization* and *socialization*, the process of community and society can be pointed out with Max Weber.[7]

Late-20th-century *communitarianism*, which became as multilayered as it was prominent, has unquestionably led to a reevaluation of the thinking about community after its purported loss, which had been proclaimed as far back as Tönnies.[8] In the process, a historical difference has to be taken into consideration insofar as the "spirit of community" in the United States has attained a more positive application (because it is comparatively historically unencumbered). In Europe, and particularly in Germany, this was and is no longer so easy in the wake of the atrocities of National Socialism. Characteristically, in thought about community that is inspired by communitarianism, adherence to an identity and strict identification with it must constitute a common object.[9] In psychoanalytical terms, this is in lieu of the ideal ego, which has retained its structure despite its historical-social variations. A subject who is situated and held in the society will behave as he or she wants to be seen from the perspective of the ideal ego (nation, family, etc.). The associated concepts fell apart (and lost legitimacy) in the transition from modernity to postmodernity but did not disappear entirely in the social reality. However, their echoes remain in a negative sense, namely the invocation of "ethnic communities" or frequently militantly executed acts of so-called "ethnic cleansing" in the name of the homogeneous nation.

In contrast to communitarian attempts to revalue community, the discourse around "post-traditional"[10] communities or communalizations[11] points toward new facets in the conceptualization of empirical communities:

> The point of departure for the concept of post-traditional communities is the empirically supported assumption that people's habitually predetermined and emotionally based relationships tend to dissipate or at least become devalued and that another type of social communalization has developed, which is simply called post-traditional. This type can roughly be described as temporary participation in a single-issue community or lifestyle group for which membership arises through enticement to participate in more or less communicative events, to consume, and to engage in distinctive collective action and staging practices.[12]

These and other similar efforts to determine the new forms of community/communalization need to be distinguished from an entirely different discourse around community, namely that of French and Italian philosophy in the outgoing 20th century.

2. *Aesthetics/Politics of Community*

Late-20th-century French and Italian postmodern and poststructural writers in search of poetic-aesthetic and political forms of community, above all Jacques Derrida (2006), Jean-Luc Nancy (1991), and Jacques Rancière (1999), proceeded from the dissatisfaction with and attendant renunciation of communitarian attempts to revalue community, which were admittedly sometimes quite divergent. This would also include certain works by Giorgio Agamben (2009) and Roberto Esposito (2010).[13] All of these authors, who are quite distinct from one another in the details, plead for greater consideration of alterity, or rather of the (radical) other in the conception of community (2.1). They also combine the search for alternative, aesthetico-ethical, and (in the broadest sense) political forms of community. Along with Nancy, Agamben and Rancière in particular are also leading figures (2.2). Based on those discussions, Thomas Claviez developed the idea of a "metonymic community/society"; I will conclude my reflections in this section by outlining its fundamental features (2.3).

2.1. ALTERITY AND COMMUNITY With Jacques Derrida, Jean-Luc Nancy described the search for an "origin" of the communal as a futile endeavor. According to him, the idea that community had been lost was a myth. Correspondingly, it was not only unnecessary but in fact historically and politically wrong to call for community to be recovered and revalued.[14] Derrida and Nancy did not take identity-, consensus-, or unity-based considerations as their point of departure, but rather assumed a radical alterity and exposure on the part of the community member:

> We are alike because each one of us is exposed to the outside that *we* are *for ourselves*. The like is not the same [*le semblable n'est pas le pareil*]. I do not rediscover *myself*, nor do I recognize *myself* in the other: I experience the other's alterity, or I experience alterity in the other together with the alteration that 'in me' sets my singularity outside me and indefinitely delimits it. Community is that singular ontological order in which the other and the same are alike [*sont le semblable*]: that is to say, in the sharing of identity.[15]

The idea, in the context of the present discussion, of a "community without a community," as Derrida outlined, for example, in his examination of a "New International" in *Specters of Marx*, was an investigatory formula that was both interesting and shared by both Derrida and Nancy. By comparison with older movements, this New International marks a break on at least two points that appear to be quite useful in the search for new forms of community. One is that the emphasis is not on cohesion—that is, unity—but on the disparate and the contingent. The other is that such thinking no longer relies on the clarity of demands and their underlying political motives, precisely with respect to politico-ethically motivated efforts. Ultimately we encounter a (seemingly paradoxical) idea of *community-free community*, which is distinguished by its insistence on alterity and the manifestation of the communal in a tertiary interstice. The imputations of alterity and identity follow from precisely this (always precarious and tentative) interstice and thereby ensure a (potential) interminability for their members, who are characterized by their singularity. Compared with affirmative approaches that evoke homogeneity and uniformity (such as communitarianism and communism), deconstructive approaches to community/the communal have the benefit of pointing out and (politically) targeting interruptive and fragmenting moments in the community form. On one hand, this has a desymbolizing effect and, on the other, disputes and rejects dangerous, forced identity formation (as ideologically motivated).[16]

2.2. POLITICS AND POLICIES OF COMMUNITY The aesthetico-poetic approaches pursued by Giorgio Agamben, Jacques Rancière, and Jean-Luc Nancy contain an eminently political dimension. In his work *The Coming Community*, Agamben therefore emphasized the problematic with which singularities confront the state at precisely the moment when society can no longer invoke affiliation or act in the interest of a "negative community."[17] Subsequently, for Agamben, the "coming politics" is not a struggle for the state or control of it but a struggle between the state and the non-state, or humanity:

> Whatever singularity, which wants to appropriate belonging itself, its own being-in-language, and thus rejects all identity and every condition of belonging, is the principal enemy of the State. Wherever these singularities peacefully demonstrate their being in common there will be a Tiananmen, sooner or later, the tanks will appear.[18]

Starting from a radical and ultimately ineluctable equality of all, Jacques Rancière thinks of political conflict as a manifestation of at least two parties that encounter one another in the production of a common situation, frequently belligerently and anything but voluntarily. In that process, *la part des sans-part* ("the part of those who have no part") plays a central role insofar as it struggles for potential participation, not least of all because it is at risk of exclusion and sharelessness:[19]

> Whoever has no part—the poor of the ancient times, the third estate, the modern proletariat—cannot in fact have any part other than all or nothing. On top of this, it is through the existence of this part of those who have no part, of this nothing that is all, that the community exists as a political community—that is, as divided by a fundamental dispute, by a dispute to do with the counting of the community's parts even more than of their 'rights'. The people are not one class among others. They are the class of the wrong that harms the community and establishes it as a 'community' of the just and the unjust.[20]

Speaking for others in accordance with (democratic) representation also comes up for criticism here because there is a danger of appearing on the political stage as a representative of (groups of) others and not meeting their singular demands in the process, for instance, when the state-organized police, as an element of the political, represent order and deny or exclude unorderly demands by non-established groups.[21] The proclaimed alterity of the members of the political community does not abolish this directly through unification, but it does ensure the possibility of a debate.[22] Community is therefore seen as inherently different just as its members must be conceived of as inherently different.

In turn, Nancy's *literary communism* can be expanded into an "urban communism" because the co-dissemination of documents/literature and the social sharing of goods and artifacts always precede thoughts of an actively produced community—and that is specifically a result of equality and fairness. Achieving this co-dissemination or extracting just one part of it would, in the worst-case scenario, result in totalitarianism or an unjustifiable (because it is unjust) division of material goods.[23]

2.3. METONYMIC COMMUNITY/SOCIETY Following on Giorgio Agamben and Jean-Luc Nancy, albeit critically, a metonymic society, as Thomas Claviez has most recently outlined, is a matter of spatial participation that eliminates the (rigid) difference between community and society:

> A metonymic society should be conceived as one in which 'co-being' is regarded as a common-being without common-having; in the form of, as Nancy writes, a 'self-opposing community, with we who oppose one another, the *with* in opposition to the *with*', a 'co-being' of singularities

between which, as Nancy noted in *Being Singular Plural*, there is contiguity but no continuity.[24]

What is important here is that such a "co-being" exists before there is any identification or even any form of identification, whereas the metonymic society is dependent on an "ethic of hospitality" in the sense of Lévinas and Derrida. More precisely, this means "an ethic that is not based on an assumed commonality (as all moral-philosophical conceptions in the Western metaphysical tradition have done from Aristotle to Kant to Bentham) but on recognizing otherness (with which I share a space) as a point of departure for community."[25] With the resulting form of a radical non-integration into a community, which is now as completely impossible as it is undesirable because of the otherness of its members, the transition to the societal mode of existence of the (indifferent) members becomes fluid.

3. *New Forms of Community?*

The thought and literature about new forms of community described in the previous section, which must be classified as fundamentally sociophilosophical-aesthetic endeavors, leads to a multifaceted deconstruction of thinking of and about communities (whereby the—historically regarded—conceptual antipode "society" also changes). In these hardly coincidental, minimally sociological contexts, community is no longer understood via the figure of the third party in the sense of an expansion of the dyadic structure as a hinge for society,[26] but as a largely spatial and transitory (and therefore fluid) mode of existence that is not based on actively producing or actualizing society. Instead, it can be described by using the terms/concepts of *contingency* and *contiguity*. Behind them lie manifestations that arise incidentally yet are spatially and chronologically directly adjacent to one another.

3.1. OCCUPY: A POSTMODERN COMMUNITY MOVEMENT? Occupy is a (protest) movement that appeared on the scene with Occupy Wall Street and the occupation of Zuccotti Park in New York City on September 17, 2011, and would (seemingly) disappear again just as quickly. The enduring impact of Occupy Wall Street is indisputable insofar as the problematic of increasing social inequality has been (likewise increasingly) on the political and national agenda:

> On September 17, 2011, people from all across the United States of America and the world came to protest the blatant injustices of our times perpetuated by the economic and political elites. On the 17th we as individuals rose up against political disenfranchisement and social and economic injustice. We spoke out, resisted, and successfully occupied Wall Street. Today, we proudly remain in Liberty Square constituting ourselves as autonomous political beings engaged in non-violent civil disobedience and building solidarity based on mutual respect, acceptance, and love. . . . [27]

According to an epigraph such as this one, Occupy was never limited to a single country. Instead, movement hot spots followed in various cities around the world. Characteristics that might be defined as "postmodern" can be identified[28] because of the activation of the network structure of the Internet, which is famously oriented to the principles of structural indeterminacy, essentially endless expansion, sustainability, and distribution of intensities as well as the rejection of any center. The uncanny thing about this postmodern movement is precisely its ghostly appearance and disappearance (which was forced by the police). In other words, Occupy can become active again at any time, anywhere in the world—and that is precisely what makes the movement so difficult for the political establishment to contend with. In connection with this, American literary scholar Richard Grusin uses the expression "premediation of financial market clientele": "#occupywallstreet opens up paths to potential futures in which the occupation of Wall Street (or the political occupation of other sites) is actualized. No matter what its goals, tactics or conclusion, #occupywallstreet successfully premediated the future occupation of Wall Street, even though such an occupation may never happen again."[29] The preparation of such possibilities is one of Occupy's important (and enduring) merits because they mean that future movements can inscribe themselves in that affective-emotional and politically prepared field and benefit from the occupations that preceded them. And if that is not enough, there is more.

Occupy's targeted occupations pointed out the grievances of the world. This has to do with the matter of another critical (counter)public, as has become characteristic and significant for present-day societies.[30] Mörtenböck and Mooshammer (2014), for example, argue that regardless of the numerous actions and interventions in the urban field, a crisis of representation of the public sphere has become evident and can be felt at urban protests. On the one hand, it appears to be rooted in the altered interplay of real and symbolic spaces in the constitution of the public sphere and, on the other hand, it is due to the fact that the contemporary concentration of power in the economy effortlessly succeeds at accessing the (non-economic) representation of our coexistence. Both phenomena are occasions to consider the likelihood of a self-determined "protest public" that does not comply with the rules of the financial markets. Occupy managed to penetrate public consciousness with the slogan "We are the 99 Percent." It is interesting that the movements that arose with and from Occupy are less concerned with concrete political demands (for which Occupy was promptly criticized by the political establishment) than with the transformation of public space into a political common. For Grusin, it is precisely "because of the virtuality and resistance to the formulation of specific demands or establishing a platform"[31] that lasting success can be attributed to Occupy. Judith Butler also sees a collective emergence as an essential aspect, for instance, in the way that political demands are articulated without pursuing hasty consensus-based demands.[32]

To summarize, we can conceive of Occupy as a postmodern movement and address and (partly) actualize the essential motifs of the previously introduced sociophilosophical discourse. Alongside the structural indeterminacy of the community movement and its members (alterity), the ideas of contiguity and contingency also arise. The incidental and therefore unpredictable in community formation is just as evident as the emphasis on the spatiotemporal juxtaposition of singularities as most clearly expressed in ideas of the "metonymic community." The politico-aesthetic dimension manifests itself in concrete, on-site (protest) actions, that is, in concrete occupations, discussion forums, and so on.

3.2. SHARING ECONOMY: FLUID COMMUNITIES UNDER COMMERCIAL PRESSURE

Another conception of how communities can be formed in Western societies manifests itself in the idea and intellectual current of the sharing economy, which is being widely discussed at the moment. Traditional economies in capitalist societies (specifically as opposed to socialism or communism) are based on the accumulation of property and ownership (of means of production). Over the course of many decades, this has resulted in a consumption-oriented disposable society that either keeps objects that have been used once in private or (depending on their durability) throws them away all too quickly. Many of the items that we own, however, are constructed in such a way that we could easily share (and repair) them with others if only we wanted to. A capitalistically constituted economy's claim to exclusivity and property and the sole truly relevant exchange medium of money is disrupted (if not actually challenged) by the philosophy of mutual sharing that arises in the sharing economy. The sharing economy principle of simply "sharing, not buying" is diametrically opposed to the capitalist logic of accumulation. That principle is as simple as it is striking: People are no longer primarily concerned with owning things, but instead only want to have a share in them. The decisive factor for consumers is access to goods and services and not so much the question of property.[33] This changes consumption patterns. Or more precisely, it is a step away from individual consumption and toward forms of communal consumption: "The prospect of collaborative consumption offers refreshing ways to rethink consumption patterns and reverse the increasing atomization of society by drawing individuals back into customs of collective action."[34] Interpersonal relationships and trust are quite obviously an important ingredient for this form of collective consumption to be able to operate. Regardless of whether the subject in question is car sharing, couch surfing, co-housing, or the like, individuals must always be able to rely on others and are therefore (morally) bound to them at the same time. Consequently, a (chronologically limited) sense of community that had previously been more common in rural contexts can also arise in cities. Additionally, sharing-economy participants elude the traditional logic of the market and consumption, or at least attempt to. These alternative forms of exchange, which is ultimately what they are, often use the Internet or other social platforms to make ideas and products available and basically accessible to anyone who is interested. This results in transitory, *fluid communities* that are spatially and chronologically delimited and serve an acutely utilitarian purpose for the participants.

This idea, which is as simple as it is ingenious, is at risk of commercialization, which should come as no surprise when we take capitalism's plasticity and mutability into consideration. This can happen whenever the market discovers for itself the possibilities behind such a sharing idea and, taking inspiration from it, attempts to develop new capitalist-oriented forms of consumption (as happened, for example, with the online housing provider Airbnb).[35] When the extraction of economic benefits and calculated profit are introduced, the idea of hospitality, at least, is reassessed (if not actually reformatted) in a new form of syncretism that merges economics, culture, and the social. This is one example of how an "absolute claim" to a market society based on individual consumption can be challenged or at least disrupted by the principle of sharing. In a way that is similar to Occupy's very general and broadly nonspecific concerns before it, here another form of economy and coexistence is being pursued. A sharing economy (which, it should be noted, is a nascent concept that started in the United States) will have an effect on ways of life that are post-capitalist and post-growth fixations, and that are focused not on property accumulation and ownership but on a new form of exchange and coexistence. Admittedly, it remains to be seen whether other forms of communal economics and coexistence, possibly in conjunction with other approaches and ideas that originate from a perspective that is critical of capitalism, manage to take root.

For the sake of assessment, the heterogeneous sharing-economy movement also exhibits hackneyed ideas with respect to conceptions of new politico-aesthetic community forms. So it is transitory and spatiotemporally contingent encounters that can allow us to participate in the sharing economy. However, its organizational form is clearly more conventional than, for instance, that of Occupy and only partly immune to market or commercial recuperation. An interesting connection to "literary" or "urban communism"[36] emerges; however, this essentially pertains to the sharing of goods to which access should ideally be made available to all. The sharing economy can therefore be interpreted as a movement that is critical of capitalism and that is capable of exerting a positive influence on access and distribution structures in our societies.

4. Summary

In conclusion, I would like to briefly recapitulate the most important points in the present essay and point out what are, in my view, the central features of new, aesthetico-political community forms with respect to the two movements that are addressed here. Some criteria can be established that may, in a heuristic sense, help break down empirical events for further discussion of new (and old) forms of community.

Contiguity and Contingency: The cited conceptions of an aesthetico-political as well as a "metonymic society" emphasize the spatiotemporal aspect and the contingency of cooperation. As such, they fluctuate between what Herman Melville so wonderfully articulated in "Bartleby the Scrivener" with the words "I would prefer not to" and, in my own words, "I would prefer to." This does not (primarily) pertain to creating community but to fundamental ideas of perpetually co-disseminating things, spaces, and people. These central moments of contiguity and contingency can be seen both in Occupy and in the sharing economy.

Interplay and Processuality of Community and Society: To make more recent social movements and initiatives comprehensible, it is worth noting the dovetailing between communalizing and socializing processes. Occupy and the sharing economy oscillate between the two because, on the one hand, they are directed at affected and affecting members yet, on the other hand, lead (sooner or later) to a detached cooperation. Contrary to the rigid conception of community/society, it is worth emphasizing the processes of communalization and socialization in order to underscore the momentary and the event-bound alongside the structural conditions.

Network Structure: Structural indeterminacy, the use of different intensities, and deliberately forgoing any center (the Internet, of course, is the model here) particularly applies to Occupy's postmodern community form. In a certain way, however, these characteristics also apply to the idea of a sharing economy, which is organized in a decentralized way and also uses a network structure to enable participation. As I have suggested, this does put it at risk of commercialization; however, I do not want to deny the advantages of this intellectual current.

Between Identification and Disidentification: More recent social movements are thoroughly affectively attuned assemblages that are characterized nonetheless by their preliminarity and unpredictability. Their members oscillate between moments of identification and disidentification and expose themselves in their singularity.[37] The idea of "urban communism" can function here as a concrete materialization to the extent that, in Occupy as well as in the sharing economy, questions of justice and allocation, or rather issues of access and participation, are of central importance.

NOTES

1. Cf. Ferdinand Tönnies, *Community and Society.*

2. Cf. Jürgen Habermas, *Theorie des kommunikativen Handelns.*

3. Cf. Dietmar Wetzel, *Diskurse des Politischen: Zwischen Re- und Dekonstruktion* and "Gemeinschaft—oder: Vom Unteilbaren des geteilten Miteinanders."

4. The literature about this is, of course, endless. The following authors are considered milestones (classics) in the sociological and sociophilosophical discussion: Ferdinand Tönnies (2002 [1887]), Max Weber (1980 [1921]), Georg Simmel (1995 [1908]), and Helmuth Plessner (2003 [1924]).

5. Cf. Tönnies, *Community and Society.*

6. Cf. Wolfgang Eßbach, "Gemeinschaft—Rassismus—Biopolitik."

7. "A social relationship will be called 'communal' [*Vergemeinschaftung*] if and so far as the orientation of social action . . . is based on a subjective feeling of the parties, whether affectual or traditional, that they belong together. A social relationship will be called 'associative' [*Vergesellschaftung*] if and insofar as the orientation of social action within it rests on a rationally motivated adjustment of interests or a similarly motivated agreement, whether the basis of judgment be absolute values or reasons of expediency" (Weber 1978, 40–41, my translation).

8. For more on this, see my own remarks in *Diskurse des Politischen: Zwischen Re- und Dekonstruktion* and "Gemeinschaft—oder: Vom Unteilbaren des geteilten Miteinanders." On the controversy between communitarian and liberal thinkers, see Axel Honneth, *Kommunitarismus: Eine Debatte über die moralischen Grundlagen moderner Gesellschaften.*

9. Embodied, for instance, in an "imagined community," as Benedict Anderson described it in *Imagined Communities: Reflections on the Origins and Spread of Nationalism.*

10. Cf. Ronald Hitzler, Anne Honer, and Michaela Pfadenhauer, eds., *Posttraditionale Gemeinschaften: Theoretische und ethnografische Erkundungen.*

11. Ibid.

12. Krotz in Hitzler, *Posttraditionale Gemeinschaften*, 151 (my translation).

13. Joseph Vogl's outstanding anthology *Gemeinschaften: Positionen zu einer Philosophie des Politischen* provides a good overview of the most important positions.

14. Nancy, *The Inoperative Community.* For more on this, see my earlier reflections on Derrida and Nancy with an eye toward alterity, community, and hospitality (Wetzel 2004).

15. Nancy, *The Inoperative Community*, 33–34.

16. See Joseph Vogl, *Gemeinschaften: Positionen zu einer Philosophie des Politischen.*

17. In his examination of Nancy in *The Unavowable Community*, Blanchot emphasizes the interminability of community and its members: "If, as the principle of

community, we had the unfinishedness or incompleteness of existence, now as the mark of that which raises it up so high it risks disappearance in 'ecstacy,' we have the accomplishment of community in that which, precisely, limits it, we have sovereignty in that which makes it absent and null, its prolongation in the only communication which henceforth suits it and which passes through literary unsuitability, when the latter inscribes itself in works only to affirm the unworking that haunts them, even if they cannot not reach it" (20).

18. Girgio Agamben, *The Coming Community*, 86.

19. Rancière (2002), 22.

20. Ibid., 9.

21. Susan Fainstein, *The Just City*.

22. Jacques Rancière, "Die Gemeinschaft der Gleichen."

23. Wolfgang Eßbach, "Die Gemeinschaft der Güter und die Soziologie der Artefakte."

24. Thomas Claviez, "Die Rückkehr des Mythos—das Ende der Aufklärung? Überlegungen zu einer metonymischen Gesellschaft" (my translation).

25. Ibid., 53 (my translation).

26. Georg Simmel, *Soziologie: Untersuchungen über die Formen der Vergesellschaftung*.

27. http://www.nycga.net/resources/priniciples-of-solidarity/

28. Mörtenböck and Mooshammer, *Occupy: Räume des Protests*, 90.

29. Richard Grusin, "Die Prämediation von Finanzmarktpublika: Der Fall #occupywallstreet," 220 (my translation).

30. See Langenohl and Wetzel, *Finanzmarktpublika: Moralität, Krisen und Teilhabe in der ökonomischen Moderne*.

31. Richard Grusin, "Die Prämediation von Finanzmarktpublika: Der Fall #occupywallstreet," 221 (my translation).

32. Judith Butler, "For and Against Precarity."

33. See Jeremy Rifkin, *The Age of Access*.

34. Angelique Edmonds, "Collaborative Consumption and the Remaking of Local Resilience: Reflecting upon Enabling Solutions," 90.

35. Byung-Chul Han (2014) sees the sharing economy as a movement toward a "total commercialization of life." The contemporary form of flexible capitalism might even be able to use communist ideas to generate profits. Here Han points to Dave Eggers' novel *The Circle*, in which maxims like "sharing is caring" or "searching for community" line the paving stones on the road to company headquarters.

36. In the words of Jean-Luc Nancy and Wolgang Eßbach.

37. Cf. Jean-Luc Nancy, *The Inoperative Community*.

ACKNOWLEDGMENTS

The essays collected in this volume derive from the first three "Distinguished Lectures Series" that took place at the Center for Cultural Studies (CCS, now Walter Benjamin Kolleg) of the University of Bern, Switzerland, between 2010 and 2012. Thanks go to the University of Bern and its Philosophical-Historical Faculty for financially supporting a series that meanwhile has achieved a unique status worldwide, in that it not only gathers three renowned scholars per semester to provide their views on a fixed topic, but also to offer workshops that are of inestimable value for the postdocs and Ph.D. and advanced students from all over Switzerland and beyond. Thanks also go out to them for having made these workshops lively fora and sites of critical exchange.

I would also like to acknowledge the support of the Burgergemeinde Bern for the 2012 series.

I'd like to express my special gratitude for the untiring and conscientious work of my two assistants, Viola Marchi and Ryan Kopaitich, who not only edited this book in an expert manner, but also offered their critical input and conversation throughout the development of this project. Thanks also go to Rahel Braunschweig for her conscientious work on the indexes.

Finally, and above all, I would like to thank my wife, Cecilie, and my daughter, Cora, for mustering so much patience through even more evenings and nights than usual spent in preparing both the lecture series and this publication.

WORKS CITED

Agamben, Giorgio. *The Coming Community*. Translated by Michael Hardt. Minneapolis: University of Minnesota Press, 2009.

Agee, James. *Let Us Now Praise Famous Men*. Boston: Houghton Mifflin, 1960.

Albo, Greg, Sam Gindin, and Leo Panitch, eds. *In and Out of Crisis*. Oakland, CA: PM Press, 2010.

Anderson, Benedict. *Imagined Communities: Reflections on the Origins and Spread of Nationalism*. Revised Edition. London: Verso, 1991.

Arendt, Hannah. *The Origins of Totalitarianism*. New York: Meridian Books, 1958.

———. "Thinking and Moral Considerations: A Lecture." *Social Research* 38.3 (Autumn 1971): 441–44.

———. *The Human Condition*. Chicago: University of Chicago Press, 1998.

Asad, Talal. *On Suicide Bombing*. New York: Columbia University Press, 2007.

Auden, W. H. "In Memory of W. B. Yeats." In *Another Time*. London: Faber & Faber, 1945. 107–10.

———. "September 1, 1939." In *Another Time*. London: Faber & Faber, 1945. 112–15.

———. *New Year Letter*. London: Faber & Faber, 1946.

———. "New Year Letter." *Collected Longer Poems*. London: Faber & Faber, 1968.

Bakker, Isabella, and Steven Gill, eds. *Power, Production and Social Reproduction*. New York: Palgrave MacMillan, 2003.

Balzac, Honoré de. *The Magic Skin, or The Wild Ass's Skin*. Translated by Herbert J. Hunt. Harmondsworth, England: Penguin Books, 1977.

Barthes, Roland. *Mythologies*. Translated by Annette Lavers. New York: Hill & Wang, 1972.

Bataille, Georges. *Georges Bataille. Visions of Excess: Selected Writings, 1927–1939*. Edited by Allan Stoekl. Minneapolis: Minnesota University Press, 1985.

———. *The Obsessions of Georges Bataille: Community and Communication*. Edited by Andrew J. Mitchell and Jason Kemp Winfree. Albany: SUNY Press, 2009.

Bauman, Zygmunt. *Community: Seeking Safety in an Insecure World*. Cambridge: Polity Press, 2001.

Beck, Ulrich. *Risk Society. Towards a New Modernity*. Translated by Mark Ritter. London: Sage Publications, 1992.

———. *The Cosmopolitan Vision*. Translated by Ciaran Cronin. Cambridge: Polity Press, 2006.

Benjamin, Walter. *The Arcades Project*. Cambridge, MA: The Belknap Press of Harvard University Press, 1999.

Berman, Jessica. *Modernist Fiction, Cosmopolitanism, and the Politics of Community*. Cambridge: Cambridge University Press, 2001.

Biesecker, Adelheid, and Sabine Hofmeister. "(Re)productivity: Sustainable Relations Both Between Society and Nature and Between the Genders." *Ecological Economics* 69 (2010): 1703–11.

Blanchot, Maurice. *The Unavowable Community*. Translated by Pierre Joris. Barrytown, NY: Station Hill Press, 2000.

———. *Infinite Conversation*. Translated by Susan Hanson. Minneapolis: University of Minnesota Press, 2011.

Blumenberg, Hans. *Work on Myth*. Cambridge: MIT Press, 1988.

Borges, Jorge Luis. *Other Inquisitions, 1937–1952*. Edited by Ruth L. C. Simms. Austin: University of Texas Press, 1964.

———. "Kafka and His Precursors." In *Other Inquisitions, 1937–1952*. Edited by Ruth L. C. Simms. Austin: University of Texas Press, 1964.

———. "Pierre Menard, Author of the Quixote." In *Collected Fictions*. Translated by Andrew Hurley. New York: Viking, 1998. 88–95.

Borradori, Giovanna. *Philosophy in a Time of Terror: Dialogues with Jürgen Habermas and Jacques Derrida*. Chicago: University of Chicago Press, 2003.

Bourdieu, Pierre. "La précarité est aujourd'hui partout." *Contre-feux I*. Paris: Éditions Raisons d'agir, 1998. 95–101.

Brodsky, Joseph. "On 'September 1, 1939' by W. H. Auden." In *Less Than One: Selected Essays*. New York: Farrar, Straus and Giroux, 1986.

Burke, Ulick Ralph. *A History of Spain, from the Earliest Times to the Death of Ferdinand the Great*. London: Longmans, Green & Co., 1895.

Butler, Judith. *Precarious Life*. London: Verso, 2004.

———. "For and Against Precarity." *Tidal—Occupy Theory, Occupy Strategy* 1 (December 2011): 12–13.

———. "Precarious Life, Vulnerability, and the Ethics of Cohabitation." *Journal of Speculative Philosophy* 26.2 (2012): 134–51.

Casanova, Pascale. *La république mondiale des lettres*. Paris: Seuil, 1999.

Castoriadis, Cornelius. "Reflections on Racism." *Thesis* 11.32 (1992): 1–12.

Chatterjee, Partha. *The Nation and Its Fragments: Colonial and Postcolonial Histories*. Princeton, NJ: Princeton University Press, 1993.

———. "Community in the East." *Economic and Political Weekly* (February 7, 1998): 277–82.

Clark, Bruce. *Twice a Stranger: How Mass Expulsion Forged Modern Greece and Turkey*. London: Granta, 2006.

Claviez, Thomas. *Grenzfälle: Mythos—Ideologie—American Studies*. Trier: Wissenschaftlicher Verlag Trier, 1998.

———. *Aesthetics and Ethics: Otherness and Moral Imagination from Aristotle to Levinas and from "Uncle Tom's Cabin" to "House Made of Dawn."* Heidelberg: Winter, 2008.

———. "Die Rückkehr des Mythos—das Ende der Aufklärung? Überlegungen zu einer metonymischen Gesellschaft." *Perspektiven der Aufklärung: Zwischen Mythos und Realität*. Edited by Dietmar Wetzel. München: Fink, 2012. 43–56.

———. "Traces of a Metonymic Society in American Literary History." *American Studies Today*. Edited by Winfried Fluck et al. Heidelberg: Winter, 2014. 299–321.

Comte, Auguste. *System of Positive Polity*. Vol. 1. London: Longmans, Green, & Co., 1875.

Damrosch, David. *What Is World Literature?* Princeton, NJ: Princeton University Press, 2003.

d'Aurevilly, Barbey. "L'Éducation sentimentale." *Le Constitutionnel*. 19 novembre 1869.

Delanty, Gerald. *Community*. London: Routledge, 2003.

Deleuze, Gilles. "Bartleby; Or, the Formula." In *Essays Critical and Clinical*. Translated by Daniel W. Smith and Michael A. Greco. Minneapolis: University of Minnesota Press, 1997. 68–90.

Deleuze, Gilles, and Felix Guattari. *A Thousand Plateaus*. Translated by Brian Massumi. Minneapolis: University of Minnesota Press, 2004.

de Pontmartin, Armand. "Le Roman bourgeois et le roman démocratique. MM. Edmond About et Gustave Flaubert." *Nouvelles causeries du Samedi*. Paris: Michel-Lévy, 1859.

Derrida, Jacques. "Structure, Sign and Play." *Writing and Difference*. Translated by Alan Bass. Chicago: University of Chicago Press, 1978.

———. "What Does It Mean to Be a French Philosopher Today?" *Paper Machine*. Translated by Rachel Bowlby. Stanford, CA: Stanford University Press, 2005. 112–20.

———. *Specters of Marx*. Translated by Peggy Kamuf. New York: Routledge, 2006.

Dobkin, Marjorie Housepian. *Smyrna 1922: The Destruction of a City*. New York: Newmark Press, 1998.

Edmonds, Angelique. "Collaborative Consumption and the Remaking of Local Resilience: Reflecting upon Enabling Solutions." In *Designing for Zero Waste: Consumption, Technologies and the Built Environment*. Edited by S. Lehman and R. Crocker. London & New York: Routledge, 2012. 89–111.

Eggers, Dave. *The Circle*. New York: Vintage Books, 2014.
Elson, Diane. "Gender Justice, Human Rights, and Neo-Liberal Economic Policies." In *Gender Justice, Development and Rights*. Edited by Maxine Molyneux and Shahra Razavi. Oxford: Oxford University Press, 2002. 78–114.
Esposito, Roberto. *Communitas*. Translated by Timothy Campbell. Stanford, CA: Stanford University Press, 2010.
———. *Immunitas*. Translated by Zakiya Hanafi. Cambridge: Polity Press, 2011.
———. *Third Person*. Translated by Zakiya Hanafi. Cambridge: Polity Press, 2012.
———. *Terms of the Political*. Translated by Rhiannon Noel Welch. Introduction by Vanessa Lemm. New York: Fordham University Press, 2012.
Eßbach, Wolfgang. "Gemeinschaft—Rassismus—Biopolitik." *Das Fremde—Der Gast*. Edited by Wolfgang Pircher. Wien: Turia und Kant, 1993. 19–35.
———. "Die Gemeinschaft der Güter und die Soziologie der Artefakte." *Ästhetik & Kommunikation* 26.99 (1997): 13–20.
Fainstein, Susan S. *The Just City*. Ithaca, NY: Cornell University Press, 2010.
Fanon, Frantz. *Black Skin, White Masks*. Translated by Charles Lam Markmann. London: Pluto Press, 1967.
———. *Toward the African Revolution*. Translated by H. Chevalier. New York: Monthly Review Press, 1967.
———. *The Wretched of the Earth*. Translated by Richard Philcox. New York: Grove Books, 2004.
Faroqhi, Suraiya. *The Ottoman Empire and the World Around It*. London: I. B. Tauris, 2004.
Federici, Silvia. *Revolution at Point Zero: Housework, Reproduction, and Feminist Struggle*. New York: PM Press, 2012.
Folbre, Nancy. *The Invisible Heart: Economics and Family Values*. New York: The New Press, 2001.
Fraser, Nancy. *Scales of Justice: Reimagining Political Space in a Globalizing World*. New York: Columbia University Press and Polity Press, 2008.
———. "Marketization, Social Protection, Emancipation: Toward a Neo-Polanyian Conception of Capitalist Crisis." In *Business as Usual: The Roots of the Global Financial Meltdown*. Edited by Craig Calhoun and Georgi Derlugian. New York: New York University Press, 2011. 137–58.
———. *Fortunes of Feminism: From State-Managed Capitalism to Neoliberal Crisis*. London: Verso, 2013.
———. "Between Marketization and Social Protection: Feminist Ambivalences in the Context of Capitalist Crisis." *Fortunes of Feminism: From State-Managed Capitalism to Neoliberal Crisis*. London: Verso, 2013. 227–41.
Freud, Sigmund. *Inhibitions, Symptoms and Anxiety*. Stamford, CT: Psychoanalytic Institute, 1927.

Fuller, John. *W. H. Auden: A Commentary.* Princeton, NJ: Princeton University Press, 1998.

Geroulanos, Stefanos. *An Atheism That Is Not Humanist Emerges in French Thought.* Stanford, CA: Stanford University Press, 2010.

Gibson, Andrew. *Joyce's Revenge: History, Politics and Aesthetics in* Ulysses. New York: Oxford University Press, 2001.

Gilroy, Paul. *Between Camps.* London: Penguin Books, 2000.

Gobodo-Madikizela, Pumla. "Alternatives to Revenge: Building a Vocabulary of Reconciliation Through Political Pardon." In *The Provocations of Amnesty: Memory, Justice and Impunity.* Edited by Charles Villa-Vicencio and Eric Doxtader. Trenton, NJ: New World Press, 2003. 51–60.

Grant, Cy. *A Member of the RAF of Indeterminate Race: WW2 Experiences of a Former RAF Navigator and POW.* Bognor Regis: Woodfield Publishing, 2006.

Grusin, Richard. "Die Prämediation von Finanzmarktpublika: Der Fall #occupywallstreet." *Finanzmarktpublika. Moralität, Krisen und Teilhabe in der ökonomischen Moderne.* Edited by Andreas Langenohl and Dietmar Wetzel. Wiesbaden: VS-Verlag, 2014.

Habermas, Jürgen. *Neue Unübersichtlichkeit.* Frankfurt am Main: Suhrkamp, 1985.

———. *Theorie des kommunikativen Handelns.* Zwei Bände. Frankfurt am Main: Suhrkamp, 1988.

Hacking, Ian. *Taming Chance.* Cambridge: Cambridge University Press, 1990.

Hall, Stuart. "The Multicultural Question." *Un/settled Multiculturalisms: Diasporas, Entanglements, Transruptions.* Edited by Barnor Hesse. London: Zed Press, 2000. 209–41.

Haraway, Donna. *When Species Meet.* Minneapolis: University of Minnesota Press, 2008.

Harvey, David. *The Enigma of Capital.* New York: Oxford University Press, 2010.

Hegel, G. W. F. *The Philosophy of Right.* Translated by T. M. Knox. Cambridge: Cambridge University Press, 1967 [1821].

Heidegger, Martin. "The Origin of the Work of Art." In *Basic Writings: From Being and Time (1927) to the Task of Thinking (1964).* Edited by David Farrell Krell. San Francisco: Harper, 1993. 137–212.

———. *Being and Time.* Translated by John Macquarrie and Edward Robinson. New York: Harper Perennial Modern Thought, 2008.

Henderson, Ian, and Philip Goodhart. *Man Hunt in Kenya.* Garden City, NJ: Doubleday, 1958.

Hitzler, Ronald, Anne Honer, and Michaela Pfadenhauer, eds. *Posttraditionale Gemeinschaften: Theoretische und ethnografische Erkundungen.* Wiesbaden: VS-Verlag, 2009.

Hobbes, Thomas. *Elements of Law, Natural and Politic.* Edited by J. C. A. Gaskin. Oxford: Oxford University Press, 2008.

Hochschild, Arlie. "Love and Gold." In *Global Woman: Nannies, Maids, and Sex Workers in the New Economy*. Edited by Barbara Ehrenreich and Arlie Hochschild. New York: Henry Holt, 2002. 15–30.

———. *The Commercialization of Intimate Life: Notes from Home and Work*. San Francisco: University of California Press, 2003.

Honneth, Axel, ed. *Kommunitarismus: Eine Debatte über die moralischen Grundlagen moderner Gesellschaften*. 2. Auflage. Frankfurt am Main: Campus Verlag, 1994.

Hoskyns, Catherine, and Shirin Rai. "Recasting the Global Political Economy: Counting Women's Unpaid Work." *New Political Economy* 12.3 (2007): 297–317.

Joyce, James. *Ulysses*. London: Bodley Head, 1960.

Kadir, Djelal. "To World, to Globalize: Comparative Literature's Crossroads." *Comparative Literature Studies* 41.1 (2004): 1–9.

———. "World Literature: The Allophone, the Differential, and the Common." *Modern Language Quarterly* 74.2 (2013): 293–306.

Kafka, Franz. "The Cares of a Family Man." In *Franz Kafka: The Complete Stories*. New York: Schocken, 1971. 427–29.

Kant, Immanuel. "On the Different Races of Man." In *Race and the Enlightenment: A Reader*. Edited by Emmanuel Eze and translated by Katherine Faul. Oxford and Malden: Blackwell Publishers, 1997. 38–48.

Kovel, Joel. *The Enemy of Nature*. London: Zed Books, 2007.

Krugman, Paul. *The Return of Depression Economics and the Crisis of 2008*. New York: W. W. Norton & Company, 2008.

Lacoue-Labarthe, Philippe. "Transcendence Ends in Politics," *Social Research* 49:2 (Summer 1982): 405–40.

Le Sueur, James D. *Uncivil War: Intellectuals and Identity Politics during the Decolonization of Algeria*. Philadelphia: University of Pennsylvania Press, 2001.

Levinas, Emmanuel. *Collected Philosophical Papers*. Translated by Alphonso Lingis. Dordrecht: Martinus Nijhoff Publishers, 1987.

Lévi-Strauss, Claude. "The Structural Study of Myth." In *Structural Anthropology*. Vol. 1. Translated by Clair Jacobson and Brooke Grundfest Shoepf. New York: Basic Books, 1963. 206–31.

Liddell, Henry George, and Robert Scott. *A Greek-English Lexicon*. Oxford: Clarendon Press, 1940.

Lindqvist, Sven. *A History of Bombing*. Translated by Linda Haverty Rugg. New York: The New Press, 2001.

Lohmann, Larry. "Neoliberalism and the Calculable World: The Rise of Carbon Trading." In *Upsetting the Offset: The Political Economy of Carbon Markets*. Edited by Steffen Böhm and Siddhartha Dabhi. London: MayFly Books, 2009. 25–40.

Lübecker, Nikolaj. *Community, Myth and Recognition in Twentieth-Century French Literature and Thought*. New York: Continuum, 2011.

Lugard, Frederick John Dealtry. *The Dual Mandate in British Tropical Africa*. London: W. Blackwood and Sons, 1922.

Mallarmé, Stéphane. "Conflit." *Oeuvres Complètes*. Paris: Gallimard, 1945.

Marcuse, Herbert. *One-Dimensional Man*. Boston: Beacon Press, 1964.

Margalit, Avishai. *The Ethics of Memory*. Cambridge: Harvard University Press, 2009.

Marx, Karl. *Capital*. Vol. 3. New York: Penguin, 1993.

———. "Critique of Hegel's Dialectic and General Philosophy." In *The Economic and Philosophic Manuscripts of 1844 and the Communist Manifesto*. Translated by Martin Milligan. New York: Prometheus Books, 1988. 141–70.

Marx, Karl, and Frederick Engels. *The German Ideology*. Edited by C. J. Arthur. New York: International Publishers, 1970.

Mazower, Mark. *Salonica, City of Ghosts: Christians, Muslims and Jews*. New York: Harper, 2005.

Megill, Kenneth A. "The Community in Marx's Philosophy." *Philosophy and Phenomenological Research* 30.3 (1970): 382–93.

Melville, Herman. "Bartleby, the Scrivener: A Story of Wall-Street." *Great Short Works of Herman Melville*. New York: Harper Perennial Modern Classics, 2004. 39–74.

Milton, Giles. *Paradise Lost: Smyrna 1922: The Destruction of Islam's City of Tolerance*. London: Sceptre, 2009.

Moretti, Franco. "Conjectures on World Literature." *New Left Review* 1 (2000): 54–68.

Mörtenböck, Peter, and Helge Mooshammer. *Occupy: Räume des Protests*. Bielefeld: transcript, 2012.

———. "Strittige Öffentlichkeiten: Die Besetzung der Ökonomie." In *Finanzmarktpublika. Moralität, Krisen und Teilhabe in der ökonomischen Moderne*. Wiesbaden: VS-Verlag, 2014.

Nancy, Jean-Luc. *The Inoperative Community*. Translated by Peter Connor et al. Minneapolis: University of Minnesota Press, 1991.

———. *Being Singular Plural*. Translated by Robert D. Richardson and Anne E. O'Byrne. Stanford, CA: Stanford University Press, 2000.

———. "The Confronted Community." Translated by Amanda Macdonald. *Postcolonial Studies* 6.1 (2003): 23–36.

Nolan, Emer. *James Joyce and Nationalism*. London: Routledge, 1995.

Nussbaum, Martha. *For Love of Country?* Boston: Beacon Press, 2002.

O'Connor, James. "Capitalism, Nature, Socialism: A Theoretical Introduction." *Capitalism, Nature, Socialism* 1.1 (1988): 11–38.

———. "On the Misadventures of Capitalist Nature." *Is Capitalism Sustainable? Political Economy and the Politics of Ecology*. Edited by Martin O'Connor. New York: Guilford Press, 1994. 125–51.

O'Donoghue, Bernard. *Selected Poems*. London: Faber & Farber, 2008.

Palumbo-Liu, David, Bruce Robbins, and Nirvana Tanoukhi, eds. *Immanuel Wallerstein and the Problem of the World: System, Scale, Culture*. Durham, NC, and London: Duke University Press, 2011.

Pelczynski, Z. A., ed. *The State and Civil Society: Studies in Hegel's Political Philosophy*. Cambridge: Cambridge University Press, 1984.

Pierce, Gareth. *Dispatches from the Dark Side: On Torture and the Death of Justice*. London: Verso, 2010.

Plessner, Helmuth. "Grenzen der Gemeinschaft: Eine Kritik des sozialen Radikalismus." *Macht und menschliche Natur*. Edited by Günter Dux et al. Frankfurt am Main: Suhrkamp, 2003 [1924]. 7–133.

Polanyi, Karl. *The Great Transformation*. 2nd ed. Boston: Beacon Press, 2001 [1944].

Quintilian. *Institutio Oratoria*. Edited and translated by Harold Edgeworth Butler. Cambridge: Harvard University Press; London: William Heinemann, Ltd., 1922.

Rai, Shirin. *Gender and Political Economy of Development: From Nationalism to Globalization*. Cambridge: Polity Press, 2002.

Rancière, Jacques. "Die Gemeinschaft der Gleichen." In *Gemeinschaften. Positionen zu einer Philosophie des Politischen*. Edited by Joseph Vogl. Frankfurt am Main: Suhrkamp, 1994. 101–32.

———. *Disagreement: Politics and Philosophy*. Translated by Julie Rose. Minneapolis: University of Minnesota Press, 1999.

———. *The Flesh of Words: The Politics of Writing*. Translated by Charlotte Mandell. Stanford, CA: Stanford University Press, 2004.

———. *The Politics of Aesthetics*. Translated by Gabriel Rockhill. London: Continuum, 2005.

———. *On the Shores of Politics*. Translated by Liz Heron. London: Verso, 2007.

———. *The Aesthetic Unconscious*. Translated by Debra Keates and James Swenson. Cambridge: Polity Press, 2009.

———. *Dissensus: On Politics and Aesthetics*. Edited and translated by Steve Corcoran. New York: Continuum, 2010.

Reclus, Onésime. *France, Algérie et colonies*. Paris: Hachette, 1886.

———. *Le plus beau royaume sous le ciel*. Paris: Hachette, 1899.

Rifkin, Jeremy. *The Age of Access*. New York: Tarcher/Putnam, 2000.

Robotham, Don. "Afterword: Learning from Polanyi." In *Market and Society: The Great Transformation Today*. Edited by Chris Hann and Keith Hart. Cambridge: Cambridge University Press, 2009. 280–81.

Rose, Nikolas. *The Politics of Life Itself*. Princeton, NJ: Princeton University Press, 2007.

Rosenfeld, Michel. "Hegel and the Dialectics of Contract." *Cardozo Law Review* 10 (1989): 1199–1269.

Ruggie, John G. "International Regimes, Transactions, and Change: Embedded Liberalism in the Postwar Economic Order." *International Organization* 36.2 (1982): 379–415.
Said, Edward. *Beginnings*. New York: Basic Books, 1975.
———. *Edward Said and the Work of the Critic: Speaking Truth to Power.* Edited by Paul Bové. Durham, NC, and London: Duke University Press, 2000.
Sekyi-Out, Ato. *Frantz Fanon's Dialectic of Experience*. Cambridge: Harvard University Press, 1996.
Shiva, Vandana. "Life Inc: Biotechnology and the Expansion of Capitalist Markets." *Sostenible? 2 La Biotecnologia* (2000): 79–92.
Sidwa, Bapsi. *Ice Candy Man*. London: Heinemann, 1988.
Simmel, Georg. *Soziologie: Untersuchungen über die Formen der Vergesellschaftung.* Frankfurt am Main: Suhrkamp, 1995 [1908].
———. "Conflict and the Structure of the Group." *Conflict and the Web of Group-Affiliation*. Translated by Kurt H. Wolff and Reinhard Bender. New York: The Free Press, 1955. 87–123.
Singer, Peter W. *Wired for War: The Robotics Revolution and Conflict in the 21st Century.* New York: Penguin Books, 2009.
Singh, Kushwat. *Train to Pakistan*. New York: Grove Press, 1956.
Skidelsky, Robert. *Keynes: The Return of the Master.* New York: Public Affairs, 2009.
Smith, Neil. "Nature as Accumulation Strategy." *Coming to Terms with Nature. Socialist Register* 43 (2007): 16–36.
Sorel, Georges. *Reflections on Violence*. Edited by Jeremy Jennings. Cambridge: Cambridge University Press, 1999.
Spivak, Gayatri C. *Death of a Discipline*. New York: Columbia University Press, 2005.
Stalin, Joseph. *Marxism and the National and Colonial Question*. London: Martin Lawrence, 1936.
Tanoukhi, Nirvana. "The Scale of World Literature." In *Immanuel Wallerstein and the Problem of the World: System, Scale, Culture*. Edited by David Palumbo-Liu, Bruce Robbins, and Nirvana Tanoukhi. Durham, NC, and London: Duke University Press, 2011. 78–98.
Taylor, Charles. *Multiculturalism and the Politics of Recognition: An Essay.* Princeton, NJ: Princeton University Press, 1992.
Tokar, Brian. *Earth for Sale*. Cambridge, MA: South End Press, 1997.
———. *Redesigning Life*. London: Zed Books, 2001.
Tönnies, Ferdinand. *Community and Society.* Translated by Charles P. Loomis. Mineola, New York: Dover Publications Inc., 2002.
Vogl, Joseph, ed. *Gemeinschaften. Positionen zu einer Philosophie des Politischen.* Frankfurt am Main: Suhrkamp, 1994.

Ware, Vron. "Infowar and the politics of feminist curiosity." *Cultural Studies* 20.6 (November 2006): 526–51.

Weber, Max. *Economy and Society.* Berkeley: University of California Press, 1980 [1921].

Wetzel, Dietmar. *Diskurse des Politischen: Zwischen Re- und Dekonstruktion.* München: Fink, 2003.

———. "Gerechtigkeit—Alterität—Gemeinschaft: Bestimmungsversuche mit Jacques Derrida und Jean-Luc Nancy." In *Zwischen Ausgrenzung und Hybridisierung.* Edited by Antonia Napp et al. Würzburg: Ergon-Verlag, 2003. 263–84.

———. "Vom Anderen des Politischen. Über 'postmoderne Ethik' und ihre Grenzen." *PostModerne De/Konstruktionen.* Edited by Susanne Kollmann and Kathrin Schödel. Münster: LIT-Verlag, 2004. 29–44.

———. "Gemeinschaft—oder: Vom Unteilbaren des geteilten Miteinanders." In *Poststrukturalistische Soziologien.* Edited by Stephan Moebius and Andreas Reckwitz. Frankfurt am Main: Suhrkamp, 2008. 43–57.

Whitman, Walt. *Democratic Vistas.* New York: The Liberal Arts Press, 1949.

———. *Leaves of Grass.* Modern Library Edition. New York: Random House, 1940.

Williams, Raymond. *Keywords: A Vocabulary of Culture and Society* [1976]. Revised Edition. London: Fontana Press, 1983.

———. "The Importance of Community." In *Resources of Hope: Culture, Democracy, Socialism.* Edited by Robin Gable. London: Verso, 1989. 111–19.

Woolf, Virginia. *To The Lighthouse.* Edited by Margaret Drabble. Oxford: Oxford University Press, 1992.

———. *Modern Fiction. The Essays of Virginia Woolf.* Edited by Andrew McNeillie. London: Hogarth Press, 1994.

———. *Mrs. Dalloway.* Ware: Wordsworth Classics, 1996.

Wright, Richard, and Edwin Roskam. *12 Million Black Voices: A Folk History of the Negro in the United States.* London: Lindsay Drummond, 1947.

Young, Jock. *The Exclusive Society.* London: Sage, 1999.

Young, Robert J. C. "Postcolonial Remains." *New Literary History* 43.1 (Winter 2012): 19–42.

Žižek, Slavoj. "Neighbors and Other Monsters: A Plea for Ethical Violence." In *The Neighbor: Three Inquiries in Political Theology.* Edited by Slavoj Žižek, Eric L. Santer, and Kenneth Reinhard. Chicago: University of Chicago Press, 2005. 134–90.

———. *Violence: Six Sideways Reflections.* London: Profile Books, 2008.

CONTRIBUTORS

Homi K. Bhabha is the Anne F. Rothenberg Professor of English and American Literature and Language, and the Director of the Humanities Center at Harvard University. Bhabha's work has significantly formed and influenced postcolonial studies. By introducing concepts of poststructuralism and Lacanian psychoanalysis into postcolonial thought, and coining key concepts such as hybridity, mimicry, ambivalence, difference, and the Third Space, Bhabha has established himself as one of the leading theoreticians in postcolonial studies. He has written numerous works exploring postcolonial theory, cosmopolitanism, and cultural change and power, among other themes. Among his most influential titles are *Nation and Narration* (1990), *The Location of Culture* (1994), and *Edward Said: Continuing the Conversation,* which he co-edited with W. J. T. Mitchell in 2005. Forthcoming books are *A Global Measure* and *The Right to Narrate.*

Thomas Claviez is Professor of Literary Theory at the University of Bern. He is the author of *Grenzfälle: Mythos—Ideologie—American Studies* (1998) and *Aesthetics and Ethics: Otherness and Moral Imagination from Aristotle to Levinas and from "Uncle Tom's Cabin" to "House Made of Dawn"* (2008). He has published essays on pragmatism, ecology, American studies, American literature, ethics and aesthetics, and Native American literature. He is the editor of *The Conditions of Hospitality: Ethics, Politics, and Aesthetics on the Threshold of the Possible* (2013); the co-author of *Zur Aktualität von Jacques Rancière* (forthcoming 2015, with Dietmar Wetzel); and he is currently working on a monograph with the title *The Metonymic Society: Toward a New Poetics of Community.*

Nancy Fraser is the Henry A. and Louise Loeb Professor of Political and Social Science and Professor of Philosophy at the New School for Social Research in New York City. Fraser's fields of expertise include social and political theory, feminist theory, and contemporary French and German thought. Her work focuses on conceptions of justice in contemporary political contexts in the tradition of feminist thinkers. In order to avoid a reductive treatment of the complex concept of justice, she argues for a synthesis of critical theory and poststructuralism that should bring social theorists to a fuller understanding of the social and political issues with which both approaches are concerned. Fraser's most recent publications in this field include *Fortunes of Feminism: From State-Managed Capitalism to Neoliberal Crisis* (2013), *Scales of Justice: Reimagining Political Space in a Globalizing World* (2008), and *Redistribution or Recognition? A Political-Philosophical Exchange* (2003), co-authored with Axel Honneth.

Paul Gilroy is Professor of American and English Literature at King's College London. He is the author of *Darker Than Blue: On the Moral Economies of Black Atlantic Culture* (2010). Earlier and influential books include *Ain't No Black in the Union Jack* (1987), *Small Acts* (1993), *The Black Atlantic: Modernity and Double Consciousness* (1993), *Between Camps* (2000), *After Empire* (2004), and *Postcolonial Melancholia* (2005). Gilroy's work has exerted an enormous influence on the burgeoning field of Transatlantic Studies, as well as contributed to the study of African diasporic intellectuals and political exchange. Moreover, his work on the politics of race, nation, and racism in Britain has been and continues to be of great relevance to academic and public debates on these issues.

Djelal Kadir is Edwin Erle Sparks Professor Emeritus of Comparative Literature at Penn State University. He is the author of *Memos from the Besieged City: Lifelines for Cultural Sustainability* (2010), as well as of *The Other Writing: Postcolonial Essays in Latin America's Writing Culture* (1993) and *Columbus and the Ends of the Earth: Europe's Prophetic Rhetoric as Conquering Ideology* (1992). He has co-edited, with David Damrosch and Theo D'Haen, the *Routledge Companion to World Literature* (2011). In a long-standing commitment to literary theory, Kadir's work revolves around world literature, comparative literature, and globalization, as well as Latin American writing and postcolonial literature. In his most recent book, *Memos from the*

Besieged City, by looking at world historical crossroads, Kadir examines the importance and influence of unconventional writing on literacy, culture, and intellectual commitment.

Jean-Luc Nancy is Professor Emeritus of the University of Strasbourg and holds the Georg Wilhelm Friedrich Hegel Chair at the European Graduate School in Saas-Fee. He is a leading French philosopher whose work is deeply invested in European philosophy, with influences ranging from Georges Bataille and Maurice Blanchot to René Descartes, G. W. F. Hegel, Friedrich Nietzsche, and Martin Heidegger. He is the author of *La communauté désœuvrée* (*The Inoperative Community*, 1982), in which he examines community as an idea that has dominated modern thought and traces its relation to concepts of experience, discourse, and otherness. Further publications include *Être singulier pluriel* (*Being Singular Plural*, 1996) and his latest book, *What's These Worlds Coming To?* (2014), co-authored with Aurélien Barrau.

Jacques Rancière is Professor of Philosophy at the European Graduate School in Saas-Fee and Professor Emeritus at the Université de Paris (St. Denis). He has written and published on pedagogy, the writing of history, philosophy, cinema, aesthetics, and contemporary art. His work cannot easily be classified because it attempts to break the borders of disciplinarity. Rancière's comparison of works and thinkers goes across centuries, and he has compared works by well-known thinkers with those of relatively unknown ones, operating from the presumption or idea of equal intelligence. His main interests focus on politics and aesthetics. Among Rancière's more recent translated texts are: *Mute Speech: Literature, Critical Theory, and Politics* (2011); *Mallarmé: The Politics of the Siren* (2011); and *Aisthesis: Scenes from the Aesthetic Regime of Art* (2013).

Dietmar Wetzel is Research Coordinator for the project "The Distribution of Security in Cities: Reflections on Justice" at the International Centre for Ethics in the Sciences and Humanities at the University of Tübingen. He is also Fellow at the Center for Cultural Studies of the University of Bern. Wetzel's work concentrates on ethics, politics and culture, social theories, and economic and cultural sociology, and he is the author of *Diskurse des Politischen: Zwischen Re- und Dekonstruktion* (2003) and of *Soziologie des*

Wettbewerbs—eine kultur- und wirtschaftssoziologische Studie zur Marktgesellschaft (2013). He is co-author, with Thomas Claviez, of the forthcoming *Zur Aktualität von Jacques Rancière* (2015).

Robert J. C. Young is Silver Professor of English and Comparative Literature at New York University. He is one of the early pioneers and most influential scholars in the field of postcolonial literatures, an interdisciplinary field involving research that includes areas of history, theory, philosophy, anthropology, and translation studies. Young has gained international renown with *White Mythologies* (1990) and *Colonial Desire* (1995). He is also the editor of *Interventions: International Journal of Postcolonial Studies* and was a founding editor of *The Oxford Literary Review*. Prime concerns in his work are people and culture, margins and peripheries, and the knowledge and experience such communities produce.

INDEX OF NAMES

SUBJECT INDEX

COMMONALITIES

Timothy C. Campbell, series editor

Roberto Esposito, *Terms of the Political: Community, Immunity, Biopolitics.* Translated by Rhiannon Noel Welch. Introduction by Vanessa Lemm.

Maurizio Ferraris, *Documentality: Why It Is Necessary to Leave Traces.* Translated by Richard Davies.

Dimitris Vardoulakis, *Sovereignty and Its Other: Toward the Dejustification of Violence.*

Anne Emmanuelle Berger, *The Queer Turn in Feminism: Identities, Sexualities, and the Theater of Gender.* Translated by Catherine Porter.

James D. Lilley, *Common Things: Romance and the Aesthetics of Belonging in Atlantic Modernity.*

Jean-Luc Nancy, *Identity: Fragments, Frankness.* Translated by François Raffoul.

Miguel Vatter, *Between Form and Event: Machiavelli's Theory of Political Freedom.*

Miguel Vatter, *The Republic of the Living: Biopolitics and the Critique of Civil Society.*

Maurizio Ferraris, *Where Are You? An Ontology of the Cell Phone.* Translated by Sarah De Sanctis.

Irving Goh, *The Reject: Community, Politics, and Religion after the Subject.*

Kevin Attell, *Giorgio Agamben: Beyond the Threshold of Deconstruction.*

J. Hillis Miller, *Communities in Fiction.*

Remo Bodei, *The Life of Things, the Love of Things*. Translated by Murtha Baca.

Gabriela Basterra, *The Subject of Freedom: Kant, Levinas*.

Roberto Esposito, *Categories of the Impolitical*. Translated by Connal Parsley.

Roberto Esposito, *Two: The Machine of Political Theology and the Place of Thought*. Translated by Zakiya Hanafi.

Akiba Lerner, *Redemptive Hope: From the Age of Enlightenment to the Age of Obama*.

Massimo Cacciari, *Europe and Empire: On the Political Forms of Globalization*. Edited by Alessandro Carrera, Translated by Massimo Verdicchio.

Adriana Cavarero and Angelo Scola, *Thou Shalt Not Kill: A Political and Theological Dialogue*. Translated by Margaret Adams Groesbeck and Adam Sitze.

Emanuele Coccia, *Sensible Life: A Micro-ontology of the Image*. Translated by Scott Alan Stuart, Introduction by Kevin Attell.

Thomas Claviez (ed.), *The Common Growl: Toward a Poetics of Precarious Community*.